THE MASORAH OF
BIBLIA HEBRAICA STUTTGARTENSIA

The Masorah of *Biblia Hebraica Stuttgartensia*

Introduction and Annotated Glossary

Page H. Kelley
Daniel S. Mynatt
Timothy G. Crawford

William B. Eerdmans Publishing Company
Grand Rapids, Michigan / Cambridge, U.K.

255 Jefferson Ave. S.E., Grand Rapids, Michigan 49503 /
P.O. Box 163, Cambridge CB3 9PU U.K.

Printed in the United States of America

02 01 00 99 98   5 4 3 2 1

Library of Congress Cataloging-in-Publication Data

Kelley, Page H.
The Masorah of Biblia Hebraica Stuttgartensia : introduction and annotated glossary / Page H. Kelley, Daniel S. Mynatt, Timothy G. Crawford.
p.   cm.
Includes bibliographical references and index.
ISBN 0-8028-4363-8 (paper : alk. paper)
1. Masorah. 2. Bible. O.T. — Criticism, Textual. 3. Masorah — Indexes.
4. Biblia Hebraica Stuttgartensia. I. Mynatt, Daniel S.
(Daniel Stephen), 1962- . II. Crawford, Timothy G., 1957- . III. Title.
BS718.K38 1998
221.4′46 — dc21   97-42457
CIP

For Our Families

Vernice

Marcy, Joshua, & Caleb

Janet & Hannah

Table of Contents

The Masorah of *Biblia Hebraica Stuttgartensia*: Introduction and Annotated Glossary

Preface

Students of Biblical Hebrew are often confused by the strange looking notes printed in the margins of Hebrew Bibles. These notes, otherwise known as the Masorah, constitute a veritable library of information about the Hebrew text in its formative period. Recent research in this area has made this information more accessible than ever before. Serious students of the Hebrew Bible can no longer afford to ignore it.

At the same time, one should have no illusions about the complexities of this vast field of study. It would require a lifetime to master it. The difficulties are accentuated by the fact that the marginal notes are written in a form of abbreviated Aramaic that must first be deciphered.

For these and other reasons, the aim of this book is a modest one. It is to help students understand the significance of the study of the Masorah, to acquaint them with the tools necessary for such a study, and to demonstrate the use of these tools in deciphering a wide range of Masoretic notes taken from the Hebrew Bible. In recognition of the fact that even students with a good working knowledge of Biblical Hebrew might not be adept at reading Aramaic abbreviations, the book includes a virtually complete glossary of the Masoretic terms appearing in the margins of the *Biblia Hebraica Stutt–gartensia*(*BHS*). Each term is translated into English and furnished with a detailed examination of its actual usage in one or more passages in *BHS*. With this glossary, students not able to read Aramaic on their own will still be able to work through the Masoretic notes in the Hebrew Bible.

Scholars agree that the Ben Asher family of biblical texts is the most reliable. It is represented today by the Aleppo Codex (A) (lacking the Pentateuch), the British Museum Codex Or. 4445 (B) (covering the Pentateuch), the Cairo Codex (C) (covering the Prophets), and the Leningrad Codex B19a (L) (the only complete representative of the Ben Asher tradition available today).

The third edition of Kittel's Hebrew Bible (1937), known as BHK^3, abandoned the eclectic Ben Hayyim text of 1524–25, also known as the Bomberg Bible, the *Second Rabbinic Bible*, or the *Textus Receptus*, in favor of the Leningrad Codex B19a. Kittel's original intention was to provide readers of BHK^3 not only with the text of L but also with its complete Masorah, placing the Masorah parva (Mp) notes in the outer margins of the printed pages, and supplementing these with an alphabetic arrangement of Masorah magna (Mm) notes in a separate volume. These plans were only partially fulfilled. While the Mp or marginal notes were reproduced exactly as they appeared in L, the separate volume would only appear in 1971, and then only as a companion volume to the fourth edition of *BHK*, otherwise known as *Biblia Hebraica Stuttgartensia* (*BHS*).

Professor Gérard E. Weil was entrusted with the task of editing both the Mp and Mm notes of *BHS*. He set out to give a complete and integrated version of the Mp notes of L. This meant that the terminology and abbreviations of parallel notes were made consistent wherever they occurred. It also meant that where a note was missing from one or more of a series of related passages in L, it was supplied in the margins of *BHS*. Weil thus introduced order and consistency into the Masorah parva of L.

He also edited a companion volume to *BHS* under the title *Massorah Gedolah*, vol. I (1971). It consisted of the lists of the Mm notes found in the upper and lower margins of the pages of L. These were arranged in accordance with their initial occurrence in L and supplied with numbers from 1 to 4271. Each of the numbered lists was correlated with the Mp notes in the margins of *BHS* by a concordant apparatus, with each note keyed to its respective list by a raised index number. Thus the reader of *BHS* who had access to Weil's *Massorah Gedolah* was now able to go from the text through the Mp to the Mm and back to the text. The possibilities that this opened for the interpreter were stressed by James A. Sanders in his presidential address at the annual meeting of the Society of Biblical Literature in New Orleans on November 19, 1978 (see "Text and Canon: Concepts and Method," *JBL* 98/1 [1979] 5–29).

One of the barriers involved in teaching students of Hebrew about the Masorah is the lack of introductory literature on the subject. Although there is a lot of information about the Masorah available in print, most of it is in technical professional journals or encyclopedia articles. Scattered about in disparate sources, often not in English, this literature is easier to ignore than it is to incorporate into Hebrew classes. Our book attempts to remedy this situation by providing 1) a clear and concise introduction to the field of Masoretic studies, and 2) a glossary of Masoretic terms used in *BHS*.

1) Chapters 1–4 are intended to be an overview of the field of Masoretic Studies. Chapter 3 (The Proto–Masoretic Text) and Chapter 2 (History of the Masorah) provide background information concerning the work of the Masoretes and the state of the Hebrew text with which the Masoretes began. We recognize that anybody with a good Masoretic bibliography and a large library could access most of the information incorporated into these chapters, but we also recognize that most students of Hebrew will not do this. Thus, these chapters should be helpful in setting the context for the Masorah of L.

There have been other attempts at providing this background, the best known of which is Yeivin's *Introduction to the Tiberian Masorah* (trans. E.J. Revell, 1980). Yeivin's work is very useful, and we refer to it often. Introductory students often complain, however, that one must already understand Masoretic studies before Yeivin's book is really beneficial. We hope that these chapters will provide a true introduction to the field for students unfamiliar with the Masorah.

Hebrew grammars generally mention the contribution of the Masoretes, but there is no discussion of how to read the Masorah. Most technical literature on the Masorah presupposes that the reader already knows how to use the notes. Chapter 1 (Introduction) and Chapter 4 (Working with Masoretic Notes) are an attempt to fill this gap. These chapters provide the student with a practical orientation to reading and deciphering Masoretic notes. They are "how to" chapters, with the goal of teaching the reader the basic skills and approaches necessary for comprehending the Masorah of *BHS*. We assume that the reader knows nothing about those curious little circles above the Hebrew words in the text, and then we systematically move the student through the various sigla in *BHS* and the various types of notes one will encounter there. To our knowledge, there is no other systematic practical guide to the Masorah of *BHS* available.

2) The Prolegomena to *BHS* (pp. L–LV) provides a list of the most frequently used Mp terms, but the list is incomplete and its definitions are given only in Latin. There are no illustrations of how the terms are used, and the terse definitions that are given frequently can be more confusing to new students than helpful. Weil had projected additional volumes to accompany his *Massorah Gedolah*, including a full commentary on the Mm lists, an analysis of the Mp notes that had no accompanying Mm lists, and a full treatment of the Final Masorah (Mf) of L. The addition of these volumes would have helped immensely in clarifying both the list of terms and the Masorah of L itself; however, Weil's premature death cut short his work and his research has been allowed to languish.

There are other Masoretic glossaries available. Yeivin's glossary in *Introduction to the Tiberian Masorah* is comprehensive and has the advantage of illustrating the terms by way of actual examples, but, as mentioned above, the work is too advanced for students who are newly initiated into the ways of the Masorah. Furthermore Yeivin, and all the others before him who wrote glossaries of the Masorah, drew most of their examples from sources other than L. Since *BHS* is the standard critical edition of the Hebrew Bible in English-speaking countries, used widely by scholars and students alike, what was needed was a complete glossary of the Masorah of L as represented in *BHS*.

In this book, we have attempted to provide such a glossary, complete with annotations and examples drawn directly from *BHS*. The glossary covers almost all of the terms that are used in the Mp of *BHS*, which is the part of L's Masorah most accessible to students. The glossary will naturally assist the reader in wading through the larger vocabulary of the Mm, but no attempt has been made to catalog every term that appears there. The sample Mp notes appearing in the glossary have been chosen because we felt that they were good illustrations of the terms involved. We admit at the outset that we have been unable to resolve every question raised by every sample note. The fact that not every mystery has been solved is testimony to the complexities of the Masorah.

All of this book was the outgrowth of a series of graduate seminars that began to be offered at The Southern Baptist Theological Seminary in the fall of 1981. These seminars continued for more than a decade. They provided opportunity for students to explore the vast field of Masoretic studies and to investigate the life and work of outstanding Masoretes from the earliest beginning to more recent times. My colleagues in the completion of this project are Professors Daniel S. Mynatt and Timothy G. Crawford. Both developed an interest in Masoretic studies as participants in the seminars. They have pursued this interest through their careers as college professors and by participation in the International Organization for Masoretic Studies (IOMS). The words of Elias Levita appended to his *Massoreth Ha-Massoreth* seem apropos at this point:

> Forsooth I have committed errors, for there is no man who does not err, so that my error cleaves to me. I pray, therefore, that whoever understands and knows them, may correct my errors according to his wisdom.

Page H. Kelley, Louisville, Kentucky (1997)

Second Preface

Page H. Kelley died unexpectedly on March 13, 1997 at the age of 72. He had been planning this book for over a decade because he was well aware that there was none like it available. Dr. Kelley felt passionately that the Masorah could be unlocked for beginning students of Hebrew if they only had the right introduction. Obviously, we were both very honored when he asked us to write this book with him. We are grieved that Dr. Kelley did not live to see the end result of his efforts; fortunately, our work was in its final stages, and we were able to complete the volume without his guiding hand.

Not only did we lose a colleague and co–author, we suffered the loss of a mentor and friend. Dr. Kelley introduced both of us to the ways of the Masorah and showed us the value of studying those notes which previously we had been taught to ignore. Our careers and professional interests would have taken different turns had it not been for the influence of Page Kelley. He was recognized as one of the few specialists in the study of the Masorah in the United States. Thus, we are grateful that we had the opportunity to study with Dr. Kelley and to have his legacy passed on to us.

The *BHS* (copyright 1971) masoretic annotations cited in this volume, prepared by G. Weil, have been reproduced by permission from the United Bible Societies (New York) and the Pontifical Biblical Institute (Rome). Weil's *Massorah Gedolah* (copyright 1971) is also cited with the permission of the Pontifical Biblical Institute (Rome).

Daniel S. Mynatt, Anderson, South Carolina
Timothy G. Crawford, Bluefield, Virginia

Chapter 1
Introduction

What Is Masorah?

The term Masorah is ordinarily used in modern biblical studies to refer to the body of marginal notes (i.e., Masoretic notes) which are transmitted with the text, either in a manuscript or in a printed edition. However, this is the narrow sense of the word. In its broadest sense, Masorah refers to traditions and rules, passed down in Judaism for generations, which regulate all aspects of the copying and use of Bible manuscripts,

The Masorah in this broad sense could be oral or written. Written Masorah is the collected body of information transmitted with the text of the Hebrew Bible. It includes everything transmitted with the consonantal text except the consonants themselves (even vowel and accent signs). Thus, the Masorah in the narrow sense (the Masoretic notes) is really only one small part of the Masorah taken as a whole. Nevertheless, it is this aspect of the Masorah which is the topic of this book. Unless otherwise noted, we have maintained the conventional use of the term Masorah, by which it refers only to the marginal notes transmitted with the traditional text of the Hebrew Bible.

The Masorah can be divided into several subdivisions. The Masorah Parva (Mp) consists of the Masoretic notes in the side margins of manuscripts (cf. *BHS*). The Masorah Magna (Mm) includes the notes in the upper and lower margins of the manuscripts (but in *BHS* they are in the supplementary volume, *Massorah Gedolah*).[1]

The Masorah Finalis (Mf) refers to the material collected at the end of a particular book, section (e.g., Torah) or manuscript. In manuscripts, the Mf consists of summary lists, such as the number of verses, *sedarim*, etc., and information of this type is included in *BHS* at the end of books. Other data for which there was no room in the margins of a manuscript could also be included in the Mf. This information includes lists of various types, such as differences between the Eastern and Western Masoretes (which is at the end of L). This information is not in *BHS*. The term Mf also refers to the edited lists collected by Jacob ben Chayyim which are found at the end of the *Second Rabbinic Bible* (discussed in Chapter 2).

The term Masorah is sometimes used to designate the Masorah of the *Second Rabbinic Bible*, especially in older literature ("Printed Masorah" always has this referent). This usage leaves the impression that the Masorah is a unified body of material transmitted uniformly with all manuscripts, which is clearly not true anywhere except in the *Second Rabbinic Bible*. The content of the Masorah varies from manuscript to manuscript, although much of it is overlapping in manuscripts from the standard Tiberian tradition (see Chapter 2 for this term). The most precise way to refer to the Masorah is by manuscript or edition, e.g., the Masorah of L, of A, etc. In this chapter, characteristics of the Masorah are described in general terms, but all specific references are to the Masorah of L as given in *BHS*, unless otherwise noted.

The purpose of the Masorah (in the broad sense) was rooted in the attitude toward the use of the Bible in Judaism. The Hebrew Bible, and especially the Torah, held a special place of sacredness and holiness in Judaism because it was the foundation of all legal traditions. Thus, the text of the Bible needed to be carefully guarded, even to the minutest detail, so that the Bible would not be altered in any way.

The purpose of the Masorah in the narrow sense was to preserve the integrity of scripture precisely, so that nothing would be added to the text or taken away. The Masoretic notes gave specific instructions regarding words and phrases where an error in writing might occur. This was a form of quality control by which the text was preserved without significant change. In the broad sense of Masorah, the purpose included, not only writing, but also the proper pronunciation of Scripture. The vowel and accent signs preserved the correct reading tradition and intonation of the words.

The etymology of the word Masorah has been the subject of considerable debate, and scholarship has not reached a consensus on the issue. A minority opinion holds that the word is related to the Hebrew root אסר, "to bind." The Masorah is instructions for the text which are bound and gathered. Most scholars relate Masorah to the Hebrew word מסר, "to hand over" or "to transmit." Thus, the Masorah consisted of instructions and traditions about the Bible which were handed down from generation to generation. Recent scholars have offered explanations of the term Masorah based on other nuances of the root מסר.[2]

Similarly, the English spelling of the word Masorah is found in various forms: Masora, Massorah, etc. All of these differences are derived from the manner in which the word is spelled in Hebrew and transliterated into English. The spelling "Massorah," with a doubled s, is based on a doubling of the *samech* in Hebrew: מַסּוֹרָה. The presence or absence of the ה in English reflects differing methods of transliterating a final *he* in Hebrew. In this book, we have adopted the spelling Masorah throughout, based on the Hebrew מָסוֹרָה.[3]

Why Study the Masorah?

In a review of *BHS*, James Barr largely approved of the arrangement of its Masorah, and he also offered this insightful commentary regarding the study of the Masorah:

Conversely, experts in the Masorah, myopically concentrated upon their

> own detailed and complicated specialism, have not generally been able to explain what they are doing in a way that is helpful to the average student of the Bible. Not a few scholars, faced with this greatly improved version of the Masoretic material, have been tempted to wish that it was not there at all.[4]

Barr's observations are unfortunately very true, and they raise two important questions. First, what is involved in the study of the Masorah? Second, and more important, why bother with the study of the Masorah at all? The answer to the first question is what this book is all about. By working through this volume, the reader should come to a good knowledge of the methods and problems involved in deciphering the Masorah. The Masorah can indeed be complicated at times, but it is not the barrier which it is frequently reputed to be. The study of the Masorah, like anything worthwhile, does take effort, but the effort will not go unrewarded, as the answer to the second question should show.

Why study the Masorah? Scholarship of the Hebrew Bible places great value on the standard Tiberian tradition of the Masoretic text; it forms the basis of all printed editions, scholarly commentaries, etc. Thus, the most obvious answer to the question is that students of the Hebrew Bible can come to a better understanding of this revered Masoretic text by mastering the Masorah, the device created to establish quality control over it. An enormous storehouse of learning, spanning at least a millennium, is deposited in the Masoretic notes. Through studying these notes, the modern scholar can become keenly familiar with what constitutes the standard tradition.

Furthermore, the study of the Masorah can move the student beyond technical matters of grammar and textual tradition. The Masorah was a rudimentary form of literary criticism. Word frequency had already been established. Unusual meanings and spellings had already been discovered. Distinctive vocabulary and spelling in particular sections of the Bible had already been noted. To be sure, these features of the text were recorded for the primary purpose of preserving the textual tradition. Nevertheless, the modern scholar can use this information to find answers to related critical questions.

Last, but by no means least in importance, a better understanding of the Masoretic text can be achieved by learning about the crucial stage in the history of the text when important features were being fixed. The text of the Hebrew Bible as we have it today, with vowels, accents, etc., was the product of the Masoretic scholars. Who were these people? What was the process that led to the final product? Does the uniformity in the Masoretic text result from uniformity among the Masoretes? Is the wording that was established by the Masoretic vowel points and word division less trustworthy than the consonantal text simply because the consonantal text was earlier?[5] These types of questions can only be answered through a study of the Masoretic period.

Basic Tools

What materials are required for one to undertake a study of the Masorah? First, the student needs an edition of the Hebrew Bible which is annotated with Masoretic notes. In modern scholarship, this is most frequently *BHS* since it is easily accessible. Furthermore, the editor of the Masorah in *BHS*, G. E. Weil, has revised the notes from their original form in L to make them easier to use. The extent of the revision will be addressed in Chapter 4. If *BHS* is used, then the companion volume *Massorah Gedolah* is also important, since it contains the lists of the Mm. Unfortunately, *Massorah Gedolah* has been out of print for several years. Therefore the student may be able to get access to this volume only through a library.

Second, the student will need a complete Hebrew concordance. Even-Shoshan's *A New Concordance of the Old Testament* will probably be the most accessible. Two other Hebrew concordances are commonly used. Mandelkern's *Concordance on the Bible* was for many years the standard concordance for scholarship, and Lizowsky's *Konkordanz zum Hebräischen Alten Testament* is also helpful, but its format differs from the others. Errors can occur in all concordances. Thus being aware of the various concordances can be helpful when an error is suspected in any one of them.

Third, the student must have a good glossary of Masoretic terms with explanations and sample notes cited for each term. Chapter 5 was designed to meet this need. The explanations have been prepared with the new student of the Masorah in mind. Yeivin has collected a similar glossary in his *Introduction to the Tiberian Masorah*, but students who are unfamiliar with the larger field of Masoretic Studies may find some explanations and terminology confusing. Furthermore, Yeivin does not include some terms which appear in *BHS*.

Last, the following works are helpful as references (see the Bibliography for complete information): Ginsburg, *The Massorah*; Frensdorff, *Die Massora Magna*; Mynatt, *The Sub Loco Notes of the Torah in the BHS*; and Yeivin, *Introduction to the Tiberian Masorah*. The discussion in Ginsburg and Frensdorff will help to solve some otherwise difficult problems facing the student. Mynatt's volume will be discussed in Chapter 4. Yeivin's work is a general introduction to the field, and it will be helpful to have it close by as a reference.

Basic Skills

The use of the tools mentioned above will be explained and illustrated in Chapter 4. However, before that discussion can be comprehensible, the new student must first learn the mechanics of how the Masorah works. The Masorah of *BHS* will serve as the basis for all of the examples in the following sections.

Mp Notes Without Index Numbers

The index number is the small Arabic numeral printed superscript beside many of the Mp notes. Some Mp notes lack the index number. These Mp notes will be discussed first. The purpose of this section is to teach the reader how to match an Mp note with the text that it annotates.[6]

1) An Mp note marking a single word. The notes of the Mp are in the outside margin of the pages. Each note is printed adjacent to a line of text, and within that line there is a word with which the Mp note should be matched. The word in question has a small circle (called a circule in the *BHS* Introduction) raised over it. The Mp note should be matched with the word marked by the raised circule.

Example: On page 44, in the first line of text, the reader will find the conclusion of Genesis 28:7. In the right margin (the outside margin) of the first line, the Mp note ד֗ is printed. Scanning the line of text, the reader will find a small circule raised over the word פַּדֶּ֑נָה. Thus, the Mp note should be matched with פַּדֶּ֑נָה.

2) More than one Mp note in the margin. Frequently, more than one Mp note will be in the margin for a single line of text. This tells the reader that there are two or more words which are being annotated, one for each Mp note in the margin. The Mp notes in *BHS* are separated by small dots placed like periods. They are printed in the same order that the pertinent words appear in the adjacent line.

Example: On the same page, the twenty-second line from the top is the conclusion of Genesis 28:22. There are two Mp notes in the right margin, ב֗ and ל֗, reading from right to left; notice that the notes are separated by a small dot. In the adjacent line, there are two words which have raised circules, עַשֵּׂ֖ר and אֲעַשְּׂרֶ֥נּוּ, again reading from right to left. The notes should be matched with words in the text respectively, first note with first word, second note with second word, etc. Thus, the Mp note ב֗ should be matched with the word עַשֵּׂ֖ר, and the note ל֗ should be matched with the word אֲעַשְּׂרֶ֥נּוּ.

3) An Mp note marking a phrase. Mp notes can mark phrases (i.e., word combinations) as well as individual words. When a phrase is the subject of the Mp note, a raised circule is printed between each of the words within the phrase. The number of circules marking the phrase will vary with how many words are contained in the phrase. The format of the Mp note (or notes) in the right margin, however, will be the same as before.

Example: On page 46 of *BHS*, in the thirteenth line from the top (hereafter page 46, line 13), the reader will find Genesis 29:35. There are two Mp notes in the right margin. The first note, ל֗, should be matched with the phrase אוֹדֶ֣ה אֶת־יְהוָ֔ה. Notice that there are two circules marking this phrase, one between each word in the phrase. Also notice that there is another note on this line, ג֗ for קָרְאָ֥ה. This situation is not different from 2) above, except that here one Mp note in the line is matched with a single word and another is matched with a phrase.

4) Mp notes marking a word within a phrase. Occasionally, a phrase will be the subject of an Mp note, and a shorter component of the phrase will also be the subject of another note. If the shorter component is a single word, the two notes can be distinguished easily. The circules marking the phrase will be between the words, and the circule marking the single word will be over the word.

Example: See Exodus 4:9 (page 91, line 1). The combination יִשְׁמְעוּן ˚לְקֹלֶ֑ךָ has three circules. The left margin contains three Mp notes (for the present, ignore the raised index numbers with the Mp notes). The first circule is directly over יִשְׁמְעוּן. Thus, only this particular word is in question. This circule should be matched with the first note in the margin, ה֗. The second circule is between the words in the phrase יִשְׁמְעוּן ˚לְקֹלֶ֑ךָ. Thus, the two-word phrase is at issue. It should be matched with the second Mp note in the margin, יז שמיעה לקול. The third circule is directly over לְקֹלֶ֑ךָ. Again, only this word is in question. This circule should be matched with the third note in the margin, ב֗ חס. Notice further how all three of the Mp notes in the margin are separated by dots. When there was insufficient room in the margin for the third note, it was printed below the first two.

5) Mp notes marking a phrase within a phrase. If the shorter component is a smaller phrase within the larger phrase, then the larger phrase will be marked with raised circules between the words. The shorter phrase will be marked by a second raised circule between the first two words of the shorter phrase.

Example: See Isaiah 3:15 (page 680, line 12). The phrase נְאֻם־˚אֲדֹנָי ˚˚יְהוִה ˚צְבָאוֹת is marked with a circule between each word (including words joined by *maqqefs*). Furthermore, there is a second circule between יְהוִה and אֲדֹנָי. There are two Mp notes in the right margin. The first Mp note, ד֗, should be matched with the entire four-word phrase. The second Mp note, ה֗י, should be matched with a smaller phrase within the larger phrase. The beginning of this smaller phrase is marked by the second circule between יְהוִה and אֲדֹנָי. The smaller phrase extends to the end of the larger phrase. Thus, the smaller phrase is אֲדֹנָי יְהוִה צְבָאוֹת.

This example has been chosen intentionally because it is the example used by Weil to illustrate this situation.[7] Weil comments that the smaller phrase "usually extends to the end of the group." In the preceding example, this is true, and the system of circules works. However, in some cases, the placement of the circules leaves ambiguity regarding the termination of the smaller phrase within the larger. See Exodus 9:8 (page 99, line 16). The phrase וַיֹּאמֶר ˚˚יְהוָה ˚אֶל־˚מֹשֶׁה ˚וְאֶל־˚אַהֲרֹן is marked with circules between each word in the phrase. There is a second circule between וַיֹּאמֶר and יְהוָה. Two Mp notes are in the left margin. The first Mp note is ד֗ בטע בסיפ (ignore the index number in *BHS*), and it should be matched with the entire six-word phrase.

According to the principles outlined above and explained in *BHS* Introduction, the second note should also be matched with the entire six-word phrase (since the second circule is between the first two words of the entire phrase). Clearly, this cannot be the case. Although the beginning of the smaller phrase can be determined (the words which have the second circule between them: יְהוָה and וַיֹּאמֶר), we cannot tell from the placement of the circules where it ends. In this case, the shorter phrase is only the two words וַיֹּאמֶר יְהוָה, but this information cannot be ascertained from the arrangement of the circules.

Important Note: In lines where there are several Mp notes, the new student may have difficulty associating the correct note with the correct textual item in the line. This is particularly true in crowded lines which also contain marked phrases or words within a phrase. One way to clarify the situation is to remember that usually the number of Mp notes in the margin (separated by dots) equals the number of textual units in the line. Starting with the first note in the margin, the new student should attempt to pair up each Mp note with its appropriate textual unit. By doing this systematically, the student will be able to clear up some of the ambiguity in a crowded line.

The student needs to be aware that two Masoretic accents, *Telisha magnum* and *Telisha parvum*, are also composed of circules. These accents can be distinguished from the Mp circules by remembering two characteristics: 1) The accent marks have small lines extending from the circules; the Mp circules do not. 2) The accents appear either at the beginning or the end of the word; the Mp circules appear either centered above the word or between words.

Example: See Genesis 31:37-38 (page 50, line 19). How many textual units should the student be looking for? There are five Mp notes in the margin. Thus, there are only five textual units to match with the Mp notes. There are six circules in the line, but the circule over זֶה has a small line attached to it, and it is situated at the left edge of the word. This circule is an accent and should be disregarded when matching Mp notes with their appropriate textual units.

Mp Notes With Index Numbers

Mp notes with index numbers are matched with words and phrases in the text in the same way as those without index numbers. The only difference is that, in addition, the index number refers the reader to the bottom of the page to the Masoretic apparatus, which is located just above the text-critical apparatus. Various kinds of information are given in the Masoretic apparatus pertinent to the Mp notes with index numbers. The purpose of this section will be to describe the different types of information that the reader will encounter in the apparatus.

The index numbers in the apparatus run consecutively within a chapter. A new series of index numbers begins with each new chapter. Thus, when one chapter ends and another begins on the same page, the index numbers in the apparatus (and in the Mp notes) are repeated. In this case the Masoretic apparatus designates the notes for the new chapter by prefacing the first with "Cp" followed by the new chapter number (cf. Lev. 11–13, p. 176). Since the same index number may be used more than once on a single page (for different chapters), the reader must take extra caution to match the index number of a given Mp note with the index number of the apparatus entry within the chapter to which it refers.

1) Mm notes. Most of the index numbers refer the reader to an entry in the apparatus which contains an Mm list number. The reader must then go to Weil's *Massorah Gedolah* to find the Mm list. The Mm lists in *Massorah Gedolah* are numbered consecutively, based on the order of their occurrence in L. Thus locating the appropriate list in *Massorah Gedolah* is very easy. Mm 1 is the first list, Mm 2 is the second, and so on. The editorial signs (brackets, etc.) encountered in *Massorah Gedolah* are the conventions which Weil used to mark his emendations to the Mm of L. They are discussed in the Introduction to *Massorah Gedolah*. This Introduction is in French, which may be a barrier to the English user, but most of the signs can be deduced with a little experience.

Example: See Genesis 1:4 (page 1, line 4). The word וַיַּבְדֵּל has a raised circule over it and should be matched with the only Mp note printed in the margin for that line, [11]גׄ. The raised 11 next to the note is the index number. The reader is directed to the Masoretic apparatus below to entry number 11. There, the reader will find Mm 6. Next, the reader needs to turn to list number 6 in *Massorah Gedolah*. The Mp note tells the reader that this word occurs 3 times, and the entry in *Massorah Gedolah* identifies the location of the 3 occurrences.

2) Multiple Mm notes. Occasionally, two or more Mm notes will be signified in one Mp note. The two Mm notes are given separate index numbers and, thus, separate entries in the apparatus and separate lists in *Massorah Gedolah*. The reader will need to treat each Mm note signified in the Mp note according to the explanation in 1) above.

Example: See Genesis 1:1 (page 1, line 1). The word בְּרֵאשִׁית is annotated with the note הׄ גׄ[1] ר״פ ובׄ[2] מ״פ. This note tells the reader that the word בְּרֵאשִׁית occurs 5 times in all (הׄ). It occurs 3 times at the beginning of a verse (גׄ[1] ר״פ). Index number 1 refers the reader to the first entry in the apparatus: Mm 1. This entry signifies the first list in *Massorah Gedolah*, where the list of occurrences will be found. The final section of the Mp note tells us that the word בְּרֵאשִׁית occurs twice within a verse (ובׄ[2] מ״פ). Index number 2 refers the reader to the second entry in the apparatus: Mm 2. This entry signifies the second list in *Massorah Gedolah*, where the list of occurrences will be found.

The reader needs to be aware that the Mm lists in the original manuscript of L are written in the upper and lower margins of the pages, not in a separate volume. Thus, if the student should consult L, a different situation will be found. This aspect of Weil's editorial activity, and his other changes, will be discussed in Chapter 4.

3) Mp ב̇ with an index number. The Mp note ב̇ indicates that the word or phrase occurs twice. Multiple occurrences of a word marked by an Mp note can be referred to as parallel passages, and so the two occurrences marked by the Mp note ב̇ are parallels. In the original manuscript of L, when a word or phrase is marked with the Mp note ב̇, the parallel passage is sometimes (but not always!) referenced by a short identifying excerpt from the verse in which the parallel is found. The identifying excerpt is located under the ב̇.

In *BHS*, this situation is handled by an index number. The Mp note ב̇ will be assigned an index number referring the reader to the apparatus. The identifying excerpt for the parallel is not reprinted in the Mp. Instead, the parallel reference is indicated in the apparatus. The reference is given, not in Hebrew, but by an abbreviation of the book followed by a chapter and verse number.

Example: See Genesis 24:28 (page 35, line 8). The only Mp note on this line is [28]ב̇, matched with the phrase לְבֵית אִמָּהּ. The apparatus entry for index number 28 has "Ru 1,8." Thus, the Mp note informs the reader that the phrase לְבֵית אִמָּהּ occurs twice. The reference in the apparatus gives the location of the second occurrence of the combination: Ruth 1:8. If the reader turns to Ruth 1:8, the same situation will be found, except that the reference in the apparatus directs the reader to Genesis 24:28.

4) Mp ל̇ with an index number. The Mp note ל̇ denotes that a word or phrase occurs only once in a particular form. When a word or phrase is marked ל̇ in L, another similar form, also occurring once, is sometimes (but not always!) given in the Mp note. Just as in the situation with ב̇, the similar form is given under the ל̇. Although this other form is very similar to the word in question in the Mp note, there is always some significant difference. The difference between the form marked ל̇ and the form in the Mp can be observed by closely comparing the two. The similar form also acts as an identifying excerpt, pointing the reader to the verse in which the form is found.

In *BHS*, this situation is also handled by an index number. The Mp note ל̇ will be assigned an index number referring the reader to the apparatus. The similar form does not appear in the Mp. Instead, it is printed in the apparatus, introduced by the formula וחד "and once," and followed by the book, chapter, verse reference.

Example: In Genesis 32:20 (page 52, line 20), there are two Mp notes in the right margin. The second is [21]ל̇. This note should be matched with the second textual unit marked by a raised circule in the adjacent line, אֶת־הַשֵּׁנִי. The index number refers to apparatus entry 21 where the statement "וחד ואת השני Lv 5,10" is found. This entry tells the reader that the similar form וְאֶת־הַשֵּׁנִי is located in Leviticus 5:10. The difference in the similar form is the addition of the *vav*. If the reader turns to Leviticus 5:10, a similar situation can be found, except that the reference is for Genesis 32:20 and the appropriate form is given.

5) Other information in the apparatus. Occasionally, Weil has used the apparatus system to communicate other information. Usually this information is not contained in the Masorah of L but instead is an observation on the text or Mp which Weil felt was relevant to the situation. These apparatus entries are varied in nature. Sometimes they note differences in the readings of the Eastern (Babylonian) or Western (Palestinian) Masoretes. Sometimes they call attention to an ancient Masoretic commentary. Sometimes they tell the reader about an unusual alteration Weil has made to the Mp. Of particular importance are the apparatus statements "contra textum" and "sub loco." Both of these items deserve special attention and are discussed in Chapter 4.

Example: See Genesis 33:4 (page 53, line 20). The first word in this line marked by a raised circule is צַוָּארָו. It should be matched with the first Mp note in the margin, which is צואריו[3] printed over ק̇. This is the usual format for a *Qere/Ketiv* situation (see below on *Qere/Ketiv*), except that index number 3 directs attention to the apparatus. There, the statement "Q addidi, cf. Gn 45,15 et Mp sub loco" is found. "Q addidi" tells the reader that this *Qere* has been added by Weil. "Cf. Gn 45,14" refers to another example of this form in Genesis 45:14. "Mp sub loco" will be discussed in Chapter 4.

6) Mp ° with an index number. On rare occasions, the Mp note in the margin will not contain Hebrew letters but instead will only consist of a circule. This circule, like any other Mp note, should be matched to the appropriate circule in the adjacent line. In such cases, Weil desired to make some kind of comment about the text or Masorah, but there was no Mp note to serve as a basis. Thus, the circule in the margin serves as the Mp note. It is simply Weil's device for footnoting some element that needs discussion. The circule invariably has an index number directing attention to the entry in the apparatus where Weil's comment on the situation can be found.

Example: In Genesis 24:14 (page 34, line 14), there are two Mp notes in the right margin. The second Mp note is a circule with index number 18 raised beside it ([18]o). This note should be matched with the word marked by the second circule in the adjacent line, הַנַּעֲרָ. The index number refers the reader to the apparatus where, in entry 18, an extensive comment can be found about the text.

Important Note: In the previous examples, only one series of index numbers was printed on the page. This will not always be the case. See page 176, which contains text from three chapters, Leviticus 11–13. Index numbers 1 and 2 are used in both chapter 12 and chapter 13. The reader must show caution not to match the index numbers in the Mp notes with the entries in the apparatus for the other chapter bearing the same index number. Thus, in Leviticus 12:4, the note ... י̇ז̇[1] should be matched with the appropriate entry in the apparatus for chapter 12, Mp sub loco. The note י̇א̇[1] in Leviticus 13:1 should be matched with the first entry in the apparatus for chapter 13, Mm 852.

***Qere/Ketiv* Notes**

Qere/Ketiv notes occur in situations where the reading tradition, the traditionally accepted pronunciation, differs from the pronunciation which the letters of the text would normally suggest. In order to avoid errors in reading, the Masoretes developed the *Qere* notes to instruct the reader regarding what is proper to be read for a particular text.

The *Qere/Ketiv* notes may very well be the most problematic issue in Masoretic studies, and a tremendous amount of literature has been generated on the questions involved.[8] No one is certain how these notes originated or what was the basis for the difference between the *Qere* and the *Ketiv*. The problem is complicated by the fact that there is no unified body of *Qere/Ketiv* notes marked in manuscripts, and there were various methods for marking the notes and the proper pronunciation of the *Qere*.[9] The instructions below represent the method in *BHS*, which is also usual practice among other printed editions and manuscripts.

Qere is Aramaic for "read," indicating what should be read. *Ketiv* is Aramaic for "written," denoting what is written in the text. In *BHS*, the *Ketiv* is written in the text, just as any other word. A circule is printed above the word. The *Ketiv* is pointed with the vowels that belong with the *Qere*. The consonants of the *Qere* are given in the margin with the other Mp notes. These consonants are printed above the letter קׄ (which stands for *Qere*). The reader must associate the consonants in the margin with the vowels in the text. Thus, in form and system the *Qere/Ketiv* notes are very similar to the other Mp notes. The distinguishing factor for the *Qere/Ketiv* notes is the *Qere* marker קׄ in the margin.

Example: See Genesis 8:17 (page 12, line 7). There are two marginal notes in this line (the second occurs in Genesis 8:18). The first note is a *Qere/Ketiv* note. The *Ketiv*, marked by a circule, is הַוְצֵא. The consonants for the *Qere*, given in the margin, are היצא. The student needs to read the vowels of the *Ketiv* with the consonants of the *Qere*. Thus, the resulting form is הַיְצֵא.

The new student should be aware that sometimes in *BHS*, *Qere/Ketiv* notes are combined with other Mp notes (Genesis 12:8, page 17, line 13) or have an index number (Genesis 14:2, page 19, line 7). This additional information should not create any problem, once the principles outlined in the foregoing sections are understood.

Notes

[1]G.E. Weil, *Massorah Gedolah*, Vol. 1 (Rome: Pontifical Biblical Institute, 1971).

[2]For a more detailed discussion of the issue, see A. Dotan, "Masorah," *Encyclopedia Judaica* (Jerusalem: Macmillan Co., 1971) XVI:1418–19.

[3]For more information on the development and pronunciation of the word Masorah, see W. Bacher, "A Contribution to the History of the Term 'Massorah'," *Jewish Quarterly Review* 3 (1890-91) 785–90.

[4]James Barr, review of *Biblia Hebraica Stuttgartensia*, ed. by K. Elliger and W. Rudolph, *Journal of Theological Studies* 30 (1979) 213.

[5]The preeminence of the consonants over the vowels, etc., is an often-held opinion; however, scholars of the Masorah generally argue that this position represents a misunderstanding of the Masoretes and their work. See E.J. Revell, "Masoretic Text," *The Anchor Bible Dictionary* (New York, NY: Doubleday, 1992) IV:599.

[6]For Weil's treatment of this mechanism, cf. *BHS* Introduction, pp. XVII–XVIII.

[7]See the *BHS* Introduction, p. XVIII.

[8]For a good introduction to the study of *Qere/Ketiv*, see W.S. Morrow, "*Kethib* and *Qere*," *The Anchor Bible Dictionary* (New York, NY: Doubleday, 1992) IV:24–30.

[9]On these two issues, see Israel Yeivin, *Introduction to the Tiberian Masorah*, trans. and ed. E.J. Revell, The Society of Biblical Literature Masoretic Studies, No. 5 (Missoula, MT: Scholars Press, 1980) pp. 52–56.

Chapter 2

History of the Masorah

Differing Masoretic Traditions

There were three broad traditions of Masoretes in antiquity, corresponding to three different pronunciation traditions and three different graphic systems for the vowels and accent signs: Palestinian, Babylonian, and Tiberian. The Tiberian tradition eventually gained dominance over the other two, and it is the tradition best known today. The information in this book concerns the Tiberian tradition, unless otherwise noted, since *BHS* is based on a manuscript in the Tiberian tradition.

Within the Tiberian tradition, there were various subsystems which differed from one another to a lesser or greater degree. For example, much discussion has been occasioned by the graphic system witnessed in Codex Reuchlinianus (written in Italy around 1105) and similar manuscripts. Scholarship has not even settled on a good name for this system. It is sometimes called the Expanded Tiberian system or the Tiberio-Palestinian system, but the more frequent name in the prominent literature for students of the Masorah in English is the Tiberian Non-Receptus system[1] or the Non-Conventional Tiberian system.[2]

This system uses Tiberian graphic signs (e.g., vowels) in a manner that is inconsistent with the standard Tiberian system, such as in L. Dotan gives a detailed analysis of the differences from the standard Tiberian system.[3] Scholars are divided as to whether this system represents a different pronunciation tradition. Dotan believes it does, whereas Goshen-Gottstein does not.[4]

The point is that, even within the Tiberian system, there were differences. Thus, we can distinguish between the standard Tiberian system and non-standard systems.[5] The Non-Conventional Tiberian system is a good example, if a bit extreme, of a non-standard system. Other non-standard manuscripts differ from the standard system in matters such as the liberal use of vowel letters or the modification of the vowel signs to reflect the pronunciation tradition in the scribe's community.

The standard Tiberian tradition is the topic of this book. Even within the standard tradition there were differences among various Masoretes, such as the differences between ben Asher and ben Naphtali discussed below. These differences amount to insignificant details when compared to another vocalization system, but they are of interest in tracing the history of the standard Tiberian tradition.

The Masorah in Talmudic Literature

Although the Talmudic period is prior to that of the Masoretes, certain information which would become the subject of Masoretic notes is already mentioned in Talmudic literature. The following are simply some examples. 1) There are references to the number of verses in books or sections (*Kiddushin* 30a, but note that the totals disagree with the Masoretic totals). 2) There are references to plene and defective spellings (*Bereshit Rabba* 12:6). 3) There are references to the irregular features of the text, such as the extraordinary points (*Sifre Numbers* 69), large and small letters, (*Megillah* 16b), and the *Itture Sopherim* (*Nedarim* 37b–38a).

Furthermore, the Talmudic literature often makes observations on the text employing terminology characteristic of the Masorah, even formulated in a manner very similar to the Masorah. Yeivin has collected a variety of statements from Talmudic literature which sound like expressions from the Masorah.[6]

Nevertheless, this type of information which is found in Talmudic literature does not always agree with the Masorah. Probably the most celebrated example of this (apart from the number of verses cited above) is the fact that Talmud refers to Psalms 1 and 2 as a single psalm (*Berakot* 9b–10a). However, the Masorah, for example in L, treats Psalm 1 and 2 as separate psalms.[7]

Thus, interest in material which we would call Masoretic began in the Talmudic period; however, there is no indication that the Masorah as such existed at this time. Furthermore, the scholars who dealt with such matters seemed to be interested primarily in the *halakah* involved; there is no evidence of interest in the textual tradition for its own sake.[8] It would be accurate to say that discussions in the Talmudic period established the foundations for the Masoretes, but Masoretic activity in the specialized sense flourished only later.

The Beginning of the Masoretic Period

Isolating a starting date for the Masoretic Period is a difficult and somewhat arbitrary problem. It is difficult because there is very little evidence about the early Masoretes and their activity. We know almost nothing about how the Masorah got its start because, by its very nature, the Masorah is concerned with the preservation of the text, not with the scholars who instituted the system of preservation.

Isolating a starting date for the Masoretic period is arbitrary because, as we have seen, there is prior evidence of interest in Masoretic phenomena in the Talmud. We argued above that there is no evidence for Masorah or Masoretes in the Talmudic period; however, it is only a small step from these Talmudic discussions to Masoretic activity in the proper sense. Thus, it is somewhat artificial to fix an absolute starting date for the Masoretic Period. As Yeivin has noted, the work of the Masoretes probably started during the end of the Talmudic period.[9]

Another approach to this question is to isolate a time period during which the Masorah first began to be committed to writing. Most scholars believe that the consonantal text was standardized around 100 C.E., and the reading tradition is also very old, but the graphic signs representing the vowels and accents of that tradition are a Masoretic convention.[10] We can narrow the beginning of the use of graphic signs for vowels and accents to the time period 600–750 C.E.[11]

The lower limit can be established from the fact that the Babylonian Talmud (generally agreed to have been closed about 600 C.E.) never mentions the vowel signs. Jerome, about a century earlier, even mentions that Jews did not have signs to mark vowels.[12] Thus, we can assume that the vowel signs did not exist before 600 C.E.

To mark the upper limit, Dotan cites the activity of a few early Masoretes about whom we have some knowledge. For example, Asher the Elder (discussed below) lived in the second half of the eighth century, and his work included matters of vowel and accent signs.[13] Thus, these must have been introduced by this time. The oldest known dated codex, the Cairo Codex of the Prophets (discussed below), dates from 895 C.E. It has the vowel and accent signs fully developed and marked. Their institution must have preceded the codex by a considerable period, a century or more. Therefore, the middle of the eighth century (ca. 750 C.E.) is appealing as the latest possible date for their first use.

This line of argument is supported by materials from the Cairo Geniza.[14] Scroll fragments were found there with some Masoretic material included with the text. Yeivin dates the earliest fragments, with Palestinian pointing, to the eighth or ninth century C.E. He also notes one Karaite document listing the names of the vowels which may date from the eighth century C.E.[15]

The question of whether the vowel and accent signs were introduced simultaneously or in stages is problematic, and there is little evidence to support any firm conclusion. The prevailing assumption had always been that the vowel signs and accents were part of an integrated system and were added to the text at approximately the same time. Recently, however, Dotan has argued from the Babylonian and Palestinian systems and from Rabbinic evidence that the accents were introduced prior to the vowel signs.[16] Apart from specific evidence that Dotan cites, the basic rationale for his argument is that the intonations and pauses marked by the accents were more difficult to preserve than the vowel sounds. Thus, the need for accent signs was more urgent and immediate than vowel signs. Dotan even argues that there may be some references in the Talmud to written accent signs (but not vowel signs), although the evidence is not conclusive.[17]

We can assume that, once the vowel and accent signs were introduced into the text, the Masoretic notes would also be introduced. Yeivin has observed that, in the Cairo Geniza, there are texts which have vowel and accent signs but few or no Masoretic notes. Thus, he speculates that the writing of the Masorah in the narrow sense was slightly later than the vowel and accent marks.[18] However, since most of the Masoretic notes deal with consonants and not vowels, the creation of most of the notes themselves should probably be dated earlier than the origin of the vowel and accent marks.[19]

Bearing in mind the general time argued above, we can speculate about the beginning of the Masorah. Approximately 600 C.E. (and probably somewhat earlier), the work on the Masorah began. Scrolls which contain markings apart from the sacred text are considered unfit for liturgical use.[20] This general prohibition probably kept the work of the first Masoretes from being copied into scrolls. Thus, at first, the Masoretic notes were transmitted orally. We can speculate that this information might have also been gathered into independent Masoretic treatises or notebooks. We know of such treatises from later dates, and it is logical that they would have existed from earlier times but no datable examples are extant. As time passed, it became acceptable to enter vowel and accents signs and Masoretic notes into scrolls intended for private use. This accounts for the scroll fragments in the Cairo Geniza which contain small amounts of these materials.

Weil, on the basis of ancient manuscripts and fragments, argues the evidence a little differently. After a period of oral transmission, the notes were first copied into manuscripts above and below the pertinent words. As the mass of notes grew, they were moved into Masoretic catalogues. At a later date, the vowels were invented, and after the vowels were stabilized in the text, the Masoretic material was added in the margins. The Mp was devised to reference the material contained in the Mm.[21]

The introduction of the codex among the Jews assisted greatly in the development of the Masorah. The wide margins (top, bottom, and sides) allowed sufficient room for annotating the text with greater amounts of material, and thus the Masorah could be written systematically. The use of the codex among the Jews probably did not begin until about 700 C.E.[22] However, after its introduction, scrolls began to be used less and codices more. Eventually, scrolls were used primarily for synagogue worship and codices were the primary media for writing the Bible text for non-liturgical use.

In summary, we can estimate that the Masoretic period began during the sixth century C.E. We know very little about the early Masoretic activity. We do not know who created the Masorah or how it was accomplished. We do not know who invented the various vocalization systems, including the standard Tiberian system. About the only thing we can say about the Masorah in absolute terms is that it is largely anonymous.

Individual Masoretes

Masoretic notes will occasionally cite the name of a Masorete as an authority for a particular reading. In these cases, we know the name of the Masorete and what opinion he held in the particular case (if the note is accurate). But beyond this, we know very little about individual Masoretes.

Most of the Masoretes cited by name are probably from the latest generations of scholars. Many are cited because of their opinions on matters of vocalization or accents, and so they cannot have been earlier than the graphic signs themselves (e.g., Mp to Job 32:3). Most are probably from much later, although it is impossible to know for sure.

A treatise on the *shewa* which is both anonymous and without title mentions several members of ben Asher's family (discussed below) and the names of several other Tiberian Masoretes. The treatise gives their opinions on various questions, but again, we know little more than their names.

Of interest to students of L and *BHS* are the opinions of Masoretes cited in L as sources of authority. Diaz Esteban published an interesting study which compares the references to Masoretes cited in the Mm of L to other sources.[23] In the limited texts he surveys, Diaz-Esteban notes references to ben Naphtali, ben Asher, the Teachers of Tiberias, the Men of Tiberias, and Phinehas, Head of the Academy. Ben Asher and ben Naphtali will be discussed below.

Phinehas, Head of the Academy, is cited frequently in Masoretic materials. He lived in the first half of the ninth century, or perhaps earlier (Snaith believes about 750 C.E.).[24] He was known for his system of marking vocal *shewas* and his unusual views, but no specific personal information about him is given.[25]

The Teachers of Tiberias and the Men of Tiberias may refer to the same group of individuals. Although the expression is general, Diaz-Esteban believes that it refers to a particular group of Tiberian Masoretes, not the Tiberian school as a whole. He also believes that this group probably predated Moses ben Asher (discussed below).[26] Other names could be mentioned which are cited in L or elsewhere, but information on them is highly speculative.[27]

In the same way that individuals are cited as authorities, manuscripts are also cited. These manuscripts were prepared by learned Masoretes, and they were undoubtedly revered in their time as accurate sources of information (and thus good authorities to cite). Usually these manuscripts are cited by name, but we know nothing about them other than their names and the readings presented by their authority. For example, L cites the readings of *Mahzor Rabba*.[28] Würthwein discusses what little is known about a few of the most often cited manuscripts, such as Codex Hillel and Muga.[29]

The Ben Asher Family

The most famous Masoretes were the members of the ben Asher family. The dynasty began with Asher the Elder, who lived in the second half of the eighth century. The untitled treatise on *shewa* mentioned above notes five generations of ben Ashers, concluding with Moses ben Asher and his son Aaron ben Asher. More information is known about the ben Asher family because they came to be considered outstanding among the various Tiberian parties. The tradition of the last member of the family, Aaron, eventually was revered as best representative of the Tiberian tradition.

Details regarding the life of Moses ben Asher are not known. He probably lived during the last half of the ninth century. Moses ben Asher's most notable accomplishment was the production of a model codex, which we now call the Cairo Codex of the Prophets. The colophon claims that the codex was written in 895 C.E. by Moses ben Asher. This codex has the distinction of being the oldest dated codex known to scholarship. The authenticity of the colophon has been greatly debated, because it appears that the system of vocalization in the Cairo Codex is closer to ben Naphtali than to ben Asher (on the difference, see below). However, Goshen-Gottstein and others have argued that the two systems were very close, and Moses ben Asher probably followed a system different from that of his son, which was still a ben Asher tradition.[30] A facsimile edition of the Cairo Codex is available, as well as a critical edition.[31]

Another codex, British Museum 4445, is also commonly associated with Moses ben Asher because its Masorah occasionally refers to him. This codex is usually dated to sometime in the first half of the tenth century, and there is considerable debate whether Moses was still alive when the codex was written. Moses ben Asher did not write the codex, but it is generally considered to be a good representative of the ben Asher tradition.

The last member of the family, Aaron ben Asher, was the most famous because his system of vocalization, accents, and Masorah eventually gained fame as the best. Aaron lived during the first half of the tenth century, and details about his life are unknown. His accomplishments in preserving the textual tradition, however, are revered until today, and there is a significant amount of material associated with his name.

The *Diqduqe ha-Te'amim* is a Masoretic treatise traditionally attributed to Aaron ben Asher. All of the rules and principles articulated in the *Diqduqe ha-Te'amim* did not originate with Aaron; he collected them and adapted them to his system from manuscripts and other independent treatises. No doubt, he also included some original material in order to elaborate his tradition. The *Diqduqe ha-Te'amim* deals with matters of vocalization and accentuation, particularly with problems concerning *shewa* and *ga'ya*. This treatise is notable, not only because it outlines many principles of Aaron's system, but also because it stands on the border between Masorah and grammar. The treatise is not simply a collection of Masoretic lists; it deals with rules of pointing and the use of *dagesh* in certain forms. These are matters which describe the grammar of the language. The best edition of the *Diqduqe ha-Te'amim* was prepared by Dotan.[32]

Two important manuscripts are associated with Aaron ben Asher. According to its colophon, the Leningrad Codex (L) was prepared in 1008 C.E. by Samuel ben Jacob from exemplars written by Aaron ben Asher. Many erasures are present in the manuscript, probably resulting from corrections intended to bring the codex closer to the tradition of Aaron ben Asher. The reliability of L has been questioned, but it is usually considered a good representative of the Ben Asher tradition. Although this codex was not written by Aaron ben Asher himself, it is probably the most famous of the ben Asher codices because it was chosen as the text for the *BHK*³ and *BHS*. Two facsimile editions of L are available.[33]

The colophon of the Aleppo Codex claims that the text was written by Solomon ben Buya'a, but the vowels, accents, and Masorah were written by Aaron ben Asher himself. Subsequent research has decided that this codex is the best representative of Ben Asher tradition available.[34] Most scholars agree that A dates from the first half of the ninth century. The codex originally contained the whole Hebrew Bible, but portions were lost during a 1947 riot at the synagogue in Aleppo where the codex was kept. Subsequently, it was brought to Jerusalem, where it forms the basis for the Hebrew University Bible Project.[35] There is a tradition that A was the codex cited by the Jewish scholar Maimonides (1135–1204) as exemplary when he was discussing certain matters related to the writing of scrolls. This tradition has been laboriously scrutinized by Goshen-Gottstein.[36] A facsimile edition of the A is available.[37]

The Differences Between Ben Asher and Ben Naphtali

Another Tiberian Masorete who was contemporary with Aaron ben Asher was Moses ben David ben Naphtali. Moses ben Naphtali held to a different tradition of the Bible text, still within the standard Tiberian tradition, and the differences between ben Asher and ben Naphtali are frequently cited in manuscripts and independent treatises. Through the course of time, many lists of the differences between these two Masoretes were created, but often they are full of errors. Since the ben Asher text was viewed as the best, readings which deviated from it were often ascribed to ben Naphtali; however, ben Naphtali did not hold to all of the opinions which were ascribed to him.

The most authoritative treatise on the differences between ben Asher and ben Naphtali was compiled by Mishael ben Uzziel. The treatise was originally in Arabic, entitled *Kithab al-Khilaf*, and the Hebrew version is *Sefer ha-Hillufim* (The Book of the Differences). This treatise is found in various manuscripts, and a critical edition was published by Lipschütz.[38] Although the date of the treatise is disputed, eleventh to twelfth century is a good estimate.[39] Thus, the treatise was compiled from extant sources close to the time period in which the two Masoretes lived, but certainly after their deaths. Most scholars hold that *Kithab al-Khilaf* is the only reliable source we have for the ben Naphtali text. No biblical manuscript is known which consistently adheres to the ben Naphtali readings and principles (the Cairo Codex is the closest; see above).

The treatise opens by outlining eight general rules which were sources of dispute for ben Asher and ben Naphtali. However, the bulk of the work is lists of particular instances, in the order of the Bible text, where the two masters disagreed. Also included are instances where ben Asher and ben Naphtali agreed in opposition to other Masoretes.

Most of the differences are matters of vocalization and accentuation. The two only differed in eight instances regarding the consonantal text.[40] The best known difference between the two deals with the pronunciation of the inseparable prepositions ב,כ, and ל when joined to certain words beginning with יִ, e.g. יִשְׂרָאֵל. Ben Asher pronounced the word בְיִשְׂרָאֵל whereas ben Naphtali pronounced it בִישְׂרָאֵל.[41]

The differences between ben Asher and ben Naphtali are minuscule; the two systems are certainly representative of small variations within the standard Tiberian tradition. In this vein, Goshen-Gottstein commented, "I am afraid...that the vast majority of present-day Bible scholars would not notice without special study any difference in a Ben Naphtali manuscript (if there were one in existence)." Goshen-Gottstein argues further that the similarity between the two systems accounts for the fact that ben Naphtali readings were able to enter subsequent manuscripts of the ben Asher tradition.[42] In essence, the two systems were so close, unobservant (or unaware) scribes could copy ben Naphtali readings into a ben Asher text without noticing any difficulty.

Earlier in this century, Kahle had identified the Non-Conventional Tiberian system with the ben Naphtali system, based on superficial similarities between the two. This led to the view that the systems of ben Asher and ben Naphtali were radically opposed to one another. However, scholarship generally no longer subscribes to this theory, and the prevailing view emphasizes the closeness of ben Asher and ben Naphtali.

The Bible text of Aaron ben Asher did not gain supremacy immediately. As we saw above, the Non-Conventional Tiberian system was still being preserved at the beginning of the twelfth century in Codex Reuchlinianus. Furthermore, statements in Masoretic treatises (discussed below) indicate that, for a time, no preference was given to ben Asher or ben Naphtali. It was only through the course of several centuries that the Aaron ben Asher text was recognized as the authoritative version. Maimonides' great appreciation for Aaron ben Asher's Bible text probably contributed greatly to its ascendancy.

Independent Masoretic Treatises

During the Masoretic Period, independent Masoretic treatises were written, separate from the Masoretic notes transmitted in the margin of manuscripts. Although the material contained in these treatises no doubt originated in the marginal annotations made in manuscripts, these large collections were independent collations, transmitted separately or at the end of manuscripts.

The largest and best known of these treatises is *Okhlah we-Okhlah*. This collection contains about 400 lists, and the treatise gets its title from the first word-pair in the first list. The lists are a mixture of ancient and recent material, making the date of the treatise difficult to determine. Dotan contends that it was not edited before the tenth century, while Yeivin argues for the ninth century.[43] Most of the lists are known from other sources, but the material in *Okhlah we-Okhlah* is more exhaustive.

The lists are arranged alphabetically, and most of the material is topical (that is, the lists deal with the Bible text by topic instead of in the order of the text). Some of the lists are simply fairly routine categories (e.g., *Qere/Ketiv*), but others fall into the category of what Yeivin calls "collative" masorah.[44] Although collative masorah can take different forms, two frequent types of lists are a) words or phrases which are different (and frequently hapax) but share some common category or detail, and b) pairs of words which are similar but differ from one another in some detail. An example of a) is list 72 in Frensdorff's edition, listing words which occur in doublets (i.e., the same word repeated immediately). An example of b) is the first list, an alphabetic list of pairs of unique words, the first one without prefixed *vav*, the second with prefixed *vav*.

Okhlah we-Okhlah was known and used for many centuries, even up to the time of Jacob ben Chayyim and Elias Levita (discussed below). However, after that time the treatise appears to have been forgotten, for we no longer find references to it until recent times. In 1864, Frensdorff published an edition of it based on a manuscript found in Paris.[45] Another edition was published in 1975 by Diaz-Esteban based on a more comprehensive manuscript found in Halle.[46] Both of these are cited in the Masoretic apparatus of *BHS*; the Frensdorff edition is referenced by "Okhl" and the Diaz-Esteban edition by "Okhl II."

In addition to *Okhlah we-Okhlah*, fragments from other treatises of this type were found in the Cairo Geniza. In fact, before the discovery of the Cairo Geniza, *Okhlah we-Okhlah* was the only treatise of this type known to exist. It is possible that some of these treatises are very old, and they, or others like them, were used to collect Masoretic material in the time when it was not allowed to write the material in the margins of scrolls. Some of the Geniza fragments contain collections of material in the order of the biblical text, while others, like *Okhlah we-Okhlah*, are topical.[47]

Masorah Approaches Grammar

Toward the end of the Masoretic Period, treatises were written which approach the line between Masorah and grammar. Masorah is a description of the Hebrew biblical text (i.e., lists of textual peculiarities), and grammar is the description of the Hebrew language itself.[48] The two areas share material in common. Thus, it is not surprising that the Masoretes would become interested in work which we would label by the term Hebrew Grammar. Mention has already been made of the *Diqduqe ha-Te'amim* by Aaron ben Asher. Certainly that treatise falls into this category.

The untitled and anonymous treatise on the *shewa* also can be included here. This treatise is in Arabic, and it is usually dated to the tenth century. Besides giving us some historical data, alluded to above, the treatise also gives us an understanding of the function and problems associated with the use of *shewa* in the Tiberian tradition. Some of the information is known from other sources, but this treatise is distinguished by its comprehensive treatment of the topic. Another notable aspect of this treatise is that it does not choose between ben Asher and ben Naphtali, but instead encourages the reader to "conform to one of the two opinions."[49] The only modern publication of this treatise was prepared by Levy.[50]

Perhaps the most important grammatical treatise is an Arabic work called *Hidayat al-Qari* (The Direction to the Reader). This treatise was adapted and translated several times, with the result that it appears in many different forms, under different titles, and included in other later works. The date of the original work is uncertain, but the tenth century is frequently suggested.[51] The Hebrew versions are called *Horayat ha-Qore* and appear in a number of manuscripts.

This treatise contains many grammatical rules, based on earlier Masorah. It is notable for its systemization, and also for the fact that it does not favor ben Asher over ben Naphtali. In fact, many scholars believe that its rules are closer to ben Naphtali.[52] One version of the treatise was included in the important grammatical work *Adat Devorim*, written by Joseph ha-Qostandini, which Dotan dates to no earlier than the second half of the eleventh century.[53] Another version of the treatise was published by Dérenbourg.[54]

The Close of the Masoretic Period

The Masoretic Period closed with the end of the activity of ben Asher and ben Naphtali (ca. 950 C.E.). By this time, the Tiberian tradition had been fixed with regard to the consonantal text and the vowel and accent signs. Variations within the Tiberian tradition existed, but these were minor details. As we have seen, the last of the Masoretes

iae. Their relative uniformity is a testimony to how monolithic the
tion had become, even by their time. The standard Tiberian tradition
l all other vocalization systems, and the ben Asher system was
curate representative of the Tiberian tradition.
rom the time period 950 to 1100, and obviously anything earlier,
they are rare.[55] By the end of this period, the last Masoretes were
was made to maintain their traditions. Thus, for example, L comes
th century, and it attempts to be faithful to Aaron ben Asher's

anuscripts were copied with less care. Often, several exemplars
ring the new manuscript, without any thought about the individual
i those exemplars. The result was that the new manuscript would
nt Tiberian traditions. Furthermore, Masoretic notes were added
ferent sources, and many times the notes were not consistent with
new manuscript. The result was a Masorah which disagreed with
preserve. Unfortunately, manuscripts from the twelfth century
e plentiful than earlier manuscripts; Yeivin estimates that more
These manuscripts, however, because of their mixed nature, are
of the Masorah.
y copyists had no understanding of the Masorah, and its pur-
xt tradition—was nullified. The Masoretic notes were copied in

the wrong places, were used as fillers, and worst of all, were copied into ornate patterns as decorations for the manuscripts. These manuscripts show how serious study of Masorah and text tradition had decreased toward the end of the Middle Ages.

Continuation of Work on the Masorah

Although the Masoretic Period properly concluded about 950, work on the Masorah and the preservation/clarification of the textual tradition has continued. The following is simply a short list of persons who have made significant contributions.

Meir ben Todros ha-Levi Abulafia (1180–1244) wrote the book *Masoret Siyag la-Torah*, which is concerned with the consonantal text in the Torah. The work is arranged like a lexicon, in the order of word roots. His primary topic is plene/defective spelling (based on the Masoretic material available to him), but the treatise also covers issues in the writing of Torah Scrolls (e.g. the layout of the Songs, etc.). The book had tremendous influence on subsequent copyists and publishers.

Menahem ha-Meiri (1249–1306) wrote *Kiryat Sefer*, a two-part treatise dealing first with rules for writing Torah Scrolls, and second with Masoretic matters. The second section gives rules for correct pronunciation and lists of Masoretic information, such as an account of plene/defective spellings in the Torah, etc. An appendix includes other matters of the Masorah, such as the open and closed sections and the number of words, etc., in the Bible.

Jekuthiel ha-Naqdan (dates uncertain, late twelfth to thirteenth century) wrote the treatise *'Ein ha-Qore*, a study of details affecting proper reading in the Torah, Esther, and Lamentations. This treatise is primarily concerned with vowels and accents, not spelling, and the first section is a description of the system of stress in biblical Hebrew. The second section is a collection of masoretic materials organized into the order of the biblical text. Jekuthiel's work was based on manuscripts and the work of various grammarians who preceded him. The treatise, like *Masoret Siyag la-Torah*, had tremendous influence on subsequent copyists and publishers.[57]

Students of the Masorah owe Jacob ben Chayyim ibn Adonijah (dates uncertain, late fifteenth to sixteenth century) a great debt of gratitude, because he rescued the Masorah and restored it to its original function, the preservation of the text tradition. Ben Chayyim came to Italy around 1510 to escape persecution. In Venice, Daniel Bomberg's press specialized in Hebrew books, and ben Chayyim entered his employ about 1517 as a corrector. Bomberg had already published the *First Rabbinic Bible*, edited by Felix Pratensis (1516–17), but he was planning a new edition.[58] The first edition had not been received well by Christians because of its Jewish emphasis, and Jews were not pleased that its editor, Pratensis, was a Jew converted to Christianity. Ben Chayyim, a learned Jew skilled in the Bible text, seemed an obvious choice to prepare the second edition.

Bomberg and ben Chayyim searched for good manuscripts on which to base the *Second Rabbinic Bible*, and ben Chayyim began preparing the volume. He wanted to include the Masorah in this new volume, but by this time the Masorah had fallen into disuse and was reduced to mere ornamentation in many manuscripts. Thus, ben Chayyim had to select, order, analyze, and correct the material from his sources and collate it into his new edition. The *Second Rabbinic Bible* appeared in 1524–25. Ben Chayyim converted to Christianity in 1527, leaving Bomberg with the same problem he had with Pratensis. Ben Chayyim's name was omitted from subsequent editions of the Bible.[59]

The Mm and the Mp appeared in the margins, but ben Chayyim's significant contribution and innovation was his Mf. The Mf listed the Masorah Magna material arranged in lexical order. Many of the lists, especially longer lists, were printed in their entirety. In other cases, only the heading of the list was printed in the Mf, and a cross reference was given to the location where the list was elaborated in the Mm. If a list was not elaborated in the Mm, a cross-reference was given to the Mf. Thus, the Masorah was organized into an orderly system by which the reader could find the lists either in the text or alphabetically in the Mf.

Ben Chayyim's text was received with great authority and became a sort of "textus receptus," even until the twentieth century. Likewise, his version of the Masorah, which was the first printed Masorah, came to be viewed as a codification of the Masorah, as if exclusively it were the standard Masorah (which explains why references in the older literature to "the Masorah" or "the printed Masorah" refer to the Masorah of the *Second Rabbinic Bible*). Frensdorff published an index to the Mm and Mf, and this volume contains many valuable notes on problems in the Masorah of the *Second Rabbinic Bible.*[60]

In spite of ben Chayyim's valuable work (and there was none like it before his time or for centuries afterward), the volume is not without fault. Ben Chayyim established the text which seemed most correct to him, based on the material he had, and it is close to what we know about the ben Asher text. In this respect, ben Chayyim's text is "a good representative of the Tiberian tradition."[61] However, ben Chayyim, who tells us little about his sources, had only late medieval manuscripts to work with, originating close to his own time.[62] These manuscripts represented a mixture of traditions, which were further mixed in ben Chayyim's text (and Masorah). Thus, the *Second Rabbinic Bible* is not viewed as a pure ben Asher text, and its status has diminished with the discovery of better, older manuscripts and the refinement of critical methodology.

Elias Levita (1468–1549) has been called the father of Masoretic Studies because of his immense contributions. Actually, Levita (also known by the names Elijah Bachur, Elijah ben Asher ha-Levi Ashkenazi, and a few others) was active in many areas of Hebrew literature. He was a poet, grammarian (producing several grammars, one of which was plagiarized), lexicographer, and student of the Masorah.

Throughout his life, Levita wrote and published many volumes in these various areas. His works on the Masorah come primarily from his time at Venice (1527–1540), where he worked at Bomberg's press as a corrector and editor (shortly after ben Chayyim's departure). In 1536, Levita produced a massive work entitled *Book of Remembrance*, which was a Masoretic concordance to the Hebrew Bible, but it was never published.

Levita's primary contribution to Masoretic Studies was his book *Massoreth ha-Massoreth* (1538), a guidebook and commentary on the Masorah. After some prefatory material, the book is organized into three introductions and three sections (First Tables, Second Tables, and Broken Tables.) In the third introduction, Levita argued that the vowel points did not originate in antiquity but instead were added by the Masoretes sometime after the close of the Talmud. Levita's study into the origin of the Masorah was met by a storm of controversy, since it went against the prevailing pious Jewish opinion that the vowel signs either originated at Sinai or were established by Ezra.

The rest of the work is an examination of many topics in the study of the Masorah. First Tables discusses plene and defective spellings. Second Tables is a collection of miscellaneous topics, including a discussion of *Qere/Ketiv* and significant technical terms. Broken Tables is a discussion of the abbreviations used in the Masorah and a survey of a few Masoretes known to Levita. Ginsburg republished *Massoreth ha-Massoreth* in 1867, and it was reissued in 1968, coupled with Ginsburg's version of Ben Chayyim's *Introduction to the Rabbinic Bible*.[63]

Menahem ben Judah di Lonzano (end of sixteenth century) wrote the treatise *Or Torah* in which the vowel and the accent signs in the Torah are discussed in the order of the biblical text. His work is based on various manuscripts and the work of previous scholars, such as Levita. Lonzano's work is significant because he discusses errors in the *Second Rabbinic Bible* which were corrected in subsequent editions.

Jedidiah Solomon Raphael ben Abraham of Norzi (first half of seventeenth century) wrote the treatise *Minhat Shay* (1626). This is frequently referred to as the most important Masoretic treatise ever written, because of its comprehensiveness. After an introduction, *Minhat Shay* includes notes on the whole Bible text. The notes cover the consonantal text, vowels, and accents. "His comments bear upon almost every word about which there is room for error, a variant reading, or any other problem."[64] In addition to manuscripts, Norzi based his work on the writings of the previously mentioned scholars as well as famous Hebrew grammarians. Norzi particularly revered the work of Lonzano and, like him, offered corrections to the text of the *Second Rabbinic Bible*. Because of Norzi's immense scholarship and authority in textual matters, editors used his work as a basis for making corrections in Bible editions. *Minhat Shay* was not printed until 1742, and it frequently was printed in expanded Bible editions, such as Rabbinic Bibles.

Seeligmann Isaac Baer (1825–1897) was a meticulous student of the Masorah and text tradition who published an edition of *Diqduqe ha-Te'amim* (with H.L. Strack, 1879) and other works on the accents. However, Baer's most significant publication was his edition of the Bible, commonly called the Baer-Delitzsch edition (1869–1895). This edition was very popular in the nineteenth century, and the Gesenius-Kautzsch-Cowley grammar is based on it. Baer's edition was based on other earlier editions and manuscripts, but his primary goal was to reconstruct the original ben Asher text as precisely as possible.

To that end, Baer developed his own rules for accents and *ga'yah*s based on his study of Masoretic sources and manuscripts. These rules are not unrelated to the Tiberian usage and could in fact be seen as a development of it.[65] However, Baer's system does not reflect the situation in Hebrew manuscripts, and his edition is now viewed as arbitrary and artificial. Likewise, Baer felt free to include readings (ben Asher/ben Naphtali, etc.) which do not represent manuscript tradition. Thus, although Baer's edition was enormously influential in the last century (and through Gesenius even today), it has now given way to critical editions based on good manuscripts or a single manuscript, such as *BHS*.

Christian David Ginsburg (1831–1914) can be mentioned here, if for no other reason than for the volume of Masoretic material he published. One primary contribution was *The Massorah Compiled from Manuscripts* (1880–1905), which is a massive four volume collection of Masoretic treatises and notes. In volumes 1–2, he lists in lexical order Masoretic notes that he found in manuscripts. Volume 3 is a supplement of other material. Volume 4 is a commentary on volume 1, and Ginsburg's discussions there are invaluable for deciphering difficult Masoretic notes. Ginsburg could not find financial backing for the commentary on volume 2. Unfortunately, Ginsburg was not systematic in collecting this material, his sources are not normally cited (except in volume 4), and his manuscripts were usually not very old.

Another significant contribution was his *Introduction to the Massoretico-Critical Edition of the Hebrew Bible* (1897), in which he discusses every significant issue in the study of the Masorah. The volume also describes a large number of Hebrew manuscripts and gives a history of printed editions. This book, in spite of its age, is still an essential reference for students of the Masorah.

Ginsburg also produced several editions of the Bible, and the notes on variants listed there are very helpful. They cover over 70 manuscripts and 19 printed editions. Although Ginsburg's edition is comprehensive in this respect, it suffers from the same problem as *The Massorah*. The manuscripts are not very old (primarily thirteenth century and later) and most are from the British Museum (including, however, B.M. 4445). And like Baer, Ginsburg often introduced changes in the text based on his material, and the result is a text which probably never existed.[66]

Paul Ernst Kahle (1875–1965), like Ginsburg, contributed to Masoretic Studies through his many publications. Unlike Ginsburg, however, he emphasized the necessity of distinguishing between different individual traditions and studying them separately. Kahle recognized the value of the ben Asher tradition, and he was responsible for using a single ben Asher manuscript, L, as the basis for the *BHK* 3. This was a significant departure from the usual practice of critical editions, such as *BHK* 1 and 2, which used ben Chayyim's text as their basis. Kahle also popularized the importance of studying non-standard traditions, like the Babylonian and Palestinian graphic systems, and he published many fragments from these traditions.[67]

Gérard E. Weil (1926–1986) was active in many areas of Masoretic Studies before his sudden death in 1986. He introduced the use of the computer into the field, creating a computerized version of L which he used to study its accentuation. Although Weil wrote extensively on the Masorah (see the bibliography) his most famous contribution was his edition of the Masorah of L for *BHS*. Weil systematized and completed the Masorah of L for *BHS* and published the Mm in a separate volume. This was the first time that the complete Mp and Mm of a specific manuscript had been published, and his revisions were intended to make it easier for the novice to use them.

Currently, the field of Masoretic Studies is supported by the International Organization for Masoretic Studies (IOMS), an organization founded by Harry Orlinsky in

1972. Some of the most notable scholars in the field are Aron Dotan, E. J. Revell, and Israel Yeivin.

Notes

[1]M.H. Goshen-Gottstein, "The Rise of the Tiberian Bible Text," in *Biblical and Other Studies*, ed. A. Altmann (Cambridge: Harvard University Press, 1963), p. 112 ff. Würthwein adopts this term in his popular book *The Text of the Old Testament* (Grand Rapids, MI: Eerdmans, 1995) p. 26, n. 49.

[2]A. Dotan, "Masorah," *Encyclopedia Judaica* (Jerusalem: Macmillan Co., 1971) XVI:1464–66.

[3]Ibid., col. 1461–63.

[4]Ibid., col. 1463–64; Goshen-Gottstein, "Tiberian Bible Text," p. 112.

[5]This terminology, which seems to be the clearest, is used throughout Yeivin's book *Introduction to the Tiberian Masorah*, trans. and ed. E.J. Revell, The Society of Biblical Literature Masoretic Studies, No. 5 (Missoula, MT: Scholars Press, 1980).

[6]Yeivin, *Tiberian Masorah*, pp. 132–135.

[7]This observation is evidenced in *BHS* by the Hebrew letters representing numbers below the Arabic numeral for each psalm. Psalms 1 and 2 are numbered separately. Notice, however, that Psalms 114 and 115 are treated as one, yielding 149 psalms in the book. This is the total number of psalms according to the Masorah.

[8]Yeivin, *Tiberian Masorah*, p. 135.

[9]Ibid.

[10]On the standardization of the reading tradition, see E.J. Revell, "Masoretic Text," in *The Anchor Bible Dictionary* (New York, NY: Doubleday, 1992) IV:599, who argues for a date of 500 CE or earlier.

[11]This is the time period argued by Yeivin (*Tiberian Masorah*, p. 164), but others argue for a similar period; see Dotan, "Masorah," col. 1416–17.

[12]Dotan, "Masorah," col. 1416.

[13]Ibid., col. 1417.

[14]A geniza is a storage room where worn or defective manuscripts can be kept until they can be disposed of ritually. The Cairo Geniza was such a room found in a synagogue in Old Cairo which yielded thousands of fragments. Some of the earlier fragments come from the Masoretic Period, but many are later. For brief sketches, see Würthwein, *The Text of the Old Testament*, p. 11 and Yeivin, *Tiberian Masorah*, pp. 30–31.

[15]Yeivin, *Tiberian Masorah*, pp. 123, 164.

[16]A. Dotan, "The Relative Chronology of Hebrew Vocalization and Accentuation," *Proceedings of the American Academy for Jewish Research* 48 (1981) 87–99.

[17]Ibid., pp. 10–12.

[18]Yeivin, *Tiberian Masorah*, p. 123.

[19]For an argument along these lines, see E.J. Revell, "Masorah," in *The Anchor Bible Dictionary* (New York, NY: Doubleday, 1992) IV:593.

[20]See Yeivin, *Tiberian Masorah*, pp. 36–38, for information on the rules regarding Synagogue Scrolls.

[21]G.E. Weil, "La nouvelle édition de La Massorah et l'histoire de la Massorah," *Supplements to Vetus Testamentum* 9 (1962) 270–271.

[22]This date is Yeivin's; see *Tiberian Masorah*, p. 7. Also see Dotan, "Masorah," col.

1416.

[23]F. Diaz-Esteban, "References to Ben Asher and Ben Naftali in the Masora Magna Written in the Margins of MS Leningrad B19a," *Textus* 6 (1968) 62–74. Dotan notes references in the Mp of L to many of these same individuals in "Masorah," col. 1423.

[24]N.H. Snaith, "Prolegomenon," in Ginsburg's *Jacob Ben Chayim Ibn Adonijah's Introduction to the Rabbinic Bible and the Massoreth Ha-Massoreth of Elias Levita* (New York, NY: Ktav, 1968) p. XXII.

[25]For more information on Phinehas, see Dotan, "Masorah," col. 1416, 1471; Diaz-Esteban, "References," pp. 65–66; Yeivin, *TiberianMasorah*, pp. 137–38.

[26]Diaz-Esteban, "References," pp. 65, 72–73.

[27]For information and readings of a few others, see Yeivin, *TiberianMasorah*, pp. 137–38 and Dotan, "Masorah," col. 1471–72.

[28]Diaz-Esteban, "References," p. 66.

[29]Würthwein, *The Text of the Old Testament*, p. 38.

[30]Goshen-Gottstein, "Tiberian Bible Text," p. 103–8.

[31]D.S. Loewinger, ed., *Cairo Codex of the Bible* (Jerusalem: Makor Publishing, 1971). F.P. Castro, ed. *El Códice de Profetas de al Cairo*, Pretacio, Tomos I–VIII (Madrid: CSIC, 1979–1992).

[32]A. Dotan, ed., *Sefer Dikduke ha-Te'amim* (Jerusalem: Academy of the Hebrew Language, 1967).

[33]D.S. Loewinger, *Codex Leningrad B19a* (Jerusalem: Makor Publishing, 1970) and A. B. Beck, ed., *The Leningrad Codex: A Facsimile Edition* (Grand Rapids, MI: Eerdmans, 1997).

[34]For a survey of the indicators, see Yeivin, *TiberianMasorah*, pp. 16–18.

[35]For a summary of the Project, see Würthwein, *The Text of the Old Testament*, pp. 43–44.

[36]M.H. Goshen-Gottstein, "The Authenticity of the Aleppo Codex," *Textus* 1 (1960) 17–58.

[37] M.H. Goshen-Gottstein, *The Aleppo Codex* (Jerusalem: Magnes Press, 1976).

[38]L. Lipschütz, *Kitab al-Kilaf, the Book of Hillufim* (Jerusalem: Magnes Press, 1965).

[39]Ibid., p. 1.

[40]Ibid., p. 16.

[41]See rule 7, Ibid., p. 18.

[42]Goshen-Gottstein, "Tiberian Bible Text," p. 108; quotation from 111.

[43]Dotan, "Masorah," col. 1428; Yeivin, *TiberianMasorah*, p. 130.

[44]Yeivin, *TiberianMasorah*, pp. 78–80.

[45]S. Frensdorff, *Das Buch Ochlah W'ochlah* (1864; rpt. New York: Ktav, 1972).

[46]E.F. Diaz-Esteban, *Sefer Oklah we-Oklah* (Madrid: Consejo Superior de Investigaciones Cientificos, 1975).

[47]For more information on this material, see Yeivin, *TiberianMasorah*, pp. 127–28.

[48]See Yeivin, *TiberianMasorah*, p. 149, for this distinction between Masorah and grammar and his helpful discussion on how grammatical ideas were developed in the Masorah and assisted later grammarians.

[49]Lipschütz, *Kitab al-Kilaf*, p. 3.

[50]K. Levy, *Zur Masoretischen Grammatik*, Bonner Orientalistische Studien, No. 15 (Stuttgart: Kohlhammer, 1936). See also Dotan, "Masorah," col. 1475.

[51]Yeivin, *TiberianMasorah*, p. 161; Dotan, "Masorah," col. 1475, and for a good summary

of the various transformations of the treatise, see col. 1473–75.

[52]Dotan, "Masorah," col. 1475.

[53]Ibid., col. 1474.

[54]J. Dérenbourg, "Manuel du lecteur d'un auteur inconnu," *Journal Asiatique* , 6ème série, Tome xvi (1870) 309–550.

[55]The division of manuscripts into two groups in this section is based on Yeivin's careful survey of important manuscripts. See Yeivin, *Tiberian Masorah*, pp. 12–29.

[56]Yeivin, *Tiberian Masorah*, p. 29.

[57]For a more detailed study of *'Ein ha-Qore*, see R. Yarkoni, "Yequti'el ha-Naqdan—One of the Last Masoretes or an Early Ashkenazi Grammarian," in *Estudios Masoreticos: Proceedings of the 10th Congress of IOMS* (Madrid: Instituto de Filología, CSIC, 1993) pp. 139–49.

[58]A Rabbinic Bible is an expanded version including the Hebrew text, Targum, and various commentaries; see Würthwein, *The Text of the Old Testament*, p. 39.

[59]Snaith, "Prolegomenon," p. VIII.

[60]S. Frensdorff, *Die Massora Magna* (1876; rpt. New York, NY: Ktav, 1968).

[61]Yeivin, *Tiberian Masorah*, p. 15, and see there for an evaluation of the text. Also see pp. 31–32, 125–26 for more information on the *Second Rabbinic Bible* .

[62]Yeivin estimates none were earlier than the twelfth century (*Tiberian Masorah*, p. 31).

[63]C.D. Ginsburg, *Jacob Ben Chayyim Ibn Adonijah's Introduction to the Rabbinic Bible and the Massoreth Ha-Massoreth of Elias Levita* (New York, NY: Ktav, 1968).

[64]Dotan, "Masorah," col. 1477.

[65]For a meticulous discussion of Baer's system, see Snaith, "Prolegomenon," pp. XX–XXXVI.

[66]For a good review of his Bible editions, see Würthwein, *The Text of the Old Testament*, pp. 41–2. For publication on Ginsburg's other works, including those not mentioned here, see the bibliography.

[67]See the bibliography for Kahle's most significant publications.

Chapter 3

The Proto-Masoretic Text

Introduction

The reader may notice that this chapter deals with the "Proto-" rather than "Pre-" Masoretic text. Since the work of the Masoretes was to add the vowels, accents, and Masoretic notes to the consonantal text, how can a text be "Proto-Masoretic" ("first or beginning") when it actually pre-dates the Masoretes?

The consonantal text which is the basis of the Masoretic text (𝔐) attained ascendancy over other Hebrew textual traditions during the Second Temple period and became authoritative by the second century C.E. (perhaps so designated by the synod of Jabneh[1]). Because of this dominance, 𝔐 is represented by a very large number of manuscripts. Since this established consonantal text consistently served as the basis for the Masoretes' work, it has come to be called "Proto-Masoretic" and even, occasionally, and anachronistically, the "Masoretic Text."[2] The Masoretes worked to maintain this received text tradition as faithfully as possible. At times the text tradition contained some irregularities or peculiar features. These were transmitted with utmost fidelity, just like the rest of the textual tradition. In some cases it seems they transmitted things which they did not understand fully.

The purpose of this chapter is to catalog and discuss the various types of textual irregularities which were encountered by the Masoretes and consequently passed on to modern times. Here it should be emphasized that these peculiarities were not the creation of the Masoretic scholars. Instead, they were part of the tradition which the Masoretes received (hence the title of this chapter). These features antedate the contributions of Masoretes.

These proto-Masoretic peculiarities will be discussed in two groups. First, there are some orthographic irregularities in the text itself. These are odd letters and points which were written among the characters of the sacred text. They form part of the written text tradition. Second, there are peculiarities concerning the text which do not appear among the characters themselves. These are matters of oral tradition which address the proper interpretation and reading of the text. While the items in this second category take us beyond the strict topic of "irregularities within the proto-Masoretic text," they are nonetheless important for understanding the textual oddities received by the Masoretes.

Orthographic Irregularities

When discussing orthographic irregularities of the Bible, one must carefully distinguish the text from the Masoretic additions. The Masoretes supplied accents, notes, and vocalization symbols for the text tradition, but they would not alter the text itself. The odd features discussed below are part of the text tradition itself which the Masoretes received and worked to preserve. Because these features are oddities, they are often mentioned in Masoretic treatises and other rabbinic sources antedating the Masoretes.

Many of these peculiarities are not uniform among the Masoretic manuscripts and treatises. Neither are they uniform among the rabbinic witnesses. Their number and location vary from source to source. The discussions that follow will attempt to mention all of the examples of these peculiarities that appear in *BHS*.

Nequdoth or Extraordinary Points (*Puncta Extraordinaria*)

At fifteen places in *BHS*, dots appear over the words of the text. Usually the dots occur over one or more letters of a single word. In one case, the dots appear over a group of words (Deut. 29:28); in another the dots appear both over and under a word (Ps. 27:13). The following list shows the ten times in the Torah (first listed in the halachic commentary *Sifre* 69 to Num. 9:10), four times in the Prophets, and a single time in the Writings that the extraordinary points occur and the words so marked:

passage	words with extraordinary points
Gen. 16:5	ובינך
Gen. 18:9	אליו
Gen. 19:33	ובקומה
Gen. 33:4	וישקהו
Gen. 37:12	את
Num. 3:39	ואהרן
Num. 9:10	רחקה
Num. 21:30	אשר
Num. 29:15	ועשרון
Deut. 29:28	לנו ולבנינו
2 Sam. 19:20	יצא
Isa. 44:9	המה
Ezek. 41:20	ההיכל
Ezek. 46:22	מהקצעות
Ps. 27:13	לולא

Dotan has collected many references to these points from ancient sources.[3] Evidence for some of them goes back to the second century C.E. The Babylonian Masoretes also marked these words and added some extra dotted words. Yet, the Babylonian tradition is not consistent with itself on the number and location of these other words.[4]

Yeivin grouped the proposed explanations for the extraordinary points into three categories.[5] 1) The dots indicate that the letters should be erased. Dots were used for this purpose in various early codices and in the Dead Sea Scrolls. 2) The dots indicate some doubt about the textual tradition for these words. 3) The dots relate to midrashic commentary and indicate nothing about the certainty of the text transition. They were intended to emphasize a special interpretation of the word. We should add a fourth explanation which is commonly found in the literature: these words were dotted because of doctrinal reservations.

Each of the explanations can account for one or more of the dotted words, but none of them can explain every occurrence. For example, Butin has vigorously argued theory 1: the dots indicate that the letters beneath them should be deleted. His opinion is supported by אֲשֶׁר in Num. 21:30.[6] The ר is dotted, and it is indeed omitted by the Samaritan Pentateuch and the LXX. Ginsburg agrees here, although he uses the LXX to make more radical changes to the Masoretic text.[7] This explanation also works for Num. 3:39, since ואהרן is lacking in some Hebrew manuscripts as well as the Samaritan and Syriac versions.[8]

Theory 1 does not apply so well in Num. 29:15 with וְעִשָּׂרוֹן עִשָּׂרוֹן. The only dotted letter is the second ו in the first word of the pair, and there appears to be no sufficient reason for deleting it. We could conclude that the deletion theory does not apply here. Butin, however, argues at length that, originally, dots were placed over every letter and that the one surviving dotted letter is intended to be representative of the whole word.[9] Thus, the first occurrence, וְעִשָּׂרוֹן, should be deleted.[10]

While Butin's research is thorough, the textual evidence for deleting the first word is very slight, which does not help the case. In a similar type of argument, Butin can make sense of Genesis 18:9 only by claiming that the dots have been misplaced.[11]

The אֶת in Gen. 37:12 defies explanation by any theory. It amounts to accepting or deleting a direct object marker. Ginsburg wanted to delete everything to the end of the verse, but that suggestion has not been generally accepted.[12]

Even if one of these theories could account for the extraordinary points, questions would still remain. Why were these words dotted and no others? Certainly the text tradition is in doubt in more places than these fifteen. Likewise, midrashic comment extends far beyond the confines of the dotted words. Furthermore, the relationship of the extraordinary points to other means of marking uncertain texts (e.g., *Ketiv/Qere*) is equally unclear. A tremendous amount of discussion has been devoted to unraveling the mystery of the extraordinary points. Perhaps this was simply a method by which the early scribes noted a variety of issues regarding the text. If this is so, the only thing the passages have in common is that there is some issue in each.

Inverted *Nun* or Isolated *Nunim* (*Nunim haphukah* or *Nunim m^e nuzarot*)

This phenomenon is designated by either of the above names. The sign assumed various forms. In some traditions it is described as כ and in Greek (especially Alexandrine) sources it is described as reversed *sigma* (antisigma).[13] In Greek texts the meaning of these signs was that the information enclosed between sigma and antisigma did not fit in its current place in the text. It was a subtle means of removing material from the larger text.[14] The inverted ׆ occurs at nine places in the Bible. In *BHS*, the sign resembles a נ turned backwards with a dot above it (׆̇).

Sources agree on the placement of the first two inverted נs. They appear after Num. 10:34 and 10:36. Apparently, they were intended to bracket out the closed paragraph composed by Numbers 10:35–36. The location of the other seven occurrences is less certain. Some manuscripts and ancient authorities place the inverted נs before Ps. 107:21–26, 40. The editors of *BHS* did not alter that arrangement.

Although ancient sources were replete with information regarding inverted נ, the situation is marked by disparity. They are frequently called "signs" (סימניות) rather than letters, indicating that these passages were not always marked by a Hebrew letter. The Jewish halachic commentary *Sifre* on Numbers, section 84, relates that Num. 10:35–36 "is dotted (נקוד) before it and after it because this is not its place."[15] This quotation implies that the passages in question were designated by dots, not letters.

Since the exact form of the sign was not prescribed, it assumed various shapes. The name for the phenomenon varied as well. Eventually, the shape of the sign developed into a reversed נ. When this occurred, the name was interchanged with other instances of reversed נ, a phenomenon not occurring in L (and so not reproduced in *BHS*) and unrelated to the isolated letters.[16]

Why did the נ sign develop out of this diverse history and plethora of sigla? It has been suggested that ׆̇ is an abbreviation for נקוד, "dotted."[17] The persons responsible for ׆̇ knew of the tradition that these passages were once distinguished by dots. Perhaps they knew the *Sifre* Numbers tradition directly. In any case, the dots were deemed insufficient to distinguish the passages adequately. Thus they were replaced with the first letter of the word designated a dotted word or passage, a נ for נקוד. They were turned backwards to distinguish them from the letters of the text itself.

Ginsburg followed one of the explanations in the *Sifre* Numbers passage to explain the purpose of the inverted נ for Num. 10:35–36: the signs were intended to show that the text was dislocated, not in its proper place.[18] This suggestion is supported by the LXX where verses 35–36 have been inserted between verses 33 and 34 (i.e., the order is

33, 35, 36, 34). But *Sifre* Numbers 84 also makes the suggestion that the passage is set off in this way to show that "when the ark set out..." should be treated as a separate scroll.[19] Tov says this indicates that the two scribal traditions indicate a similar situation, i.e., uncertainty.[20]

Ginsburg also championed this explanation for Ps. 107:40. He argued that verse 40 should be inserted between verses 38 and 39. With this transposition, the subject for verse 39 is supplied and the logic of the passage is improved.[21] We should note that *BHS* also suggests this transposition in note [a] for verse 39. No adequate suggestion has been made for the purpose of the other occurrences of ׆ in this passage.[22]

Suspended Letters (Litterae Suspensae אותיות תלויות)

Four letters in the Bible are written above their normal position and are thus called suspended letters. The Masoretic manuscripts are uniform in marking these instances. In spite of the uniformity in position, these letters appear to perform a variety of functions. The suspended letters can be found in Judg. 18:30; Ps. 80:14; Job 38:13 and 15.

The נ in מְנשֶׁה (Judg. 18:30) appears to be an insertion intended to change the name of Moses to Manasseh. The motive was to spare Moses the bad reputation involved in having an idolatrous priest for a grandson (Jonathan). (Compare the *Tiqqune Sopherim* regarding Moses later in this chapter.) Ginsburg demonstrates that many of the ancient interpreters knew better anyway.[23]

All of the other three instances involve suspended ע. The ע in מִיָּער (Ps. 80:14) has generally been explained as calling attention to the middle letter of the Psalms. This suggestion may be true, although large letters are generally found elsewhere fulfilling that function. Others have noticed that the ע may have originally been a large letter which was subsequently mistaken for a suspended letter.[24] Ginsburg cleverly argues that the ע was a true suspended letter. He begins by noting that the weak letters ע and א were frequently not written in the consonantal text. The original form of the word would have been מיר. He then quotes rabbinic evidence to show that this word was subsequently understood in two ways by different traditions, one reading an א ("river") and the other reading an ע ("forest"). His conclusion is that the ע is suspended to conserve the variant traditions.[25]

Ginsburg argues less effectively for a similar situation standing behind the two suspended עs in Job 38:13 and 15.[26] Along very different lines, Yeivin suggests that the letters may simply represent a correction where the ע, once omitted, was added above the line. He claims that this was a common form of correction in the Dead Sea Scrolls, especially with ע.[27] Thus, Ginsburg's theory of linking the suspended letters with two interpretive traditions may need to be reevaluated. Tov says that all of these suspended letters were meant as corrections to the text.[28] McCarthy, on the other hand, maintains that the four did not have a common origin, pointing out that in the earlier sources which mention them, they are not related to each other.[29]

Large Letters

The use of letters larger than usual was never legally fixed. Thus, instances of large letters varies among the manuscripts. Older manuscripts generally have fewer of these than later manuscripts.[30] L only has three large letters. The editors of *BHS* have added one more, although the critical notes often mention others. The following list gives the location of these.

passage	word	L	*BHS*
Lev. 11:42	גָּחוֹן		x
Num. 27:5	מִשְׁפָּטָן	x	x
Deut. 6:4	שְׁמַע	x	x
Deut. 6:4	אֶחָד	x	x

Yeivin notes three categories for the function of the large letters: 1) the letter stands at the beginning of a book or at the beginning of a new section; 2) the letter draws attention to a significant statistical point, e.g., the large letter in Lev. 11:42 marks the middle of the Torah in letters; 3) the letter shows that the reading must be precise.[31] This is probably the function of the large letters in Deut. 6:4. In other cases, like Num. 27:5, the reason for the large letter is lost.

Small Letters

Some of what was said for the large letters holds for the small letters as well: the manuscripts vary, and the older manuscripts show fewer instances. The number of small letters is consistently less than the number of large letters. There are only three in L, all of which are reproduced in *BHS*. These three cases each involve final ן and are called נונין זעירין in the Mp. The list below gives their locations. It has been suggested, though, that the small letters may have served one of two purposes: 1) the letters hint at an alternative textual tradition, or 2) the letters were intended as corrections but their meaning was forgotten.[32] The differences between the various printed editions and their notes may be seen by comparing Gen. 2:4 in *BHS* and *BHK*³. In *BHS*, the word בְּהִבָּרְאָם carries the editor's note "frt l בְּבָרְאָם אֱלֹהִים." The reader might easily think the only difference is the addition of אֱלֹהִים. But *BHK*³ has a fuller note, "mlt MSS ה min; l בְּבָרְאָם אֱלֹהִים." This note informs the reader that a variant tradition is noted by the presence of a small ה (ה minusculum), which would change the infinitive from a Nif'al to a Qal.

passage	word
Isa. 44:14	אֹרֶן
Jer. 39:13	וּנְבוּשַׁזְבָּן
Prov. 16:28	וְנִרְגָּן

One of the basic difficulties with treating the large and small letters in this section comes in determining whether these instances are part of the Proto-Masoretic tradition at all, or whether they are the work of the Masoretes themselves.

Other Orthographic Peculiarities

Some manuscripts have other letters formed oddly, but historical information on many of these is lacking. At times, the information known about the character is limited to its name. Most of these letters do not appear in L or *BHS*.[33]

Yeivin suggests that some of these odd features may only be a matter of the *taggim* (crowns), strokes used to decorate certain letters.[34] If so, then the letters themselves represent no true textual irregularity. This could be the case for "rolled-up פ," found frequently in Yemenite manuscripts, and the two instances of "attached ק" (Exod. 32:25; Num. 7:2).

In some manuscripts Gen. 11:32 contains an inverted נ which is actually part of a word. Other orthographic irregularities are "broken ו" (Num. 25:12), "crooked נ" (Exod. 3:19), and "מ *apertum*" (medial מ where ם is expected, Num. 2:13). "ם *clausum*" occurs in the word לםרבה (ם where מ is expected, Isa. 9:6) and is preserved in *BHS*.

Irregularities Mentioned in Oral Tradition

Some textual oddities which the Masoretes received do not appear in the written text; they are not orthographic irregularities. Instead, they are matters of oral tradition that give directions concerning the proper interpretation or reading of the text. This category, like the former, is also characterized by inconsistency among the historical sources with regard to the specifics of these peculiarities.

***Tiqqune Sopherim* (The Emendations of the Scribes)**

A Masoretic tradition lists eighteen passages which have been emended for theological reasons. These changes were attributed to earlier scribes who designed the emendations to remove irreverent expressions concerning God. One of these emendations removes an irreverent expression concerning Moses (Num. 12:12).

The most complete lists are found in the Masorah to certain manuscripts. Ginsburg discusses the particular Masoretic manuscripts.[35] Rabbinic sources also mention some of the emendations.

These alterations were made through slight changes in the text. The change may be the omission of one consonant or, occasionally, more than one. The emendations were also effected through the transposition of consonants. In other cases, the word order has been altered.

A good example of the *Tiqqune Sopherim* occurs in Gen. 18:22. The text states that "Abraham stood before Yahweh." The list of emendations tells us that the text originally stated that "Yahweh stood before Abraham." Since the idiom of "standing before" someone may also imply service before that person or homage, thus denoting a state of inferiority, this statement was deemed irreverent when applied to God. The word order was changed to have Abraham standing before Yahweh. The *Tiqqune Sopherim* preserves the original text and thought of the verse.

All this being said, the tradition is complicated by several factors. On the Masoretic level, the extant lists frequently do not agree with one another. They are inconsistent in the areas of 1) the number of emendations, 2) the order of presentation, 3) the precise passage under question, and 4) the proposed "original" reading which was changed by the scribes.

Some Masoretic manuscripts flag all of the *Tiqqune Sopherim*, while others note only some of them. Some manuscripts, like the Aleppo Codex (A), do not mention the *Tiqqune Sopherim* at all. Likewise, the *Tiqqune Sopherim* are not noted in the Mp of *BHS* (or that of *BHK*^{3}).

The text-critical apparatus of *BHS* mentions some of the *Tiqqune Sopherim*, using the sigla *tiq soph*; however, some are conspicuously absent. The following list gives the location of all eighteen passages (in *BHS* order), indicating whether or not the passage is mentioned in the textual apparatus of *BHS*. Ginsburg (*Introduction to the Massoretico-Critical Edition of the Hebrew Bible*) gives a detailed discussion of each of these, and the specific page numbers in Ginsburg are noted below where *BHS* has omitted a reference.[36]

passage	omitted from *BHS*, Ginsburg reference
Gen. 18:22	
Num. 11:15	
Num. 12:12	
1 Sam. 3:13	
2 Sam. 16:12	omitted; Ginsburg, p. 355
2 Sam. 20:1	omitted; Ginsburg, p. 355–56
1 Kgs. 12:16	omitted; Ginsburg, p. 355–56
Jer. 2:11	
Ezek. 8:17	

Hos. 4:7
Hab. 1:12
Zech. 2:12
Mal. 1:13
Job 7:20
Job 32:3
Lam. 3:20
2 Chr. 10:16 omitted; Ginsburg, p. 355–56

The titles of the lists in Masoretic documents also vary. Some of the headings have "Emendations of the Scribes." Others bear the heading "Euphemisms of the Scribes." This title betrays the belief that the text was never really emended. Instead, the text had always expressed itself euphemistically, meaning something it did not actually state. The scribal lists simply relate what the text would have stated, and thus its original intention, had it not expressed itself euphemistically in the first place.

Moving beyond the Masoretic level to the rabbinic/Talmudic traditions, one will find many of the same problems. The number and order of the emendations vary, and both the "emendation" and "euphemism" interpretation are found. The scribal lists were probably intended to be representative of this phenomenon, not exhaustive. Thus, they represent only a portion of the emendatory activity.

McCarthy has claimed that some of the *Tiqqune Sopherim* are true emendations.[37] Through literary criticism (context and grammar) and textual criticism (comparison of witnesses), she has argued that the "original" reading is sometimes the best one. Such is the case in 1 Sam. 3:13 and Job 7:20 where the emended reading is supported by the LXX. Other passages have no critical evidence to support that an emendation ever took place.

McCarthy speculates that the history of the *Tiqqune Sopherim* occurred along these lines. There were some authentic emendations, and the list preserved for us represents only a part of these. Yet, the climate of ancient Judaism, especially as the text was being standardized, was such that not all authorities sanctioned or recognized the emendatory activity. It was not discussed openly in certain circles. This restrictive atmosphere yielded the "euphemism" interpretation for the proper emendations.

Since the phenomenon was somewhat covert, it was open to contamination. False emendations (in that an "original text" never existed) crept into the *Tiqqune Sopherim* tradition. Eager rabbis interpreted the text euphemistically, and a variant reading was established, although the received text had never been changed. Thus, these emendations are really no more than midrashic commentary on the received text and do not represent text history. Some of these false emendations probably occurred very early in the *Tiqqune Sopherim* tradition.

When modern readers encounter one of the *Tiqqune Sopherim*, they must then decide whether or not the passage is an authentic emendation. If so, the original reading will represent an earlier stage of the text history. If the emendation is false, readers must ask a) did the text intend to express itself euphemistically in the first place (the text does not mean what it says), or b) is the text expressing itself directly? Since the *Tiqqune Sopherim* lists are probably not exhaustive, readers will find other passages showing signs of theological emendation although these passages do not appear on any official list. McCarthy argues this case for a number of specific passages.[38]

***Itture Sopherim* (The Omissions of the Scribes)**

A passage from the Babylonian Talmud (*Nedarim* 37b–38a) cites five instances where a ו conjunction that is expected does not appear. The passage implies that the scribes deleted the וs in these cases because they had accidentally crept into the text.[39] This tradition was included in the Masoretic material.

This phenomenon occurs four times with the word אחר (Gen. 18:5; 24:55; Num. 31:2; Ps. 68:26) and once with the word משפט (Ps. 36:7). None of these is mentioned in the *BHS* Mp. The ו issue is mentioned in the critical apparatus for each passage, but nothing is mentioned about the passages composing the *Itture Sopherim*.

A number of questions surround the *Itture Sopherim*. For example, there are many places in the Bible where a ו might be added or deleted. The use of ו differs among the various manuscripts. What makes these five cases unique? Why didn't the scribes use the *ketib-qere* system to note these passages? One answer might be that *ketib-qere* marks a passage which is to be read differently but without changing the text. Perhaps the *Itture Sopherim* mark places where the text was actually changed. Evidence to back this suggestion, however, is lacking.[40]

***Qere we-la' Ketiv* ([Words] Read but not Written)**

Nedarim 37b–38a also mentions seven passages where a word is to be read, although it is not written in the text (קר̇ ולא כת̇). The words קר̇ ("what is read") and כת̇ ("what is written") are abbreviations of the Aramaic Pe'il participles. Masoretic sources list ten passages. The following table will show the location of these passages. Note that Ruth 2:11 is included in *Nedarim* but absent from Masoretic sources.

Nedarim	Masoretic references
2 Sam. 8:3	omit Ruth 2:11
2 Sam. 16:23	add the following:
Jer. 31:38	Judg. 20:13
Jer. 50:29	2 Sam. 18:20
Ruth 2:11	2 Kgs. 19:31

Ruth 3:5	2 Kgs. 19:37
Ruth 3:17	

The difference of the reading tradition from the written tradition is usually minor. Many of the extra words in the reading have the effect of making the passage more explicit in its meaning. This is the case in 2 Sam. 8:3 where we are directed to read "Euphrates" after "at the river." This addition also brings 2 Sam. 8:3 into line with 1 Chr. 18:3 where "Euphrates" is in the text.

These words were evidently not in early manuscripts but were present in the reading tradition. We can assume that they dropped out of the text for various reasons, but the reading tradition was never altered. The text was deemed too holy to restore the words. In *BHS*, the vowels for the *Qere* words are noted, but there are no consonants. The Mp calls attention to the word which is read but not written.

***Ketiv we-la' Qere* ([Words] Written but not Read)**

This situation is the opposite of the one just described. The same *Nedarim* passage mentions five places where a word is written, but it should not be read (כת̇ ולא קר̇). Masoretic sources list eight of these passages. The following table will show their location. Note that Jer. 32:11 is included in *Nedarim* but absent from Masoretic sources.[41]

Nedarim	Masoretic reference
2 Kgs. 5:18	omit Jer. 32:11
Jer. 32:11	add the following:
Jer. 51:3	2 Sam. 13:33
Ezek. 48:16	2 Sam. 15:21
Ruth 3:12	Jer. 38:16
	Jer. 39:12

Most of the extra words are minor matters (for example, a particle of entreaty, a direct object marker, conditional particles, etc.). Some references are simply a matter of dittography. Nevertheless, early scholars evidently felt that some words which were not present in the reading tradition had erroneously crept into the text. In *BHS*, the consonants for the ketiv words are written, but there are no vowels beneath them. The Mp calls attention to the words which are written but not read.

In the categories of *Itture Sopherim*, *Qere we-la' Ketiv*, and *Ketiv we-la' Qere*, we can assume that the *Nedarim* passage never intended to be exhaustive. It simply gives representative examples. The Masoretic lists were intended to be exhaustive, but this type of activity was probably more extensive than the lists indicate.

Qere/Ketiv[42]

In the categories of *Qere we-la' Ketiv* and *Ketiv we-la'Qere* the difference of the text from the reading tradition is an issue of the presence or absence of a word. The *Qere/Ketiv* differs from these in that it deals with cases where the reading tradition records a different word or, more often, a different form of a word from the written text. The *Qere* indicates how the word should be read. In *BHS* the *Ketiv* is pointed with the vowels belonging to the *Qere* while the *Qere* (in the margin written over קׄ) remains unpointed. Other printed editions follow a different procedure. Other manuscripts also vary in the ways *Qere/Ketiv* is marked.[43]

Scholars are divided with regard to the *Ketiv/Qere* notation system. Morrow says that the *Ketiv/Qere* variations represent alternative traditions accepted in different circles, specifically, *Ketiv* represents the written tradition of the scribes; *Qere* the oral tradition of readers and synagogue schools. The Masoretes, who knew both traditions, devised this system to safeguard readings where the *Qere* varied so much from the *Ketiv* that it might affect the consonantal text, which was the Masoretes' primary concern. He bases his argument that the Masoretes were the creators of the *Ketiv/Qere* notation system on two points: 1) there is no manuscript evidence for *Ketiv/Qere* notes before the Masoretes and 2) the *Ketiv/Qere* notes are integral to the character of other Masoretic activity.[44] But there are also two alternate theories regarding the origin of the notes and these are often held together. The collation theory holds that the marginal *Qere* notes represent a method of collating variant readings from other manuscripts. The collation theory dates back to the time of David Kimhi (ca. 1160–1235) who suggested that the scribe Ezra collated the manuscripts after the exile. Objections to this theory include the question of why there are only two traditions preserved. The correction theory dates to the time of Abrabanel (ca. 1437–1508) who held that Ezra and the scribes found mistakes—carelessness, improper grammar, etc.—in the text. Against these theories, Morrow argues the strong likelihood that the *Ketiv/Qere* notes are the work of the Masoretes based on manuscript evidence and the fact that it was the primary goal of the Masoretes to preserve the consonantal text passed down to them.

But, while the notation system for *Ketiv/Qere* was probably developed by the Masoretes, some of the categories of *Ketiv/Qere* it notes likely predate the notation system and the Masoretes. Yeivin divides the *Ketiv/Qere* into six categories. He dates three of these categories as proto-Masoretic.[45] We have already examined one of these three, *Qere we-la' Ketiv* and *Ketiv we-la' Qere* which he groups together as "category 5." The other two are the sixteen *Ketiv/Qere* euphemisms (his category 1) and the perpetual *Qere* of the divine name (part of his category 6).[46] He makes the point that these are proto-Masoretic because they are mentioned in the Talmud. On the other hand, the other categories are based on elements of the text which were added later. Weil also notes the antiquity of some of the information recorded in *Ketiv/Qere*.[47]

From all of the previous categories, one can see that the proto-Masoretic text contained a variety of irregularities. Some were orthographic, and some were matters of oral tradition. The Masoretes faithfully preserved these anomalies, and their tradition continues into modern times.

Notes

[1]E.J. Revell, "Masoretic Text," *Anchor Bible Dictionary* (New York, NY: Doubleday) IV:598.

[2]E. Tov, *Textual Criticism of the Hebrew Bible* (Minneapolis, MN: Fortress Press, 1992.)

[3]A. Dotan, "Masorah," *Encyclopedia Judaica*, (Jerusalem: Macmillan Co., 1971), XVI:1407.

[4]I. Yeivin, *Introduction to the Tiberian Masorah*, trans. and ed. E.J. Revell, The Society of Biblical Literature Masoretic Studies, no. 5 (Missoula, MT: Scholars Press, 1980), p. 44.

[5]Ibid., pp. 45–46.

[6]R.F. Butin, *The Ten Nequdoth of the Torah* (New York, NY: Ktav Publishing House, Inc., 1969), pp. 88–92.

[7]C.D. Ginsburg, *Introduction to the Massoretico-Critical Edition of the Hebrew Bible* (New York, NY: Ktav Publishing House, Inc., 1966), pp. 326–28.

[8]Tov, *Textual Criticism*, pp. 55–57.

[9]Butin, *The Ten Nequdoth*, pp. 92–100.

[10]Although he makes the statement "it is certain that עשרון was not repeated in certain mss," he does not specify the manuscripts (p. 94).

[11]Ibid., pp. 63–65.

[12]Ginsburg, *Introduction*, pp. 325–26.

[13]Tov, *Textual Criticism*, pp. 54–55.

[14]Ibid., p. 54.

[15]Quoted from Yeivin, *Tiberian Masorah*, p. 46.

[16]Dotan reviews the history of the sigla and the corresponding names in "Masorah," *Encyclopedia Judaica* (Jerusalem: MacMillan Co., 1971) XVI:1408.

[17]E. Würthwein, *The Text of the Old Testament* rev. (Grand Rapids, MI: Eerdmans, 1995) p. 16.

[18]Ginsburg, *Introduction*, pp. 341–43.

[19]Dotan, "Masorah," pp. 1408. Sid Z. Leiman ("The Inverted Nuns at Numbers 10:35–36 and the Book of Eldad and Medad," *JBL* 93/3 [1974] 348–55) agrees after rejecting another solution: that these verses were from an apocryphal or pseudepigraphical book of Eldad and Medad.

[20]Tov, *Textual Criticism*, p. 55.

[21]Ibid., pp. 343–45.

[22]Tov (*Textual Criticism*, p. 55) gives no other explanation, implying that this explanation is sufficient to explain all occurrences.

[23]Ibid., pp. 335–38.

[24]W. Gesenius, *Gesenius' Hebrew Grammar*, 2nd Eng. ed., ed. E. Kautzsch, trans. A.E. Cowley (Oxford: Clarendon Press, 1983), p. 31.

[25]Ginsburg, *Introduction*, pp. 338–40.

[26]Ibid., pp. 340–41.

[27]Yeivin, *Tiberian Masorah*, p. 47. Tov (*Textual Criticism*, p. 57) agrees, "In many Qumran texts laryngeals and pharyngeals were also added supralinearly as corrections."

[28]Tov, *Textual Criticism*, p. 57.

[29]C. McCarthy, *The Tiqqune Sopherim and Other Theological Corrections in the Masoretic Text of the Old Testament*, Orbis Biblicus et Orientalis 36 (Göttingen: Vandenhoeck & Ruprecht, 1981) p. 226.

[30]Dotan, "Masorah," pp. 1408–9.

[31]Yeivin, *Tiberian Masorah*, pp. 47–48.

[32]K. Albrecht, "Die sogenannten Sonderbarkeiten des masoretischen Textes," *Zeitschrift für die Alttestamentliche Wissenschaft* 39 (1921) 167.

[33]Dotan surveys the available evidence in "Masorah," p. 1409. He also provides the locations of irregularities not present in *BHS*.

[34]Yeivin, *Tiberian Masorah*, p. 48.

[35]Ginsburg, *Introduction*, pp. 349–51.

[36]In addition, it should be noted that where the text-critical apparatus of *BHS* does not mention an occurrence of *Tiqqune Sopherim*, it was also not noted in the apparatus of *BHK*^{3}. In one case, Hos. 4:7, *BHS* has added a reference to *Tiqqune Sopherim* not mentioned in *BHK*^{3}. In one other case, Mal. 1:13, *BHS* and *BHK*^{3} differ, with *BHS* noting *Tiqqune Sopherim* on the word אוֹתוֹ in verse 13 while *BHK*^{3} notes it for the same word in v. 12. For more information on this (and the other passages), see McCarthy, *Tiqqune Sopherim*, pp. 111–15.

[37]C. McCarthy, "Emendations of the Scribes," *The Interpreter's Dictionary of the Bible, Supplementary Volume* (Nashville, TN: Abingdon Press, 1976), pp. 263–64.

[38]Ibid., p. 264. For a much fuller treatment of this phenomenon, see McCarthy, *Tiqqune Sopherim.*

[39]Ginsburg, *Introduction*, pp. 307–8, quotes the entire passage.

[40]Yeivin, *Tiberian Masorah*, pp. 51–52.

[41]Some sources will offer Deut. 6:25 as the passage which is included in *Nedarim* but omitted in Masoretic sources. Evidently, this disparity stems from a difference in interpretation regarding which verse is intended by the *Nedarim* passage. The passage directs the reader to delete the אֶת before הַמִּצְוָה. Since similar phrases occur in Deut. 6:25 and Jer. 32:11, some ambiguity is

created.

[42]This same phenomenon is also called *Ketiv/Qere*. Scholars are about evenly divided over the two labels.

[43]W.S. Morrow, "Kethib and Qere," *Anchor Bible Dictionary* (New York, NY: Doubleday, 1992) IV:25, chart KET.01.

[44]Ibid., p. 27.

[45]Yeivin, *Tiberian Masorah*, pp. 56–60.

[46]The proper names "Jerusalem" and "Issachar" are also *Qere perpetuum*. In the Pentateuch of L הִוא for הִיא is usually considered one as well although designated as קׄ four times in L, (Morrow, "Kethib and Qere," IV:24). The references are Lev. 6:18, 22; 13:20; and Deut. 13:16. *BHS* notes only the last of these and with the designation Mp sub loco. Cf. D.S. Mynatt (*The Sub Loco Notes of the Torah of Biblia Hebraica Stuttgartensia*, North Richland Hills, TX: Bibal Press, 1994) p. 197, #254 and p. 139, #161.

[47]G.E. Weil, "Qere-Kethib," *The Interpreter's Dictionary of the Bible, Supplementary Volume* (Nashville, TN: Abingdon Press, 1976) p. 719.

Chapter 4

Working With Masoretic Notes

Masorah Parva Notes

The purpose of the Masorah was to safeguard the sacred text from any additions or deletions. The Mp notes function within that larger purpose by providing the reader or copyist instant information in the margin about how a given text feature ought to appear. If the text was found to be contrary to its Mp notes, the circumstances needed investigation in order to ascertain whether an error had occurred. Without Mp notes, errors would not so readily be brought to the attention of the reader or copyist.

Although the rubrics marked by Mp notes often appear trivial to the uninitiated, there is actually a fundamental principle at work behind the text features that are annotated. Mp notes mark features in the text where an error could easily be made. Many Mp notes, for example, pertain to vowel letters, which are sometimes present (plene) and sometimes absent (defective), yielding different spellings for the same word. In such cases, the Mp marks the traditional spelling so that a letter will not be accidentally inserted or deleted where it might not be noticed otherwise.

Phrases are marked according to the same rationale, i.e., because of their similarity to other phrases. The difference between two similar phrases might be the presence or absence of a *vav* conjunction, or some other small item. Without the Mp note to distinguish the two, one phrase could easily be harmonized to another.

Two corollaries of this fundamental principle deserve mention. 1) The Masorah, and the Mp in particular, preserves the minority spelling. If a word is spelled ten times one way and three times another, the corruption most likely to occur will be that the three occurrences are harmonized to the ten. If a phrase contains a masculine verb twenty times and a feminine verb two times, it is the two times which are in danger of being lost. The Mp notes carefully mark the minority spellings and formulations in the text so they won't be adapted inadvertently to the majority.

The Mp doesn't mark the minority formulation exclusively. Some Mp notes will take notice of the number of majority occurrences and minority occurrences, thus giving a full picture of that text feature. However, the notes function to protect the minority occurrences. In any given Mp note, an interesting question to ask is "Why is this note here? What is it protecting?"

2) Mp notes tend to be based on actual cases where an error might occur, not on theoretical cases. The fact that a certain word *could* be spelled in some unusual way was not sufficient reason to create an Mp note. Generally, the basis of the notes was whether the word actually was spelled in different ways. That a word might be spelled with or without a vowel letter, with or without *he* directive, etc., is relevant to the Mp only to the extent that these variations actually do occur.

In general terms, we can speak of different types of Mp notes. The categories below delineate the different types, and examples are given for each. This division of categories is somewhat artificial, but understanding the fundamental principles behind each category should assist the student in approaching almost any Mp note. For a more thorough analysis of these types, see the examples which are worked in the *Analysis of Notes* section below.

Frequency Notes

This is the most common kind of Mp note. They tell the reader how often a given text feature occurs. For example, in Genesis 19:1, the word סְדֹמָה is annotated with the note ג̇. This note tells the reader that סְדֹמָה occurs 3 times. The most common type of Mp note is the Frequency Note ל̇, showing that a particular form occurs only once; it is hapax. In Genesis 19:2, the word אֲדֹנַי has the Mp note ל̇. This word with this spelling occurs only once. Any student familiar with Hebrew might take issue with this note: certainly the word is more common than the note indicates. The problem will be resolved below, and the result will be insight which otherwise might have gone unnoticed.

Frequency Notes are commonly qualified in some way. They count the frequency of a form in a particular section of scripture, like the Torah (see Genesis 19:14, בְּעֵינֵי: לג̇ בתור̇, "33 times in the Torah"). They count the frequency of a form with a particular spelling (see Genesis 19:34, וּבֹאִי: ד̇ ג̇ חס̇ וחד̇ מל̇, "occurs 4 times, 3 times defective and once plene"). They count the frequency of a form in a particular verse position (see Genesis 7:6, וְנֹחַ: ג̇ ר״פ, "occurs 3 times at the beginning of a verse"). The features which can be qualified are almost endless; the glossary (Chapter 5) will assist the student in understanding what the qualifiers are.

Qualitative Notes

Qualitative Notes give information about a particular text feature, but they do not give a count of how often that feature occurs. The term "qualitative" was used by Weil to describe these notes, and the title seems as good as any.[1] Like the Frequency Notes, they can be qualified in various ways. Qualitative Notes are regularly introduced by the term כל, showing that all of the occurrences appear the same way within the given parameters.

For example, in Genesis 18:18, the word גּוֹיִ֑ has the Mp note כל אורית מל̇, "all the occurrences in the Torah are spelled plene." The number of occurrences is not given, but the reader can assume that each occurrence of גּוֹיִ֑ in the Torah will be spelled plene. Index number 17 directs the reader to Mm 152, where a list can be found.

Sometimes Qualitative Notes will mention exceptions to the general rule. For example, in Genesis 5:16, the word שְׁלֹשִׁים has the note כל קריא חס ו̇ ב̇ מ̇ ד̇, "all the Bible has defective *holem* with the exception of 4 occurrences." The note is saying that שְׁלֹשִׁים is always spelled with a defective *holem*, with four exceptions. Note that index number 9 directs the reader to Mm 41, where a list of the references for the exceptions can be found.

Notes Giving Parallels

Some Mp notes give a statement regarding a particular text feature and then mention parallels or similar occurrences. Two types of notes from this category have already been discussed in Chapter 1, notes with ל̇ or ב̇ plus an identifying excerpt.

Another type of note from this category includes the term ושאר, "and the rest." This Mp note tells the reader that all other forms within the given parameters are alike, but they differ in some way from the word being annotated. In function, these notes are like Mp notes with ל̇ plus an identifying excerpt. For example, in Exodus 17:8, the phrase וַיִּלָּחֶם עִם־יִשְׂרָאֵל is matched with the note ב̇ ושאר וילחם בישראל. This note tells the reader that the combination וַיִּלָּחֶם עִם־יִשְׂרָאֵל occurs twice. But in the rest of the cases where וַיִּלָּחֶם occurs in a phrase with יִשְׂרָאֵל, the combination is וַיִּלָּחֶם בְּיִשְׂרָאֵל.

דכות Notes

These notes are used primarily when variant spellings are at issue. If one unit of the Hebrew Bible regularly has one spelling, but the rest of the Bible (or another unit of it) has another spelling as a rule, the one unit (hereafter called the focus unit) will be treated separately, and the variants will be noted for the rest of the Bible. In the first section of the note, the variants will be numbered. In the second section, introduced by וכל, the unit with the consistent spelling (i.e., the focus unit) will be mentioned. Since these notes frequently contain the term דכות ("like it, the same"), the title דכות Notes seemed appropriate for the category.

For example, in Genesis 11:5, בְּנֵי הָאָדָם has the Mp note ו̇ וכל קהלת דכות, "occurs 6 times and all occurrences in Ecclesiastes (Qoheleth) have the same form." At this point, it is helpful for the student to realize that this note is making a distinction between בְּנֵי הָאָדָם and בְּנֵי אָדָם. The note is saying that בְּנֵי הָאָדָם occurs six times outside of Ecclesiastes, but within Ecclesiastes, בְּנֵי הָאָדָם is the rule; all of the occurrences are spelled this way.

In this case, the focus unit is the book of Ecclesiastes. It is treated separately because בְּנֵי הָאָדָם is the rule within that book. Outside of Ecclesiastes, בְּנֵי אָדָם is more common, and thus the occurrences of בְּנֵי הָאָדָם, the variant expression, are enumerated. Perhaps a clearer way of expressing the note is "Ecclesiastes always has בְּנֵי הָאָדָם, and outside of Ecclesiastes בְּנֵי הָאָדָם occurs 6 additional times."

Some דכות Notes use the same formulation although there is inconsistency in the focus unit. These exceptions are noted with the same formula that was used in the Qualitative Notes to mark exceptions: x ב מ, "with the exception of x times." In Genesis 29:13, the word וַיְבִיאֵהוּ has the note ה מל וכל כתיב דכות ב מ א, "occurs five times plene and all of the occurrences in the Writings are the same with one exception." Thus, the note says that וַיְבִיאֵהוּ occurs five times spelled plene outside the Writings, but inside the Writings it is always spelled plene, with one exception. Mm 1618 gives the pertinent references (see index number 9). Notice that in this case, the focus unit is a recognized section of the Bible, the Writings.

In the examples above, the unit which was consistent in its spelling was a book, Ecclesiastes, or a section, the Writings. Thus, the focus unit is often based on traditional divisions in the Hebrew Bible, or perhaps several of them (see Genesis 19:4, עַל־הַבַּיִת: ד וכל מלכים וישעיה דכות ב מ ד, "occurs 4 times, and the books of Kings and Isaiah always have the same spelling, with the exception of 4 occurrences"). Sometimes, however, the unit will be constructed on another basis such as position within a verse, accent pattern or word combinations, as in the example below.

In Genesis 17:18, the word יִחְיֶה has the note יח וכל חיו יחיה דכות, "occurs 18 times and always in the combination חיו יחיה." The purpose of this note is to make a distinction between יִחְיֶה and other words with which it could be easily confused. In this case, the basis of the focus unit is not a section of the Bible but instead the word combination חָיוֹ יִחְיֶה. The note is saying that the word יִחְיֶה always occurs in the combination חָיוֹ יִחְיֶה, and additionally it occurs another 18 times.

For an example of accents as the basis of the focus unit, see הַקָּטָן in Genesis 27:42: ה קמ וכל אתנח וס״פ דכות, "occurs 5 times with *kamets* and always with *kamets* when the accent is *athnah* or *sof pasuq*." For an example of verse position as the basis of the focus unit, see וְכָל־הָעָם in 2 Samuel 16:15: נא מ״פ וכל ר״פ דכות ב מ ג, "occurs 51 times in the middle of a verse, and the phrase always has this form at the beginning of the verse with the exception of three times."

Another adaptation of the דכות Notes occurs when the focus unit is a book or section of the Bible and it is contrasted, not with the rest of the Bible, but with another book or section. In these cases, the note uses the same formulation, but it really relates that one spelling is the rule in one section while another spelling is the rule in the other section. In Genesis 23:18, the word לְמִקְנָה has the note ל̇ בסיפ̇ וכל ירמיה דכות̇ ב̇ מ̇ א̇, "occurs once in this book, and it is always written like this in the book of Jeremiah with one exception." This note is contrasting מִקְנָה (prefixes not significant here) with מִקְנֶה, which is more common. The note tells us that מִקְנָה is the form used regularly in Jeremiah (with one exception; see index number 11); however, in Genesis, it only occurs once. Thus, in Jeremiah, מִקְנָה is the rule with one exception, and in Genesis, מִקְנֶה is the rule with one exception.

Since this note pertains specifically to מִקְנָה, it is reasonable to ask whether there are other occurrences outside of both Genesis and Jeremiah. In other words, is this note exhaustive? In this case the note accounts for all of the occurrences of מִקְנָה in the whole Bible, and therefore it is exhaustive. However, the student should always consult a concordance to determine whether this type of note covers every occurrence, especially in notes from sources other than *BHS*.

Mnemonic Notes

Mnemonic Notes are not very frequent in the Mp when compared to the other types. Nevertheless, the reader needs to be aware of them, because otherwise they will be very confusing. In these notes, the Mp gives a mnemonic of some type so that the reader or copyist will remember something important about the text, like the location of another occurrence or the manner in which a series of words is spelled.

In *BHS*, notes of this type frequently involve the order of words which appear in varying arrangements in different texts. For example, the lists of the nations inhabiting Canaan are given in varying orders. There was always a danger that the order in a particular text might be corrupted in the process of copying. Thus, Mnemonic Notes were added to the Mp to prevent this.

In Exodus 13:5, the Mp סימן כ̇ ת̇ מ̇ ו̇ ס̇ should be matched with all the words in the adjacent line which are marked with a raised circule.[2] The words are a list of nations. The Mp is introduced by the term סימן, which here means "mnemonic sign." The letters that follow give the proper order of the nations. Each letter is a distinguishing characteristic for one of the words: כ̇ for הַכְּנַעֲנִי (the Canaanites), ת̇ for וְהַחִתִּי (and the Hittites), מ̇ for וְהָאֱמֹרִי (and the Amorites), ו for וְהַחִוִּי (and the Hivites), and ס̇ for וְהַיְבוּסִי (and the Jebusites). Thus, by following the Mp note, the correct order of nations is maintained.

For another Mnemonic Note giving a different order for the nations, see Exodus

23:23. In manuscripts, the Mnemonic Notes can take different forms and may involve some Aramaic notations. They frequently appear in the Mm. The form given in *BHS* will help the student, but notes of this type can be a great challenge to decipher. For more information on Mnemonic Notes, see the entry סימן in the Glossary, Chapter 5.

Citation of Authorities

Some Mp notes cite the authority of a great Masorete or a revered codex in support of a particular reading. The amount of this type of Mp note varies by manuscript. In comparison with the other types of Mp notes, they are few in L. For example, in Psalm 31:12, the word וְלִשְׁכֵנַי is annotated with the note כן לבן אשר, "thus according to ben Asher." In this case, the famous Masorete ben Asher is cited in support for this reading (see also the previous Mp note in *BHS*).

For a similar example, see 1 Chronicles 12:7. There, the word וְיִשִּׁיָּהוּ has the note כן לבן אשר ("thus according to ben Asher") as in the previous example. However, index number 8 sends us to the apparatus where we also find the reading of ben Naphtali for this word. This example not only cites ben Asher, but it also notes the difference from the reading of his famous disputant, ben Naphtali. This Mp note may have been intended to supplement a list of differences between ben Asher and ben Naphtali, or it may have been taken from such a collection. See Chapter 2 for a discussion of these lists.

Collative Mp Notes

These Mp notes function as notices that the word or phrase belongs to a Collative Mm Note; see below on these. They can be as varied as the Collative Mm Notes are.

Masorah Magna Notes

The Mp notes give the number of times that a particular text feature occurs. The Mm goes another step by giving references to the verses where the text feature occurs. The system of reference that we use today (chapter number and verse number) was a product of the Middle Ages. Therefore, in manuscripts, the lists of the Mm use the only reference system available at the time: identifying excerpts. Each verse or passage in the rubric annotated by the Mm note is identified by a short excerpt from it (known by the term סימן; for another usage, see under Mnemonic Notes above). Fortunately, Weil has added chapter and verse references to the lists in *Massorah Gedolah*, so the student does not have to recognize a verse by the short quotation!

There are two basic types of Mm notes (following Yeivin's categories).[3] Their common factor is that both list occurrences.

Elaborative Mm Notes

Elaborative Notes are the most frequent kind. They simply list the references where the word or phrase at issue in the Mp note can be found. In other words, they elaborate on the frequency information given by the Mp notes. For example, in Genesis 21:15, the word אַחַד has the Mp note כ̇ה (a Frequency note). The Mp note tells us that אַחַד occurs 25 times. Index number 14 sends us to Mm 187, where we find the list of the 25 occurrences.

Collative Mm Notes

These Mm notes list 1) words/phrases/verses which are different but share some common characteristic or 2) words/phrases/verses which are the same except for some distinguishing characteristic. Collative Mm lists are not very common in L and therefore not in *BHS* either.

Probably the most frequent type of Mm note in L from category 1 deals with verses. These notes list all the verses which share some common characteristic. For example, in Genesis 13:3, the Mp note to be matched with וְעַד is ג̇ פסוק ועד עד. The note marks the three verses in which the series וְעַד עַד appears. In this case, it does not matter that a word (or words) intervenes between עַד and וְעַד. Notice also that the circule is over וְעַ֯ד, the first significant word in the verse for this Mp note. In L, the circule will sometimes be over the first word of the verse (since the note deals with the whole verse). Index number 1 sends us to Mm 3938, where we find the list of verses.

Examples of this type are not hard to find in *BHS*. See Leviticus 1:8: יב̇ פסוק את את ואת ומילה חדה ביניה̇, "12 verses in which the sequence את את ואת (*tsere* or *seghol*) occurs with one word between each item." Index number 11 sends us to Mm 44 where we can find the list. See Leviticus 1:2: ד̇ פסוק מן מן ומן, "4 verses where the sequence מִן מִן וּמִן is found." Index number 4 sends us to Mm 422 where we can find the list.

In many examples, the Mp notes are present, but the Mm is lacking in the manuscript. No doubt, the Mp was originally accompanied by such a list. See Genesis 17:23: יח̇ פסוק את ואת ואת את, "18 verses in which the sequence of direct object markers אֵת וְאֵת ואת את (*tsere* or *seghol*) is found." See Genesis 13:9: ז̇ פסוק בתור̇ אם ואם, "7 verses in the Torah in which the sequence אִם וְאִם is found."

In the collative category 2, notes with the term זוגין (pairs) are good examples. These notes arrange words (or phrases) into word groups. The words are usually very similar, sometimes almost identical. But there is some characteristic which distinguishes each member of the group. Thus, the זוגין notes gather together words which are similar but differ in some way.

Very often, the word groups collected by this type of note are composed of two words which are hapax. In such cases, each word group has only two members. Thus, the word groups are commonly called "pairs." Occasionally, however, notes employing the term זוגין collect word groups involving more than two words. In these cases, the translation "pair" is misleading and "word group" is preferable.

In Genesis 17:4, the phrase לְאַב הֲמוֹן has the note ל֗4. The Mp note simply relates that the phrase is hapax. But if the student follows index number 4 through the apparatus to Mm 959, a rubric involving pairs will be found. The statement of the text feature is יד֗ זוגין קדמ֗ נסיב ל ותינ֗ לא נסיב ל, "14 pairs of phrases (or words), the first including *lamed* and the second not including *lamed.*" Each element in each pair is hapax, as the Mp note has shown us. Thus, the note has grouped together 14 pairs of hapax phrases, the first of which has a *lamed* and the second of which lacks it. The parallel for לְאַב הֲמוֹן in Genesis 17:4 is אַב הֲמוֹן in Genesis 17:5.

Mm 959 gives the phrases in question with their references. A careful examination of the references reveals some additional information. The *lamed* in each case is usually supported by *shewa*, לְ, but it does not have to be the *lamed* preposition; see לְקַח in Proverbs 20:16. Other vowels are admissible (Proverbs 21:9, לָשֶׁבֶת). The rubric includes phrases or single words (2 Samuel 18:28//2 Samuel 24:20). The *lamed* does not have to be initial in the phrase (Numbers 22:4//Numbers 22:10). Also, each pair is found within only one book, although there is more than one pair per book. Thus, the student can learn a lot about a rubric involving pairs simply by paying close attention to the pairs themselves.

Obviously, collative Mm notes do have corresponding Mp notes (referred to above as Collative Mp Notes). Although some of the Mp notes for each rubric are frequently missing in L, in *BHS* the Mp notes are regularly supplied to their proper places. Ideally, the Mp notes should restate the rubric of the Mm note, and where there is room this is done. In *BHS*, the notes about verses regularly restate the entire rubric, and the term פסוק is naturally included. In the notes about pairs (זוגין), there is rarely room in the margins of *BHS* to state the whole rubric. Thus, in many cases, Weil has shortened the Mp notes to "זוגין x," where x is the number of pairs in the rubric. The index number refers the reader to the *Massorah Gedolah*, where the rubric title is fully stated. In other cases, the Mp note contains some other information about the text but the index number still refers the reader to *Massorah Gedolah* where the rubric will be stated in terms of pairs. Thus, in the example above, the Mp ל֗ is a frequency note, showing that the phrase is hapax. The reader must follow the index number to find the information regarding the pairs.

Important Items in the Masoretic Apparatus

It was mentioned in Chapter 1 that there are some items in the Masoretic apparatus which deserve special attention. Each of these will be discussed below.

Sub Loco

The term "sub loco" is discussed on page XVII of the *BHS* Introduction. There Weil comments, "The note indicates that we have corrected an error in the Mp of L, or that the difficulty is due to the absence of a related list in the Mm of L. These instances are discussed fully in our *Massorah Gedolah*, vol. III." The intention was that future editions of *BHS* would contain a reference number instead of "sub loco," and these numbers would direct the reader to a discussion in *Massorah Gedolah*, vol. III. Unfortunately, *Massorah Gedolah*, vol. III never appeared, and the problems which Weil identified in these notes were never explained.

In *The Sub Loco Notes of the Torah in the BHS*, Mynatt has attempted to remedy this situation by analyzing the "sub loco" notes in the Torah. In most cases, "sub loco" is noted when the Mp contains an error or has otherwise been altered by Weil in the editing process. By consulting Mynatt's volume, the student can discover the original Mp of L, the problem which Weil identified, and the changes that he effected. This type of analysis is not available for the Prophets or the Writings. Thus, in order to move beyond the "sub loco" notation in those sections, the student must consult L itself and ascertain the problem by comparing the Mp of L with *BHS*.

Contra Textum

"Contra textum" means that some aspect of the Masorah of L is opposed to the text of L. When the text departed from an Mm note, Weil recorded "contra textum" in the apparatus. When the text departed from an Mp note which lacked an Mm note, Weil recorded "Mp contra textum" in the apparatus coupled with the "sub loco" statement, apparently because he intended to discuss them further in *Massorah Gedolah*, vol. III.

"Contra textum" Mp notes are significant because they depart from the usual manner by which Weil edited the Masorah of L. In most cases where Weil found an Mp note at odds with the text, he simply corrected the Mp note, either to conform to the text or the corresponding Mm note. However, when "contra textum" occurs with an Mp note, the Mp note has generally not been corrected. Thus, it appears that in these cases Weil judged the Mp note to be more accurate than the text. Weil included the statement "contra textum" in the apparatus in order to alert the reader to the contradiction between the Masorah and the text of L.

The same type of conclusions apply when Mm apparatus entries contain "contra textum." In these cases, Weil has generally edited the Mp to be consistent with the Mm, not the text. Thus, we can assume that in such cases Weil has sided with the Masorah against the text.

Contra textum situations usually involve notes dealing with vowel letters. This is because the writing of vowel letters was one aspect of copying manuscripts where mistakes could easily be made. Furthermore, the various Masoretic schools had differing traditions regarding the plene/defective spelling of words, and the accidental mixing of text traditions was a persistent danger when manuscripts were copied. However, the possibility always exists that the Masorah of L has been corrupted, not the text. Therefore, when the Masorah of L contradicts the text with regard to vowel letters, one must decide which has the most merit, the text or the description of the textual situation given in the Masorah. "Contra textum" generally indicates the opinion that the Masorah is more reliable than the text in that instance; however, by consulting other manuscripts, editions, and additional sources of Masoretic information, the student can investigate whether the Mp or the text is more reliable and make that judgment independently.

In summary, then, when "contra textum" appears in the apparatus, it is reasonable to assume that the text contains the error, not the Mp or the Mm. Otherwise, Weil would have edited the Mp to make it consistent with the text, the usual practice. The reader needs to be aware, however, that the term "contra textum" is nowhere discussed in *BHS*, and the conclusions above are based solely on the observations of the authors.

Reference	**Spelling**	**Mp Note in L**
Genesis 30:20	זְב֖לוּן	ט̇ כת̇[4]
Genesis 35:23	וּזְבוּל֖ן	No Mp Note
Genesis 46:14	זְבוּל֖ן	No Mp Note
Joshua 19:27	בִּזְב֖לוּן	ט̇ כת̇ כן
Joshua 19:39	בִּזְב֖לוּן	ט̇ כת̇ כן
Judges 4:6	זְב֖לוּן	ט̇ כת̇ כן וכל כתיב דכות̇ ב̇ מ̇ א̇
Judges 5:18	זְב֖לוּן	No Mp Note
Judges 6:35	וּבִזְב֖לוּן	ט̇ כת̇ כן
Isaiah 8:23	זְב֖לוּן	No Mp Note

The word זְבֻלוּן (Zebulun) is spelled three different ways in the Hebrew Bible: זְבוּלֻן (plene first *shureq*), זְבֻלוּן (plene second *shureq*), or זְבוּלוּן (doubly plene). Mm 218 specifies the occurrences of זְבֻלוּן (plene second *shureq*): ט֗ כת כן וכל כתיב ב֗ מ֗ חד, "occurs nine times written thus (i.e., plene second *shureq*), and this spelling always occurs in the Writings with the exception of once." Obviously, the various spellings of Zebulun could be easily confused or harmonized. The specific purpose of this note is to keep זְבֻלוּן from being harmonized to זְבוּלֻן in the Torah and the Prophets (in which זְבוּלֻן, plene first *shureq*, is the more common spelling), and vice versa for the Writings (in which זְבֻלוּן, plene second *shureq*, is more common). Prefixes, etc. are not at issue in this note, and some variation occurs.

The table above gives each of the nine occurrences where זְבֻלוּן (plene second *shureq*) is supposed to occur in the Torah and the Prophets (according to Mm 218), along with the Mp notes for those occurrences, if any. Note that in Genesis 35:23 and 46:14, the *BHS* text (and thus L) has some form of זְבוּלֻן (plene first *shureq*). Thus, the text lacks two of the nine occurrences and contradicts the Mm note.

In this instance, Weil has edited *BHS* under the assumption that the Mm note is correct and the text is wrong.[5] In *BHS*, the Mp note for all of these occurrences is ט֗ כת֗ כן וכל כתיב דכות ב֗ מ֗ א, based on the Mp of L in Judges 4:6, the Mp note with the most complete statement. He has added "contra textum" in the apparatus statements for Genesis 35:23 and 46:14 in order to call attention to the contradiction between the text and the Mp. Thus, this example demonstrates that, generally, when the Mp is wrong or incomplete, Weil corrects it, and when "contra textum" appears in the apparatus, the Masorah is favored over the text.

The Abbreviation TM

The definition for the abbreviation TM is not given in the Table of Abbreviations for the Masoretic apparatus on page L of the *BHS* Introduction. It appears to be an abbreviation for the Latin phrase "textus masoretici." Thus, TM refers to the traditional Masoretic text. The abbreviation is used in cases where the text of L is not consistent with the traditional Masoretic text as given in other manuscripts or editions, such as the *Second Rabbinic Bible*. Thus, Weil uses TM to cite what he feels to be the standard Masoretic text in the situation.

Okhlah we-Okhlah

Okhlah we-Okhlah is an ancient Masoretic collection; it was discussed in Chapter 2. On page XVII of *BHS* Introduction, Weil remarks that he will occasionally make reference to *Okhlah we-Okhlah*, and he cites both the Frensdorff (Paris manuscript) and the Diaz-Esteban (Halle manuscript) editions.[6] However, he nowhere mentions how the two manuscripts are distinguished in the Masoretic apparatus. In practice, Weil refers to the Frensdorff edition by "Okhl" and the Diaz-Esteban edition by "Okhl II."

Other Editions and Manuscripts

On page L of *BHS* Introduction, Weil lists a number of other manuscripts or editions of the Hebrew Bible which he notes in the apparatus. The student needs to be aware of these abbreviations in the apparatus. Most of these have been discussed in Chapter 2, and further information is given in the Bibliography. Unfortunately, most of these are also rare books or limited editions, and, unless students have access to a very large theological library, they will probably not be able to consult them.

The Extent of Weil's Revisions in *BHS*

It has been noted in various places throughout this book that Weil substantially revised and edited the Masorah of L when it was printed as the Masorah of *BHS*. The purpose of this section is to describe the nature and extent of those revisions.

The Masorah Magna

The most obvious revision Weil made for *BHS* was moving the lists of the Mm to a separate volume. In L, the Mm lists are written in the upper and lower margins of the pages. A particular list may be written on the same page as the corresponding Mp note, or it may be written on the page just before or after the corresponding Mp note. Since an Mm list is frequently written only once, it may not even occur with the corresponding Mp note. Weil's revisions to the Mm of L make it much easier to use. Citations to an Mm list are used each time the corresponding Mp note appears. Instead of searching for an Mm list, which would take a considerable amount of time, the list can be located easily in *Massorah Gedolah*.

Furthermore, in L, the citations in the Mm are given only by way of short identifying excerpts. This convention presumes a level of familiarity with the Hebrew Bible that is unusual today; the reader is expected to know from the excerpt the exact location of the text feature collated by the Mm note. Weil has included these excerpts, but he has also identified them by references to book, chapter, and verse.

The Completion of the Mp

In L, an Mp note indicating a certain number of occurrences for a text feature may be present in context with only a limited number of those occurrences. In many cases, the note will be absent from several (or most) of the parallel passages.

Weil "completed" the Mp reference system in *BHS*.[7] Any Mp note specifying a certain number of occurrences of a text feature will be found with all of the parallel texts in *BHS*, regardless of its presence or absence in L. Weil comments that about 70% of this data had not been indicated in L.[8] Weil's completion of the Mp reference system simply made explicit what had already been implicit, and it enabled the Mp to be used systematically.

Notes which have more than 100 occurrences form an exception to the general rule. In these cases, Weil did not supply the Mp to all the parallel passages. Mp notes which have more than 100 occurrences are found in *BHS* only in places where they are found in L.[9]

Although Weil's completion of the Mp made it much easier to use, it was complicated when words or phrases were members of more than one rubric. Weil had to contend with two or more Mp notes annotating one textual item. Instead of marking the item with several circules, Weil combined the Mp notes into one note. Thus, the textual item was marked with only one circule, but the combination of the separate Mp notes often involved rephrasing one or more of the notes in order to produce one intelligible Mp note. When the student encounters a long Mp note with several components in *BHS*, generally it has resulted from the combination of several shorter notes in L. See *BHS* Introduction, p. XVII for Weil's own discussion of this arrangement.

Weil has also corrected Mp notes where they are in error or misleading. If there is no corresponding Mm list, the corrections are generally marked "sub loco" (see above). If there is a corresponding Mm list, the error is generally not marked in any way; the reader of *BHS* cannot tell that Weil has corrected an error.

Mp ב̇ Plus an Identifying Reference

Mp notes with ב̇, plus an identifying excerpt, mark a text feature that occurs twice. The identifying excerpt, located below the ב̇ in L, gives the location of the other occurrence. See chapter 1 for instructions regarding how *BHS* treats these situations.

In L, one of the two parallel passages will frequently be marked with the ב̇ and an identifying excerpt for the parallel, but the parallel will only be marked with a ב̇. The identifying excerpt for the other passage will be absent. In *BHS*, Weil has supplied the missing information in these cases. The appropriate references have been supplied in the Masoretic apparatus for both passages.

Mp ל̊ Plus an Identifying Reference

Mp notes with ל̊, plus an identifying excerpt, mark a text feature which occurs once, but another form occurs once which is very similar yet significantly different. The similar form is given under the ל̊, and the difference between the two can be detected by close comparison. See chapter 1 for instructions regarding how *BHS* treats these situations.

In L, although one of the forms may be marked with ל̊ plus an identifying excerpt, the similar form may not be annotated with this information. The similar form usually has the Mp note ל̊, but the excerpt giving the other form is frequently missing. Weil has supplied this missing information in the Masoretic apparatus so that both occurrences are uniform.

Abbreviations

Weil has used consistent abbreviations for certain common terms which are sometimes written out in L. For example, ר״פ (the beginning of the verse) is abbreviated from the fuller statement in L, some form of ראש פסוק. The fuller statement in L appears in various forms, but in *BHS* it is consistently abbreviated ר״פ.

Standardizations

Weil has standardized the abbreviations which are used in L. For example, ק̇ is the standard abbreviation in *BHS* for קר̇ and ק̇, both of which are used in L. Furthermore, the spelling of terms has been standardized in all notes, as opposed to the various spellings for a single term which are also found in L.

Weil has also standardized the terminology and the formulations of the Mp notes in *BHS*. In L, parallel Mp notes (i.e., Mp notes which mark different occurrences of the same text feature) frequently vary in the way they are formulated and in the terminology they use (probably indicating different sources). Instead of reproducing varying terms and formulations, Weil has made parallel Mp notes consistent with one another. A set of Mp notes marking the parallel texts of a single text feature will use the same terminology; however, separate sets of notes may use different terms having the same meaning (e.g. אור̇ versus תורה, both denoting the Torah). Where a text feature is marked by notes with different terms and formulations, the most frequently occurring form was chosen for *BHS*. Obviously, this type of standardization reduces confusion and promotes clarity.[10]

Analysis of Notes

The purpose of this section is to describe for the new student how the notes of the Masorah can be approached and analyzed. In previous sections, we translated a number of Mp notes which served as illustrations of the various types. We will use many of these Mp notes again as examples so the student can see them worked to their completion. Furthermore, the student should pay close attention to the use of the basic tools already mentioned in Chapter 1.

The student needs to ask three essential questions when confronting almost any Mp note. 1) What does the note say? How should the note be translated and interpreted? Coming to a clear understanding of the information presented in the Mp is the foundation upon which the rest of the analysis rests. The types of notes outlined above should help the new student avoid confusion in answering this question.

2) What is the text feature? Which forms are being marked, and which are excluded? In other words, what is the rubric? This question can be the most difficult one of the three because Mp notes are sometimes not clear concerning the details of the rubric. Sometimes similar forms are included. Sometimes, the precise form marked by the Mp note is the only form at issue. It often takes some investigative work to narrow down the rubric as precisely as possible.

3) Where are the references? The Mp note is not solved until the student has a list of references equal to the number of forms specified by the Mp note.

Genesis 19:1: סְדֹמָה, Mp Note ג̇

As mentioned above, the note ג̇ tells the reader that this word occurs three times. This is the answer to the first question. With regard to the second question, it is essential to notice here that Sodom has the *he* directive attached to it. Thus it is likely that this form alone is at issue in the note. The student must consult a concordance to confirm or deny this suspicion, and indeed סְדֹמָה occurs three times. Only this form is at issue in the note. The three occurrences are Genesis 10:19, 18:22, and 19:1.

Genesis 19:2: אֲדֹנַי, Mp Note ל̇

As mentioned above, the note ל̇ indicates that this form is hapax. An easy error to make here, particularly in copying, would be to confuse אֲדֹנַי (my lords) with אֲדֹנָי (Lord), which occurs over 400 times. Thus, this Mp note preserves the minority spelling אֲדֹנַי and protects it from being harmonized to אֲדֹנָי. By observing the Mp note in the margin, the reader or copyist could be warned that there was something unusual about this form, and a potential error could be avoided. The form אֲדֹנַי occurs only once.

Genesis 27:14: וַיָּבֵא, Mp Note נא[12] יח מנה בתור

This note is really two Frequency notes combined into one. Its meaning is rather straightforward: "וַיָּבֵא occurs 51 times, 18 of them in the Torah." The student should first determine whether וַיָּבֵא alone is at issue here. Consulting a concordance, one will find that וַיָּבֵא does indeed occur 51 times, so only וַיָּבֵא is of interest in this note. A simpler way of ascertaining the same information would be to follow index number 12 through the Masoretic apparatus to Mm 639. There one will find the list of 51 occurrences.

The second section of this Mp note is a Frequency note qualified with regard to where the occurrences can be found. It states that 18 of the occurrences are in the Torah. Again, either the concordance or Mm 639 will show that the 18 occurrences are Genesis 2:19; 4:3; 8:9; 27:14, 25, 31, 33; 29:23; 30:14; 37:12; 43:17, 24; 47:7, 14; Exodus 4:6, 37:5, 38:7, and 40:21. Thus, all of the information suggested in this note has been obtained.

Genesis 5:16: שְׁלֹשִׁים, Mp Note כל קריא חס ו ב מ ד[9]

As mentioned above, this note relates that שְׁלֹשִׁים is always spelled with a defective *holem*, with four exceptions. In this case, defining the parameters of the rubric requires careful attention. By consulting a concordance, the student will observe that only two of the plene *holem* occurrences have the precise form שְׁלוֹשִׁים (Esther 4:11; 2 Chronicles 16:12); the other two have the definite article, הַשְּׁלוֹשִׁים (1 Chronicles 11:15; 11:25). The student can conclude that this Mp note is annotating forms of שְׁלֹשִׁים with or without prefixes, etc., and thus the plene exceptions show the same variation. The same information could be obtained by consulting Mm 41 (see index number 9) and looking up the references where the identifying excerpt fails to include the precise form.

The number of occurrences conforming to the usual spelling (defective *holem*: שְׁלֹשִׁים) is quite extensive, which is one reason this note takes the form of a Qualitative note. The references can be found in a concordance. The references for exceptional spellings (plene *holem*: שְׁלוֹשִׁים) were given above.

Exodus 17:8: וַיִּלָּחֶם עִם־יִשְׂרָאֵל, Mp Note ב ושאר וילחם בישראל

As mentioned above, this note says that the phrase וַיִּלָּחֶם עִם־יִשְׂרָאֵל occurs twice, but the rest of the occurrences are וַיִּלָּחֶם בְּיִשְׂרָאֵל, without עִם־. Obviously, one of the two occurrences is Exodus 17:8. It will be necessary to consult a concordance to find the other.

Finding the occurrences of phrases in a concordance can be frustrating, but there are some ways to work efficiently. The Even-Shoshan concordance gives an index for the occurrences of common phrases in the information at the beginning of each word or root. By consulting this information for every word in the phrase, the student may find the phrase and thus save much time. If it isn't listed, the student will have to search for the phrase manually. The student should look for the phrase by the least common word in the phrase (so that the number of entries which must be reviewed will be held to a minimum).

In this case, Even-Shoshan does not list the phrase, so we must search for it by the least common word, וַיִּלָּחֶם. Looking through the references, one will find that the second occurrence of the phrase וַיִּלָּחֶם עִם־יִשְׂרָאֵל is Judges 11:20. This information can be confirmed by looking up Judges 11:20 in *BHS*, where the Mp note ב ושאר וילחם בישראל is found once again.

The Mp note also says that in the rest of the occurrences where וַיִּלָּחֶם is in a phrase with יִשְׂרָאֵל, the combination is וַיִּלָּחֶם בְּיִשְׂרָאֵל. The references for some or all of these occurrences can be located by the same method. By looking through the references for וַיִּלָּחֶם in a concordance, several occurrences of וַיִּלָּחֶם בְּיִשְׂרָאֵל can be found, e.g. Numbers 21:1, 23; Joshua 24:9.

Genesis 11:5: בְּנֵי הָאָדָם, Mp Note ו וכל קהלת דכות

The translation of this note was given above as "occurs 6 times and all occurrences in Ecclesiastes are written like this." As in any Mp note, the student should next ask "What is the text feature at issue?" But in דכות notes, it is also helpful to ask "What is the text feature with which this word/phrase is being contrasted?" Sometimes the note will state this information explicitly, but not usually. Before any information is collected, the student may have to make an intuitive guess, and then revise that guess as the analysis proceeds.

In this case, one can began by looking up אָדָם in Even-Shoshan's concordance. The occurrences of the phrase בְּנֵי הָאָדָם are grouped together, but so are the occurrences of בְּנֵי אָדָם. Thus, a good guess is that the contrast of בְּנֵי הָאָדָם and בְּנֵי אָדָם is the issue in this note.

The next step is to identify the six occurrences of בְּנֵי הָאָדָם outside Ecclesiastes. The references given in the concordance are Genesis 11:5; 1 Samuel 26:19; 1 Kings 8:39; Psalm 33:13; 145:12, and 2 Chronicles 6:30. The occurrence in Psalm 145:12 is לִבְנֵי הָאָדָם, which demonstrates that prefixes are not relevant to the issue in this note; small variations like this among the occurrences can be expected.

The last step is to identify the occurrences in Ecclesiastes. Once again, the concordance lists these: Ecclesiastes 1:13; 2:3, 8; 3:10, 18, 19, 21; 8:11; 9:3, and 9:12. The occurrences in 1:13; 2:3; and 3:10 are spelled לִבְנֵי הָאָדָם; however, since variations can be expected in this note, these forms do not represent a problem. Thus, the information in this note has been fully extracted.

Genesis 29:13: וַיְבִיאֵהוּ, Mp Note ה֯ מל וכל כתיב דכות ב֯ מ֯ א֯[9]

This note was translated above as "occurs five times plene and all of the occurrences in the Writings are the same with one exception." Thus, the note explicitly identifies the text feature at issue and the form with which it is contrasted. The form at issue is וַיְבִיאֵהוּ, spelled with plene *hirek yod*. The contrast is the same word with a defective *hirek yod*: וַיְבִאֵהוּ.

The first step is to identify the five occurrences of וַיְבִיאֵהוּ (with plene *hirek yod*). By looking up וַיְבִיאֵהוּ under its root בוא, one will come to the precise form in question. A survey of the entries reveals that וַיְבִיאֵהוּ (plene or defective) occurs ten times outside the Writings. As the note indicates, five of these occurrences are spelled plene: Genesis 29:13; Judges 19:21; 1 Samuel 16:12; 2 Kings 4:20; and Ezekiel 17:4. The same information is given in Mm 1618.

The next step is to isolate the occurrences of וַיְבִיאֵהוּ in the Writings. Since the entries are listed in the order of the Hebrew Bible, the occurrences are easy to locate: 2 Chronicles 25:23 and 36:4. The last step is to find the one exception to the rule in the Writings, where a defective spelling occurs: וַיְבִאֵהוּ. The concordance (and Mm 1618) shows that it is 2 Chronicles 36:10.

Exodus 25:20: Mp Note י֯ד֯ פסוק על אל אל[11]

This note is an example from collative category 1. The Mp note relates that this verse is one of 14 verses which contain the sequence עַל אֶל אֶל. Fortunately, the corresponding Mm note was also written in L. Index number 11 sends us to Mm 4093 where we can find the list. Therefore, as long as the Mm list is present, the collative notes (of both categories) are easy to solve. One must simply consult the Mm to find the references.

Genesis 43:8: Mp Note י֯ב֯ פסוק גם גם גם

This is another example from collative category 1, but the Mm note is not present in the manuscript. Therefore, we do not have a list of references readily available in *Massorah Gedolah*. These notes can still be solved, but they take more effort.

In this case, the Mp note tells us that Genesis 43:8 is one of 12 verses containing the sequence גם גם גם. The easiest way to resolve this situation is to look for the note in other sources of Mp notes. One source is Ginsburg's *Massorah*. The student should look for the Mp note under גַּם, because most of the notes collected in Ginsburg's *Massorah* are arranged alphabetically according to the word with which the note is matched. Each note is numbered sequentially, starting anew with each letter of the alphabet.

The note we are searching for can be found in volume 1, page 210, list 167. The formulation is slightly different from the Mp of *BHS*: י״ב פיס׳ אית בהו׳ גַּם גַּם גַּם וסימנה׳. Ginsburg gives the list of references: Genesis 24:25; 32:20; 43:8; Exodus 4:10; 12:32; Judges 8:22; 1 Samuel 28:6; Isaiah 48:8; Jeremiah 12:6; 23:11; Ecclesiastes 9:6; 1 Chronicles 11:2. A survey of the occurrences will reveal that it does not matter whether גַּם or גַּם־ appears. In Genesis 24:25, all of the occurrences in the sequence are גַּם־. In Genesis 32:20, all of the occurrences in the sequence are גַּם. In Judges 8:22, the occurrences are mixed.

If the note in question is found in volume 1 of Ginsburg's *Massorah*, then the student should also consult volume 4, which is a commentary on the notes in volume 1. Ginsburg was never able to finish his commentary, so notes obtained from volume 2 will have no annotations in volume 4. In this case, the annotation for the note can be found in volume 4, page 246, list 167 (the list number corresponds with volume 1). Ginsburg discusses the manuscript sources in which he found this note, and he also mentions one other verse (Ecclesiastes 4:8) which may be included in this rubric. Ginsburg's annotations should always be consulted when the student is analyzing any difficult note; his insights are invaluable.

Another source for the same information is Frensdorff's *Die Massora Magna*; it is an index of the Mm and Mf of Jacob ben Chayyim's *Second Rabbinic Bible* (see chapter 2 on this work). The organization of *Die Massora Magna* is a bit confusing to the uninitiated. Although the notes are usually arranged according to the lexical root of the word with which it is matched, separate chapters are devoted to different kinds of words. Frensdorff sometimes gives comments on the Mp notes in the footnotes.

In this case, the student needs to consult the chapter devoted to particles (*Partikel* in German). The student will find the heading for the letter *gimel* and the subheading for the word גַּם. Having perused the entries for גַּם, the student will find the note in question on page 232; however, the formulation is again somewhat different from the Mp of *BHS*: י״ב פסוקין אית בהון גם גַּם גם גם. After the title, Frensdorff lists the references where this rubric is mentioned in the Mm of the *Second Rabbinic Bible*. The references marked with asterisks isolate the passages where the Mm of the *Second Rabbinic Bible* lists all of the references for the rubric: Judges 8:22, Jeremiah 12:6, and Ecclesiastes 9:6. Note also that Frensdorff lists where this rubric is mentioned in the Masorah Finalis of the *Second Rabbinic Bible* (Mf 11 גם) and where the listing can be found in his edition of

Okhlah we-Okhlah (א״אר 356). A full list of references is not given in *Massora Magna.* The student will need to consult the *Second Rabbinic Bible* (e.g., Goshen-Gottstein's edition) or *Okhlah we-Okhlah* for a full listing.

If an Mp note in *BHS* lacks a corresponding Mm note, especially for the collative notes, the student should consult one or both of these works. These two contain references and discussions for many Mp notes, and the chance of finding the note in question or some reference to it is good. Otherwise, the student must use a concordance to find the references, and that can often be a rigorous, time-consuming process.

Numbers 23:16: וַיִּקָּר יְהוָה, Mp Note ג זוגין[20]

This note is an example from collative category 2. The full statement of the text feature can be found by consulting Mm 3268 (cf. index number 20): ג זוגין מן ב̇ ב̇ בחד עינין חד יְהוָה וחד אֱלֹהִים וסימנהון, "3 pairs (of phrases) occurring twice in one context, the first with יְהוָה and the second with אֱלֹהִים, and their signs (references)." This statement means that וַיִּקָּר יְהוָה is one member from one of three pairs of phrases which occur twice in a single context. The first member of each pair is a phrase containing the word יְהוָה, and the second member of each pair is an identical or similar phrase containing the word אֱלֹהִים. In this case, the second member of the pair is וַיִּקָּר אֱלֹהִים in Numbers 23:4. Thus, this note collects phrases which are similar, yet they differ on one point, יְהוָה versus אֱלֹהִים.

The full list of references can be found by consulting the list in Mm 3268. The list shows the phrases in question and the reference for each member of each pair. Observe that some of the phrases in each pair are similar to the parallel but not identical (e.g. Psalm 40:18 versus Psalm 70:6, and note that Psalm 40:18 has אֲדֹנָי not יְהוָה, but see the *BHS* text-critical apparatus).

Exodus 12:29: בְּבֵית הַבּוֹר, Mp Note ה זונין בבית בית[22]

This note is another example from collative category 2. The Mp note simply says "5 pairs בבית בית," but index number 22 sends us to Mm 3761 where we can find the full title for this rubric: ה̇ זוגין מן ב̇ ב̇ מיחדין חד בְּבֵית וחד בֵּית וסימנהון, "5 pairs of unusual phrases which occur twice, once with בְּבֵית and once with בֵּית, together with their signs (references)." The note has collected five pairs of phrases. In any particular pair, the phrases are identical except for בְּבֵית versus בֵּית, the presence or absence of the בְּ preposition. Once again, the pairs contrast texts which are almost identical, yet they differ in some way. Mm 3761 gives the reference for each element in the pair.

The description in the note that each phrase occurs twice is not precisely correct. Each element is actually hapax; the note refers to them as occurring twice only because the elements of the pairs are so similar. Furthermore, for some of the pairs, other phrases exist which are no more different from the elements than the elements are different from each other. For example, the third pair is בְּבֵית רָשָׁע (Proverbs 3:33) versus בֵּית רָשָׁע (Micah 6:10), but there is also לְבֵית רָשָׁע (Proverbs 21:12). Thus, a better statement of the text feature would be "5 pairs of hapax phrases, once with בְּבֵית and once with בֵּית."

Genesis 1:12: לְמִינֵהוּ, Mp Note יד֫ [5]

By category, this is a simple Frequency note; however, index number 5 leads to the apparatus entry "Mp sub loco." Thus, this example serves as an illustration of how to deal with a "sub loco" note. The meaning and implications of the statement "sub loco" were discussed above. In general, it indicates some kind of problem in the Mp of L which Weil has corrected or otherwise altered for the Mp of *BHS*.

The student can approach the problem by two avenues. The most difficult (but probably the most educational) method is to compare the original Mp of L with the Mp of the *BHS*. (The Mp of L can be obtained by consulting either a photographic copy of L or *BHK*[3], which usually reprints L's Mp.) The student will then need to fill the role of a private investigator. What changes were effected for *BHS*? Why were the changes necessary? What is wrong with L's Mp note?

The easiest method for dealing with notes found in the Torah is to consult Mynatt's *The Sub Loco Notes of the Torah in BHS*. In that volume, the investigative work has already been done; the student simply needs to find the correct entry and read the article about the particular Mp note in question. The entries are arranged in the order of the biblical text, so in this case, the student should turn to the entry for Genesis 1:12. This work covers only the "sub loco" notes in the Torah; for the other sections of the Hebrew Bible, students must do their own research.

The entry for לְמִינֵהוּ explains that L's Mp note is ד֫ (occurs four times), although לְמִינֵהוּ actually occurs 14 times, as *BHS* Mp note states. The easiest explanation for the error is that, in the process of copying, the scribe accidentally omitted the ten's digit (י֫), leaving the erroneous impression that לְמִינֵהוּ occurs only four times.

Genesis 35:5: סְבִיבֹתֵיהֶם, Mp Note ב֫ מל֫ [8]

This is a Frequency note which has been qualified (occurs twice plene); however, index number 8 leads us to the apparatus entry "Mm 257 contra textum." Thus, this is an example of an Mm note which is "contra textum." See above for a complete discussion of "contra textum," but essentially it means that the Masorah contradicts the text, and the Masorah is probably more accurate.

The Mp tells us that סְבִיבֹתֵיהֶם occurs twice spelled plene, but since there are several letters in the word which could be either plene or defective, the issue is still ambiguous. Consulting Mm 257, one will discover from the title of the list that the issue is the *holem*. Mm 257 prescribes that the proper spelling in this case should be סביבוֹתֵיהֶם, with the plene *holem*; however the text has the defective *holem*. Thus, Weil has placed "contra textum" in the apparatus to alert the reader to the contradiction. Evidently, the spelling in the text has resulted from a scribal error, and the Masorah provides the correct reading.

Deuteronomy 28:49: מֵרָחוֹק, Mp Note ז חס בתור̇[43]

By category, this is another Frequency note, although it has been qualified extensively (occurs 7 times spelled defectively in the Torah). However, index number 43 leads us to the apparatus entry "Mp contra textum, cf Mp sub loco." Thus, this is an example of an Mp note which lacks an Mm note and is "contra textum." The additional statement "sub loco" is almost always included in these cases. Both statements have been discussed above.

The Mp of *BHS* tells us that מֵרָחוֹק occurs seven times spelled defectively, and "contra textum" alerts us to the fact that the Mp is contrary to the text. The obvious contradiction is that the Mp note is enumerating defective occurrences, but the text is spelled plene. "Sub loco" informs us that Weil planned to comment on this note further; however, since this note is in the Torah, the student can consult Mynatt's *The Sub Loco Notes of the Torah in the BHS* for more information. The student should look for the appropriate entry under Deuteronomy 28:49.

The entry explains that the Mp notes in L for the occurrences of מֵרָחֹק in Genesis 22:4 and Exodus 24:1 indicate that the word occurs only seven times in the Torah, and all seven occurrences should be spelled defectively. Furthermore, although L has מֵרָחוֹק spelled plene in Deuteronomy 28:49, the Aleppo Codex (see chapter 2 on this) has מֵרָחֹק spelled defectively, which is the form that L's Mp notes are calling for. Thus, it seems likely that the scribe of L accidentally added a ו to the text. Weil noted "contra textum" in the Masoretic apparatus to bring this contradiction to the reader's attention.

Notes

[1]See the *BHS* Introduction, p. XVI. Weil uses the term "quantitative" to describe those notes which were called Frequency Notes above.

[2]Mnemonic Notes like this one are an exception to the general rule of one Mp note per raised circule over a single word. See Chapter 1 on the general rule.

[3]Israel Yeivin, ***Introduction to the Tiberian Masorah***, trans. and ed. E.J. Revell, The Society of Biblical Literature Masoretic Studies, No. 5 (Missoula, MT: Scholars Press, 1980) pp. 74-80.

[4]In some printings of *BHK*^{3}, the note appears to be טֹ בחֹ, but in L it is טֹ כחֹ.

[5]This appears to be a correct assessment. We have found no evidence supporting the plene first *shureq* spellings in Genesis 35:23 and 46:14. The error was probably due to scribal carelessness concerning forms which depart from the usual spelling.

[6]E.F. Diaz-Esteban, *Sefer Oklah we-Oklah* (Madrid: Consejo Superior de Investigaciones Cientificos, 1975); S. Frensdorff, *Das Buch Ochlah W'ochlah* (1864; rpt. New York: Ktav Publishing House, 1972).

[7]This is Weil's terminology; see the *BHS* Introduction, pp. XIV–XV.

[8]See the *BHS* Introduction, pp. XIV.

[9]See the *BHS* Introduction, p. XV.

[10]For Weil's comments on these standardizations, see the *BHS* Introduction, pp. XV, XVII and XVIII.

Chapter 5

A Glossary of Masoretic Terms

Introduction

Below is a sample entry from the glossary which will serve as a model for illustrating the composite parts of each entry.

ישעיה

"The book of Isaiah."

Example: 2 Sam. 13:39 [Mp to נִחַם] ו̇ פת̇ וכל ישעיה דכות "One of 6 occurrences of נִחַם with *patah* in the final syllable, and all occurrences of this word in Isaiah are like this" [Mm 1775]. The other five occurrences are listed as Ezek. 32:31; Amos 7:3, 6; Jon. 3:9; Zech. 1:17. No indication is given of occurrences of this word in Isaiah. A concordance search yields these passages: Isa. 49:13; 51:3 (2x); 52:9. Reference sources: E-S, p. 754, #63–66; Ginsburg, II:278, #187.

Each entry will have some or all of the following components:

1) The term in question, enclosed within a rectangle.

2) A definition of the term enclosed within quotation marks. The definition may offer several translations of the term, not just one (e.g., כנוי). In some cases, the definition is followed by cross-references to similar terms and/or a general explanation of the term, but this additional information is not enclosed in quotation marks (e.g., מל̇).

3) An example, or perhaps several examples, drawn from *BHS*. For each example, the scripture reference is given, followed by the word or phrase under discussion enclosed in brackets. Then the Mp note for that word or phrase is printed as it appears in *BHS*.

4) A translation of the Mp note, enclosed in quotation marks. We have attempted to make the translations a reasonably literal rendering of the note; however, some liberties have been taken so that the meaning is clear. Sometimes we have enclosed information in parentheses which has not been stated explicitly in the Mp note but is either implied or crucial to its proper understanding (e.g., שפטים).

5) The Mm list number, enclosed in brackets. This item is normally the last component of the translation. The Mm list number refers the reader to Weil's *Massorah Gedolah*, where the pertinent list for the Mp note can be found. If there is no Mm list, then the translation will conclude with "[Mm lacking]."

6) An explanation for the Mp note. In most cases, the implications of the Mp note are made explicit by way of a short explanation. The explanation usually also includes relevant scripture passages.
7) Reference sources. These are citations of reference works where additional explanations or supporting information can be located.

List of Abbreviations

2ms second person masculine singular
2mp second person masculine plural
2x occurs twice in the given verse
3fs third feminine singular, etc.
3x occurs three times in the given verse
A the Aleppo Codex
BDB F. Brown, S.R. Driver, and C.A. Briggs. *A Hebrew and English Lexicon of the Old Testament*. Oxford: Clarendon Press, 1907.
BHK^3 R. Kittel. Ed. *Biblia Hebraica*. Stuttgart: Virtembergericum Institutum Biblicum, 1937.
BHS K. Elliger and W. Rudolph. Eds. *Biblia Hebraica Stuttgartensia*. Stuttgart: Deutsche Bibelstiftung, 1967/1977.
const. construct
E-S A. Even-Shoshan. Ed. *A New Concordance of the Bible*. Grand Rapids, MI: Baker Book House, 1985.
Gesenius Gesenius, H.F.W. *Gesenius' Hebrew Grammar*. 2nd English ed. Ed. E. Kautzsch. Trans. A. E. Cowley. Oxford: Clarendon Press, 1983.
Ginsburg C.D. Ginsburg, *The Massorah*. 4 vols. New York: Ktav, 1968. (unless otherwise noted
Imv. Imperative
Inf. Infinitive
L Codex Leningradensis
Mandelkern S. Mandelkern *Concordance on the Bible*. 2 vols. New York: Shulsinger Brothers, 1955.
Mynatt D.S. Mynatt, *The Sub Loco Notes of the Torah in BHS*. Fort Worth: Bibal Press, 1994.
Okhl S. Frensdorff, *Das Buch Ochlah W'ochlah*. 1864; rpt. New York: Ktav, 1972. (See the section "Independent Masoretic Treatises" in Chapter 2.)
Yeivin I. Yeivin. *Introduction to the Tiberian Masorah*. Trans. and Ed. E. J. Revell. Masoretic Studies, No. 5. Missoula, MT: Scholars Press, 1980.

Glossary Entries

The entries are alphabetized in the order of the Hebrew alphabet. Cross-references are given where the first letter of the entry is a preposition or particle attached to another term (e.g., דחס and חס̇).

א written alone, without the diacritical point (cf. א̇), refers to the first letter of the alphabet.

Examples:

a) Josh. 10:24 [Mp to הֶהָֽלְכוּא] יב̈ יתיר א ס״ת "One of 12 cases of a superfluous א at the end of a word" [Mm 907]. (Cf. Mm 3815.)

b) Josh. 18:8 [Mp to וּפֹה] ב̇ חד כת̇ ה וחד כת̇ א "One of 2 occurrences of this word, once written with ה, and once with א (וּפֹא Job 38:11) [Mm 3556].

c) Lev. 11:43 [Mp to וְנִטְמֵתֶם] ט̇ כת̇ חס̇ א ול̈ בליש "One of 9 words lacking a (customary) א (cf. נִטְמֵאתֶם in Ezek. 20:43), and the only occurrence of this particular form" [Mm 922, this Mm list indicates that this list is restricted to the Torah].

The number "one" (cf. חד).

1) א̇ normally occurs in number combinations involving other letters. Thus י̈א = "11" (Num. 32:32); כ̈א = "21" (Num. 26:62); ל̈א = "31" (Num. 27:3); etc.

2) א̇ stands alone when it is used in the abbreviated phrase ב̇ מ̇ א, translated "with only one exception."

Examples:

a) Gen. 22:18 [Mp to בְּקֹלִי] כל אורית̇ חס̇ ב̇ מ̇ א מל̈ "Every occurrence of בְּקֹלִי in the Pentateuch is written defectively (with a defective *holem*), except for one occurrence, which is written *plene*" (בְּקוֹלִי Num. 14:22) [Mm 153].

b) Exod. 7:12 [Mp to וַיַּשְׁלִיכוּ] דׄ מלׄ וכל כתיבׄ דכותׄ בׄ מׄ אׄ "One of 4 occurrences of this form (in the Pentateuch and Prophets) written *plene* (with full *hireq-yod*) and all occurrences in the Writings are likewise written *plene*, with one exception" (וַיַּשְׁלִכוּ Neh. 9:26) [Mm 415].

3) A *hapax legomenon* (the Greek designation for a word whose given form occurs only once) is indicated in the Mp notes by לׄ and not by אׄ.

אׄ, בׄ, גׄ...תׄ

Letters of the alphabet with diacritical marks above them have several functions:

1) When placed as the final letter of a word they indicate that the word is abbreviated. Some of the more common abbreviations are מלׄ (מלא) "*plene*" (cf. Josh 16:10); חסׄ (חסר) "defective" (cf. Deut. 17:14); כתׄ (כתיב) "written" (cf. Gen. 14:2).
2) Sometimes an individual letter or series of letters having diacritical marks above them will function as abbreviated words. Examples are לׄ (לית) "one of a kind, unique," Gen. 1:11; בׄ מׄ (בר מן) "except," Gen. 3:10; קׄ (קרי) "to be read," Gen. 8:17.
3) Post-biblical scholars assigned numerical value to the letters of the alphabet and used them either alone or in combination with other letters to indicate the number of times some feature occurred in the MT. Here is a partial listing of these numbers.

אׄ = 1	יׄאׄ = 11	כׄאׄ = 21	קׄאׄ = 101
בׄ = 2	יׄבׄ = 12	כׄבׄ = 22	רׄ = 200
גׄ = 3	יׄגׄ = 13	לׄ = 30†	שׁׄ = 300
דׄ = 4	יׄדׄ = 14	מׄ = 40	תׄ = 400
הׄ = 5	טׄוׄ = 15‡	נׄ = 50	תׄקׄ = 500
וׄ = 6	טׄזׄ = 16	סׄ = 60	תׄרׄ = 600
זׄ = 7	יׄזׄ = 17	עׄ = 70	תׄשׁׄ = 700
חׄ = 8	יׄחׄ = 18	פׄ = 80	
טׄ = 9	יׄטׄ = 19	צׄ = 90	
יׄ = 10	כׄ = 20	קׄ = 100	

†(not לׄ, cf. Deut. 32: 51) Note, however, that 31–39 are formed with לׄ, as לׄאׄ (31), לׄבׄ (32), etc.

‡(in Mp, cf. Gen 23:9)

א״ב

Abbreviation for אלפיא ביתא.

1) "The Hebrew Alphabet."
   Example: Jer. 32:29 [Mp to וּבָאוּ] כוׄ פסוקׄ דאית בהון א״ב "One of 26 verses that have within them all the letters of the alphabet." [Mm lacking]

Reference Source: One list may be found in Ginsburg, II:456.

2) א״ב is sometimes used as a special designation for Ps. 119, because of its structure as an alphabetic acrostic poem. This psalm is sometimes designated as אלפא ביתא רבא "the Great Alphabet."

Examples:

a) Ps. 119:57 [Mp to דְּבָרֶיךָ] ג̇ מל̇ בא״ב "Three times in Ps. 119 (vv. 57, 130, 139) this form is written *plene*" (i.e., דְּבָרֶיךָ rather than דְּבָרְךָ) [Mm 3408].

b) Deut. 33:10 [Mp to וְתוֹרָתְךָ] ב̇ וכל א״ב דכות "The word וְתוֹרָתְךָ occurs 2 times (cf. Deut. 33:10; Ps. 40:9), and always has this form when it occurs in Psalm 119" (cf. vv. 29, 109, 113, 142, 174). [Mm lacking]

Reference source: E-S, pp. 1225f.

אדכר̇

Abbreviation for אדכרה (אדכרא). Alternate form is אזכרה (אזכרא). This term is substituted for the Tetragrammaton (יהוה) in order to safeguard its sanctity.

Examples:

a) 2 Chr. 11:11 [Mp to וַיְחַזֵּק] ה̇ וכל דסמיכ̇ לאדכרה דכות̇ "One of 5 occurrences of this form, and in all cases where it is followed by the Tetragrammaton (יהוה) it has this same form" (cf. Exod. 9:12) [Mm 1661].

b) Mal. 3:1 [Mp to וּמַלְאַךְ] ב̇ פת̇ וכל דסמיכ̇ לאדכרה דכות̇ "Twice וּמַלְאַךְ is written with *patah* (instead of the ordinary מַלְאָךְ, with *qamets*) and in all cases where it is followed by the Tetragrammaton (יהוה) it has this same form" (cf. Judg. 6:21) [Mm 3187].

אורית̇

Abbreviation for אוריתא. Alternate forms are אורי̇, אור̇, and או̇. Cf. תורה, באר̇, and בתור̇. "Pentateuch, Torah."

Examples:

a) Gen. 22:18 [Mp to בְּקֹלִי] כל אורית̇ חס ב̇ מ̇ א̇ מל̇ "Every occurrence of בְּקֹלִי in the Pentateuch is written defectively (with a defective *holem*) with one exception, which is written *plene*" (בְּקוֹלִי Num. 14:22) [Mm 153].

b) Deut. 31:30 [Mp to אֶת־דִּבְרֵי הַשִּׁירָה] ג̇ חד באור̇ חד בנביא̇ וחד בכתיב̇ "This phrase, 'the words of this song,' occurs 3 times, once in the Pentateuch, once in the Prophets (cf. 2 Sam. 22:1), and once in the Writings" (cf. Ps. 18:1) [Mm 4256].

"Letter or letters of the alphabet." Abbreviation for אותיות. Alternate form is אתין̇.

Examples:

a) Lev. 11:42 [Mp to גָּחוֹן] (with *vav* maiusculum) חצי אותיות בתור֯ "The middle of the letters in the Pentateuch."

b) Jer. 6:7 חצי המקרא באותיות "The middle of the Bible by letters" (i.e., the middle letter of the Bible. Note that the specific letter is not indicated.

c) Ps. 80:14 [Mp to מִיָּ֑עַר] ד֯ אות֯ תלויות "One of 4 raised letters." The others are found in Judg. 18:30; and Job 38:13, 15 [Mm 3557]. See chapter 3 for a discussion of this phenomenon.

d) Josh. 11:14 [Mp to וְכֹל] ג֯ פסוק֯ וכל כל וחד מן ג֯ ר״פ וכל ופ֯ אות֯ "There are 3 verses in which וכל כל כל occur and 1 of 3 occurrences of וכל at the beginning of a verse with 80 letters." This note is calling attention to two different textual phenomena: 1) there are three verses in which the words וכל כל כל occur (in this order), and 2) this is one of three verses where וכל is at the beginning of a verse which has 80 letters.

א֯ ז֯ ן֯

Abbreviations for אני "I" or אלה "these," זאת "this," and נא (particle of entreaty).

Example: Ps. 25:7 [Mp to זְכָר־] ב֯ וכל דסמיכ֯ ל א֯ ז֯ ן֯ דכות֯ "The form זְכָר־ (imperative 2ms, with *qamets* instead of זְכֹר) occurs twice (cf. Lam. 3:19), and in all cases where it is followed by and joined by *maqqef* to אני or אלה, זאת, or נא it takes this same form" (cf. Pss. 89:48; 74:18; 2 Kgs. 20:3).
Reference source: Ginsburg, I:463, #83; IV:360, #83.

איוב

"The book of Job."

Examples:

a) Prov. 18:5 [Mp to בַּמִּשְׁפָּט] ח֯ דגש֯ וכל איוב דכות֯ ב֯ מ֯ א֯ "One of 8 cases of בַּמִּשְׁפָּט with *dagesh*, and all occurrences (of this word) in the book of Job are written similarly, with one exception" (בְמִשְׁפָּט in Job 14:3) [Mm 772].

b) Ezra 1:4 [Mp to מְקֹמוֹ] ו֯ חס֯ בליש֯ וכל אורית֯ ואיוב דכות֯ ב֯ מ֯ ב֯ "One of 6 cases where מְקֹמוֹ is written defectively in this form (with 3ms pronominal suffix), and all occurrences in the Pentateuch and Job are written similarly (defectively) with two exceptions" (twice in Job it is written *plene*: מְקוֹמוֹ Job 20:9; 37:1) [Mm 489].
Reference source: Mandelkern, p. 1225.

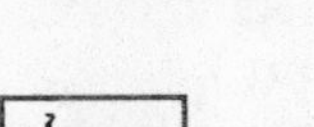

אילן

"These."

Example: Ps. 136:1 [Mp applies to the entire verse] אילן כו̇ פסוק̇ כנגד "These 26 verses (are divided into) corresponding halves."

אית

Alternate form דאית (cf. לית). "There is, there are."

Examples:

a) Gen. 5:32 [Mp to נֹחַ] ה̇ פסוק̇ דאית בהון ה̇ מילין מתאימין "One of 5 verses which have in them 5 similar words" (in each of these verses the Mp note is placed on the first of a series of five two-letter words, cf. Gen. 35:17; 1 Sam. 20:29; 1 Kgs. 3:26; Neh. 2:2) [Mm 1890].

b) Exod. 16:16 [Mp to זֶה] כ̇ו̇ פסוק̇ דאית בהון א״ב "One of 26 verses which have within them the letters of the alphabet." [Mm lacking]

אית̇

Abbreviation for איתתא. Cf. אנש. "Wife, woman."

Examples:

a) Isa. 6:6 [Mp to רִצְפָּה] ל̇ וכל שם אית̇ דכות̇ "This is the only occurrence of רִצְפָּה as a simple noun, but in all cases where it represents a woman's name it has this same form" (cf. 2 Sam. 3:7; 21:8, 10, 11). [Mm lacking]

b) 1 Chr. 8:9 [Mp to חֹדֶשׁ] ל̇ שם אית̇ "The only occurrence of חֹדֶשׁ as a woman's name" (its normal meaning is "new moon, month," cf. Gen. 7:11; etc.). [Mm lacking] A "Mp sub loco" note accompanies this entry in *BHS*.

אכילה

Cf. לשון אכילה. "Food, a meal, the act of eating."

Example: Ps 19:9 [Mp to בָּרָה] ה̇ כת̇ כן וכל לשון אכילה דכת̇ "One of 5 occurrences of בָּרָה written thus" [i.e., with final ה rather than final א (cf. Mm 3680)], "and all forms of בָּרָה meaning 'to eat' are written thus" (i.e., with ה as the third consonant of the verb root) [Mm 3680].

אמירה

"The act of saying, to say."

Examples:

a) Gen. 17:17 [Mp to וַיֹּאמֶר בְּלִבּוֹ] ו̇ אמירה פלוני בלבו "There are 6 cases where

some form of the verb אמר ('he said') is followed by בְּלִבּוֹ ('in his heart'), referring to someone saying in his heart." Note: The six passages are Gen. 17:17; 27:41; 1 Kgs 12:26; Isa. 47:10; Obad. 3; Eccl. 2:15. (Since Mm is lacking, these references have to be gathered from a Hebrew concordance. E-S, pp. 85ff. was the source used here.) The more commonly occurring form used to describe someone speaking in his heart is בִּלְבָבוֹ (cf. Deut. 7:17; 9:4; Isa. 47:8; etc.). As is normally the case, the Mp was placed here to protect the minority reading. [Mm lacking]

b) Gen. 24:50 [Mp to רַע] ט וכל אמירה יצר לשון עשייה ועין דכות ב מ ז "One of nine cases of רַע [i.e., pointed with *patah*; forms with *qamets* are far more frequent]; and רַע also occurs in all cases where the reference is to speaking evil, an evil imagination or intention, doing evil, or appearing evil in one's eyes, with 7 exceptions" [where the form is רָע]. Note: Reference is made to nine cases of רַע, but only eight are given in Mm 824. These are Gen. 24:50; 41:21; Lev. 27:10; Num. 11:1; Jer. 2:19; Ps. 7:10; Prov. 11:15; Neh. 2:1. The ninth occurrence remains in doubt (perhaps Prov. 23:6 or 28:22 was intended?). The seven exceptional occurrences of רָע in the categories listed above are Num. 11:10; 1 Sam. 29:7; Mal. 2:17; Eccl. 4:3; 8:11, 12; 2 Chr. 33:9.

Reference sources: Mm 824 (cf. Mm 3290); E-S, pp. 1080f.; Mandelkern, p. 1101; Ginsburg, II:578f., #374–76 (for variant listings from other sources).

Abbreviation for אמצע. Also used with the preposition ב as באמ֗,באמצע. Alternate forms are מצעא,מ׳צעא,מ״פ. "Within, in the middle." When it is used to contrast ר״פ or ס״פ, it may apply to any word other than the first or last word of the verse, in which case it may be abbreviated as מ״פ. In fact, this is the usual form one finds in *BHS*.

Examples:

a) Josh. 13:21 [Mp to וכל] י ר״פ וכל ומ״פ וכל "One of 10 verses with וכל both at the beginning and within the verse." The ten are Gen. 2:5; Exod. 13:13; Lev. 7:9; 15:17, 20; Josh. 13:21; 1 Kgs. 10:21; 2 Chr. 9:20; Jer. 31:40; Ezek. 12:14. [Mm lacking]
Reference source: Ginsburg, II:37f. #224.

b) 2 Chr. 24:10 [Mp to וְכָל־הָעָם] נא מ״פ וכל ר״פ דכות ב מ ג "One of 51 occurrences of וְכָל־הָעָם within a verse, and it always has this same form when it stands at the beginning of the verse, with 3 exceptions." [Mm lacking]
Reference source: Cf. Mynatt, pp. 82–83, #80.

אמ״ת

Abbreviation for the three major poetic books: אִיּוֹב מִשְׁלֵי תְּהִלִּים (Job, Proverbs, Psalms). Also designated as שלש ספרים, "the three books."

Examples:

a) Ps. 33:17 [Mp to לֹא יְמַלֵּט] בׄ בספר אמ״ת "One of two occurrences of this combination of words in the books of Job, Proverbs, and Psalms" (cf. Job 20:20). [There is no occurrence of this phrase in Proverbs.] (Cf. Amos 2:14f.) [Mm lacking]

b) Ps. 51:18 [Mp to כִּי] יׄא בטע ר״פ בשלש ספרים "The word כִּי occurs 11 times at the beginning of the verse with this accent (*mehuppak legarmeh*) in the three books (Job, Proverbs, Psalms)." (The eleven occurrences are Pss. 5:5; 16:10; 32:4; 51:18; 94:14; 96:5; Prov. 1:9; 23:7; 24:20; Job 5:6; 20:20.) [Mm lacking]
Reference source: Ginsburg, II:29, #126.

אנש

"Man," or in certain instances, "person," including females. אנש is generally used with reference to a word that can be used either as a common noun or a proper name. Cf. אי̇ת and שם.

Examples:

a) Ps. 71:3 [Mp to מָעוֹן] דׄ וכל שם קריה ואנש דכות "The word מָעוֹן occurs 4 times (as a common noun, cf. 1 Sam. 2:29, 32; Pss. 71:3; 90:1) and in all cases where it is used as the name for a city or a man, it has this same form" (cf. 1 Chr. 2:45; Judg. 10:12; etc.) [Mp lacking].
Reference source: E-S, pp. 686f.

b) 2 Sam. 17:20 [Mp to מִיכַל] לׄ וכל שם אנש דכות "The word is unique (as a common noun, meaning 'brook, stream'), but in all cases where it is used as a person's name (Michal, cf. 1 Sam. 14:49; etc.), it has this same form." [Mm lacking]

See אי̇ת.

The pausal accents *athnah*, *soph pasuq*, and *zaqqef.*"

Example: Exod. 16:33 [Mp to אַחַת] וׄ זקף פת וכל חקה מדה שנה תורה ואספ
דכות במא "The word אַחַת occurs 6 times with *pathah* accented with *zaqqef qatan*. Furthermore, the word is always written this way when it is combined with

the terms תּוֹרָה (Law), שָׁנָה (year), מִדָּה (measure), חֻקָּה (ordinance), or when it is accented with *athnah*, *soph pasuq* or *zaqqef*, with one exception" [Mm 492]. Mm 492 lists the six occurrences: Exod. 16:33; Josh. 6:14; 1 Sam. 26:8; 2 Sam. 6:19; 1 Kgs. 3:25; Zech. 5:7. The one exception is Deut. 24:5 where the combination is שָׁנָה אֶחָת. Apparently this note is not meant to be exhaustive because the word אַחַת occurs over 100 other times. Based on a comparison with Ginsburg, the note should be read ו֗ זקף פת֗ וכל חקה מדה שנה תורה דכות֗ במ֗א֗ ואס֗פ֗ דכות֗ "The word occurs 6 times with *pathah* accented with *zaqqef qatan*. Furthermore, the word is always written this way when it is combined with the terms תּוֹרָה (Law), שָׁנָה (year), מִדָּה (measure), חֻקָּה (ordinance), with one exception (שָׁנָה אֶחָת), and it is always written like this (with *qamets*) when accented with *athnah*, *soph pasuq* or *zaqqef*." The correct reading is arrived at by placing ואס֗פ֗ after במ֗א֗.

Reference source: Ginsburg, I:42, #287; IV:46, #287.

"Anger" (חמת אף).

Example: Amos 6:2 [Mp to חֲמָת] ל֗ וכל חמת אף דכות֗ "The word is unique (as a proper name), but all of the occurrences which mean 'anger' are like it." [Mm lacking]

Reference source: E-S, p. 377, #41–59.

"Lion."

Example: Jer. 39:7 [Mp to לָבִיא] ב֗ וכל לשון אריה דכות֗ "The word לָבִיא (as abbreviated form of לְהָבִיא 'to bring') occurs twice (cf. 2 Chr. 31:10), and all other occurrences of the word in this form mean 'a lion'" (cf. Gen. 49:9; Num. 24:9; Joel 1:6; Nah. 2:12; etc.). [Mm lacking]

Reference sources: E-S, pp. 158 (#2032–33), 588 (לָבִיא, #1–12); BDB, p. 522.

ארמי

Abbreviated form of ארמית. Cf. לשון ארמית. "Aramaic, the Aramaic language" (as found in Ezra and Daniel).

Examples:

a) Jer. 12:9 [Mp to הֵתָיוּ] ג֗ ב֗ מנה֗ בליש֗ וחד לשון ארמי "The word הֵתָיוּ (Hif'il imperative, 2mp, from אתה 'Bring!') occurs 3 times, twice in Hebrew (cf. Isa. 21:14) and once in Aramaic (cf. Dan. 3:13)." [Mm lacking] Although there is no Mm listing, the same Mp note occurs in Jer. 12:9; Isa. 21:14; and Dan. 3:13.
Reference sources: Gesenius, *Grammar*, §68i, p. 186; E-S, p. 141.

b) 2 Kgs. 20:3 [Mp to אָנָּה] ו֗ כת֗ ה וכל ר״פ וכל לשון ארמית דכות "One of 6 cases where אָנָּה occurs with final ה (instead of the more common אָנָּא [cf. Gen. 50:17; etc.], and all occurrences of this word at the beginning of a verse, and all forms occurring in the Aramaic portions of the Bible are written in the same way (i.e., with final ה, cf. Dan. 2:8; etc.)" [Mm 2169].
Reference sources: E-S, p. 93; Ginsburg, I:95 #918.

אשור

"Ashur/Assyria." See משיחה.

אתנ֗ח

Abbreviation for אתנחתא. "The accent *'atnah.*"

Examples:

a) Num. 11:11 [Mp to לְעַבְדֶּ֔ךָ] ז֗ וכל אתנח וס״פ דכות ב֗ מ֗ א֗ "One of 7 occurrences of this form (i.e., a pausal form accented with *zaqef* on the next to the last syllable). The form is the same when the accent is either *'atnah* or *sof pasuq* (*silluq*), with one exception (i.e., Ps. 119:65, where *sof pasuq* [*silluq*] falls on the final syllable [עַבְדְּךָ֑])" [Mm 1660].

b) Gen. 3:10 [Mp to אָנֹ֔כִי] ח֗ בטע֗ וכל זקף אתנח וס״פ דכות ב֗ מ֗ א֗ "One of 8 occurrences of אָנֹ֔כִי with the accent on the next to the last syllable (i.e., מִלְעֵיל). And in all cases where this word is accented with either a *zaqef*, *'atnah*, or *sof pasuq* (*silluq*), the accent will fall on the next to the last syllable, with one exception (cf. Job 33:9, where אָנֹכִ֑י occurs with אתנח on the final syllable)" [Mm 1571].

ב

ב

"In, into, with." A preposition that is prefixed to the following word.

Examples:

a) Jer. 13:12 [Mp to וְאָמַרְתָּ֤ אֲלֵיהֶם] ג֗ בטע֗ ר״פ בסיפ֗ "One of 3 occurrences of this phrase with this accent (*'azla*) at the beginning of a verse in this book (Jeremiah)." (Cf. Jer. 13:12, 13; 19:11.) [Mm lacking]
Reference sources: E-S, p. 86; Ginsburg, I:88, #816.

b) 1 Kgs. 16:18 [Mp to וַיְהִי] ט̇ בטע בסיפ̇ "One of 9 occurrences of וַיְהִי with this accent (*garshayim*)(at the beginning of the verse) in this book (i.e., the book of Kings, both 1 and 2 Kings)." (Cf. 1 Kgs. 3:18; 5:21; 12:2, 20; 16:18; 2 Kgs. 5:8; 10:25; 13:21; 18:9.) [Mm 1955]

"The number two."

Examples:

a) Exod. 5:1 [Mp to כֹּה־אָמַר יְהוָה אֱלֹהֵי יִשְׂרָאֵל] כ̇ד̇ ב̇ מנה בתור̇ "The phrase listed above occurs 24 times (in the Bible), 2 of them in the Pentateuch." (Cf. Exod. 32:27.) [Mm lacking]
Reference source: Ginsburg, I:26, #74; Mynatt, pp. 102–3, #108.

b) Jer. 16:16 [Mp to וְאַחֲרֵי־כֵן] ב̇ מ״פ בנבי̇א "One of 2 cases of this phrase within a verse in the Prophets." (Cf. Jer. 46:26.) [Mm lacking]
Reference source: E-S, p. 41 (#316, 318).

"Well, spring, fountain."

Example: Gen. 26:33 [Mp to שִׁבְעָה] ל̇ שם באר "The word שִׁבְעָה occurs only here as the name of a well." [Mm lacking]

בבני גד

"In the section on the sons of Gad." (Cf. 1 Chr. 5:11–22.)

Example: 1 Chr. 5:12 [Mp to וְשָׁפָט] ל̇ בבני גד "This word occurs only once in the section on the sons of Gad." [Mm lacking] It does occur outside of this section (cf. 1 Chr. 3:22).

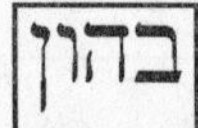

"In them, in which." (ב prefixed to הון)

Examples:

a) Gen. 5:32 [Mp to נֹחַ] ה̇ פסוק̇ דאית בהון ה̇ מילין מתאימין "One of 5 verses in which there are 5 similar words." The similarity is that in each case the five words stand in consecutive order and have two letters each. (Cf. Gen. 5:32; 35:17; 1 Sam. 20:29; 1 Kgs. 3:26; Neh. 2:2.) [Mm 1890]
Reference source: Cf. Mynatt, pp. 118–20, #132.

b) Exod. 23:13 [Mp to לֹא] ד̇ פסוק̇ דאית בהון לא לא ומילה חדה ביניה̇ "One of 4 verses in which לֹא occurs twice, with one word between them." (Cf. Exod. 23:13; Isa. 16:10; 57:11; 64:3.) [Mm 2267]

בּוֹזֹמֹיֹם

A mnemonic sign giving the correct form for certain words in Num. 29. Cf. סימן for a discussion of mnemonic signs.

Example: Num. 29:33 [Mp to כְּמִשְׁפָּטָם] סימן בּוֹזֹמֹיֹם "The sign is בּוֹזֹמֹיֹם." This mnemonic sign gives the correct form for words spelled irregularly in the passage concerning the offerings made at Succoth (the Feast of Booths, Num. 29:12–38). The offerings in this passage are specified according to the day of the festival. The first three abbreviations in the mnemonic sign are numbers that indicate by the number of the day the passages which contain an irregular spelling (בֹּ = second day [29:17–19], וֹ = sixth day [29:29–31], זֹ = seventh day [29:32–34]). The last three abbreviations are the letters creating an unusual form for one word in each of the three passages. The מֹ draws attention to וְנִסְכֵּיהֶם in 29:19 and the יֹ draws attention to וּנְסָכֶיהָ in 29:31. The usual form for this word in this passage is וְנִסְכָּה (29:16, 22, 25, 28, 34, 38). The ם draws attention to כְּמִשְׁפָּטָם in 29:33, which is otherwise spelled כַּמִּשְׁפָּט in this passage (29:18, 21, 24, 27, 30, 37). The last three letters in the mnemonic sign form the word מים ("water"), which is appropriate for a mnemonic dealing with libations.

בטעׂ

"With this accent." ב plus the abbreviation for טעם. Mp notes dealing with accents have several functions. They may indicate the position of the accented or stressed syllable within a word (cf. דמטעׂ example "b" and זקף example "a" below). Frequently they note the occurrence of a particular accent within a word or a particular sequence of accents within a verse.

Examples:

a) Gen. 1:6 [Mp to וַיֹּאמֶר אֱלֹהִים] כֹּהֹ גֹ מנה בטעׂ בעינׂ "One of 25 occurrences of this phrase (in the Bible, cf. Mm 5), three of them found in this context and having the same accents" (*munah* and *zaqef*)(cf. Gen. 1:20, 26) [Mm 7].

b) Isa. 43:16 [Mp to כֹּה אָמַר יְהוָה] דֹ בטעׂ בסיפׂ "This phrase occurs 4 times with these accents (*yetiv–munah–zaqef*) in the book of Isaiah." (All are at the beginning of a verse.) [Mm lacking] According to the Mp notes in Isaiah, the other three references are Isa. 52:4; 56:1; 66:1.

ביאה

"Going, coming, entering," from בוא.

Example: Jer. 17:27 [Mp to וּבָא] בֹּ בלשון ביאה "One of two cases where this form is used in the sense of 'going,' or 'entering.'" (Cf. Est. 5:14.) [Mm 3764]

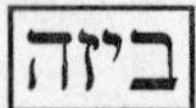

"Plunder, spoil, booty," from בזז.

Example: Gen 49:27 [Mp to עַד] ב̇ בלשון ביזה "One of two cases of עַד meaning 'booty, prey.'" The other case is Isa. 33:23. Normally, עַד is translated "as far as," "even to," "until." [Mm lacking]

Reference source: BDB, p. 723.

ביני̇ה

"Between them." Abbreviation for ביניהון.

Examples:

a) Gen. 47:19 [Mp to גַּם] י̇ פסוק בתור̇ גם גם ומילה חדה ביני̇ה "One of ten verses in the Pentateuch where גַּם appears twice with one word between them." [Mm lacking] A search of Mandelkern, p. 266, and verification of the Mp notes in *BHS*, identifies the ten occurences of גם...גם in the Pentateuch as Gen. 44:16; 46:34; 47:3, 19; 50:9; Exod. 5:14; 12:31; 18:18; Num. 18:3; Deut. 32:25.

b) Gen. 5:32 [Mp to אֶת־] י̇ב̇ פסוק את את ואת ומילה חדה ביני̇ה "One of 12 verses with את את ואת, with one word between them." The 12 references are Gen. 5:32; 6:10; 11:26; Exod. 21:5; Lev. 1:8; Deut. 3:24; 26:15; 28:20; Isa. 24:10; 29:10; Jer. 27:5; 29:17 [Mm 44].

בכיה

"Weeping, the act of weeping," from בכה.

Example: Ezek. 27:31 [Mp to וּבָכוּ אֵלַיִךְ] ג̇ בליש̇ וכל לשון בכיה על ב̇ מ̇ ג̇ "One of 3 occurrences of a form of the verb בכה in combination with the preposition אל (2 Sam. 1:24; 3:32; Ezek. 27:31); (elsewhere) the preposition accompanying a form of this verb will be על, with these three exceptions" (cf. Gen. 50:1; Judg. 14:17; Jer. 31:15; Lam. 1:16; etc.) [Mm 2898].

"In the Writings." Preposition plus abbreviation for כתיבין.

Examples:

a) Ps. 148:6 [Mp to יַעֲבוֹר] ז̇ מל̇ ג̇ מנה בכתי̇ב "One of 7 cases of יַעֲבוֹר written *plene* (with *holem-vav*), three of which are found in the Writings." (Cf. Est. 1:19; 9:27.) The other occurrences are in the Prophets (Isa. 26:20; 31:9; 40:27; Ezek. 48:14). [Mm lacking] See Mp sub loco note, probably with reference to Ezek. 48:14.

Reference source: Mandelkern, p. 817.

b) 2 Chr. 11:3 [Mp to וְאֶל כָּל־] יא בכתיב "This phrase occurs 12 times in the Writings." [Mm lacking]

בליש

"Language, form, meaning." Occasionally it means "in this and similar forms."

Preposition ב prefixed to the abbreviated form of לשון. Cf. ליש.

Examples:

a) Jer. 12:9 [Mp to הֵתָיוּ] ג ב מנה בליש וחד לשון ארמי "The word הֵתָיוּ (Hif'il imperative 2mp, from אתה, "Bring!") occurs 3 times, twice in the (Hebrew) language, and once in Aramaic." (Cf. Dan. 3:13) [Mm lacking] However, the same Mp note accompanies Jer. 12:9; Isa. 21:14; and Dan. 3:13.
Reference sources: Gesenius, §68i, p. 186; E-S, p. 141.

b) Jer. 17:17 [Mp to מַחֲסִי] ח רפי ב מנה בליש וכל אחסה דכות ב מ א "One of 8 cases where a form of the verb חסה occurs with the composite sheva (חֲ), two of which have this same form (מַחֲסִי, cf. Ps. 71:7). And all occurrences of אחסה have composite sheva under ח (אֶחֱסֶה), with one exception" (Ps. 57:2= אֶחְסֶה) [Mm 3046, 3278].

c) Exod. 15:1 [Mp to גָאֹה] יו כת ה בתור ב מנה בליש "One of 16 occurrences of a word written with a final ה (where ו would normally stand) in the Pentateuch, two of which have this form" (Exod. 15:21) [Mm 598].
Reference source: Cf. Mynatt, p. 128, #144.

d) Exod. 30:13 [Mp to גֵּרָה] ה ג כת ה וב בליש שם ברנש כת א "There are 5 occurrences of this form, 3 written with a final ה, and 2 with the meaning of a masculine name written with a final א" [Mm 1405]. The other two forms ending in ה are found in Lev. 11:3, 6. The two forms ending in א are in Judg. 3:15 and 2 Sam. 16:5. (Note that Mm 1405 distinguishes between types of occurrences.)

e) Lev. 2:4 [Mp to תַקְרִב] י חס בליש "There are 10 occurrences of this and similar forms (of the verb קרב) written defectively (with *hireq* instead of *hireq-yod*)" [Mm 667]. The remaining references are Lev. 9:9; Num. 3:4; 7:19; Deut. 1:17; Josh. 8:23; Ezek. 46:4; Dan. 3:8; 6:13 (*contra textum*); Ezra 6:17.

ב מ

"Except for, with the exception of." Abbreviation for בר מן.

Examples:

a) Gen. 23:18 [Mp to לְמִקְנָה] ל בסיפ וכל ירמיה דכות ב מ א "This is the only occurrence of מִקְנָה (a purchase) in Genesis. All the occurrences in Jeremiah are like it, with one exception." (Cf. מִקְנָה in Jer. 9:9) [Mm lacking]

b) Gen. 25:17 [Mp to וְאֵלֶּה] יז ר״פ בתור וכל תלדות דכות ב מ ד "The form וְאֵלֶּה occurs 17 times at the beginning of the verse in the Pentateuch, and whenever the phrase וְאֵלֶּה תּוֹלְדֹת (cf. Gen. 25:19) occurs, the form (וְאֵלֶּה) remains the same, except in the four cases" (אֵלֶּה) [Mm 267, 48]. Mm 48 gives the four exceptions as Gen. 2:4; 6:9; 11:10; 37:2. Note that all occur at the beginning of the verse.

במדבר

"The book of Numbers." (Cf. וידבר.)

Example: Lev. 13:6 [Mp to וְכִבֶּס] ט וכל במדבר דכות ב מ ב "This word (in this precise form, Piel Perfect 3ms) occurs 9 times, and all of the occurrences in the book of Numbers are like it with the exception of 2 (where the form is Pi'el Imperfect 3ms)" [Mm 734]. This word, in this precise form, occurs 9 times, all of which happen to be in the book of Leviticus (13:6, 34; 14:8, 9; 15:8, 11, 13, 27; 17:15). In addition, it always occurs in this form in the book of Numbers (19:7, 10, 19), with 2 exceptions where the imperfect occurs (Num. 19:8, 21).

בן אשר

"According to the Ben Asher tradition." This is usually stated in contrast to the Ben Naphtali tradition. (Cf. לבן אשר)

Examples:

a) Ps. 45:10 [Mp to בְּיִקְּרוֹתֶיךָ] ל וכן לבן אשר "This is the only occurrence of this word and it is pointed in accord with the Ben Asher tradition" [Mm 3276]. This Mm note states the difference in the pointing of this word between the Ben Asher and Ben Naphtali traditions.

בן אשר : בְּיִקְּרוֹתֶיךָ
בן נפתלי : בִּיקְּרוֹתֶיךָ

b) Job 3:5 [Mp to תִּשְׁכָּן־עָלָיו] כן לבן אשר "The form תִּשְׁכָּן is pointed according to the Ben Asher tradition" [Mm 3302]. The Mm note states the difference between the pointing of this word in the Ben Asher and Ben Naphtali traditions.

בן אשר : תִּשְׁכָּן־עליו
בן נפתלי : תִּשְׁכֹּן עליו

בנ״ך

"In the Prophets and the Writings." See נ״ך. Cf. כתיב and נביא.

"According to the Ben Naphtali tradition." This is usually stated in contrast to the Ben Asher tradition.

Example: Isa. 44:20 [Mp to הֲלֹא־] בן נפתלי הֲלֹא־ "According to the Ben Naphtali tradition, הֲלֹא־ is written with a *maqqef.*" The Ben Asher tradition is represented in the text as it now stands (הֲלֹא). [Mm lacking]

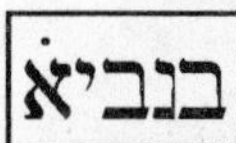

"In the Prophets." Preposition ב prefixed to the abbreviation for נביאים.

Examples:

a) Gen. 5:4 [Mp to שְׁמֹנֶה] כל קריא חס ב מ ג מל בנביא "The word שְׁמֹנֶה is written with defective *holem* in all the Bible, except for three occurrences in the Prophets where it is written *plene*" (שְׁמוֹנֶה, cf. Judg. 3:14; Jer. 52:29; Ezek. 40:31) [Mm 34].

b) Jer. 34:11 [Mp to וַיָּשׁוּבוּ] ו מל בנביא ול בסיפ "One of six cases in the Prophets where וַיָּשׁוּבוּ is written *plene* (instead of the more common וַיָּשֻׁבוּ, cf. Josh 2:23) and the only *plene* form in the book of Jeremiah." The six cases are Judg. 8:33; 21:23; 1 Kgs. 22:33; 2 Kgs. 1:5; Jer. 34:11; Zech. 1:6. The purpose of this Mp note was to protect the minority reading. [Mm lacking]
Reference source: E-S, p. 1121.

בסיפ

"In this book." (A reference to the book in which the Mp note occurs.) Preposition ב prefixed to the abbreviation for סיפרא. The form בספ in 2 Kgs. 15:38 is a typographical error for בסיפ.

Examples:

a) Ps. 92:2 [Mp to טוֹב] ג בטע ר״פ בסיפ "One of three occurrences of this accent (*revia'*) on the first word of a verse in the book of Psalms" (cf. Ps. 118:8, 9) [Mm 3400].

b) 1 Chr. 22:9 [Mp to הִנֵּה] ג ר״פ בסיפ "One of three occurrences of this word at the beginning of the verse in the book of Chronicles" (cf. 2 Chr. 2:3; 21:14) [Mm 4213].

בעינ

"In this context, pericope, section." (The biblical text had not yet been divided into chapters. ענינא generally indicates a rather loosely defined section.) The preposition

ב prefixed to the abbreviated form of ענ׳נא. The plural is ע׳ני׳ן.

Examples:

a) Gen. 1:6 [Mp to וַיֹּאמֶר אֱלֹהִים] כה ג מנה בטע בעינ "One of 25 occurrences of this phrase (in the Bible, cf. Mm 5), three of them found in this context and having the same accents" (*munah* and *zaqef*)(cf. Gen. 1:20, 26) [Mm 7].

b) Amos 1:14 [Mp to וְהִצַּתִּי אֵשׁ] ו ול בעינ "This is one of 6 occurrences of this phrase (cf. Jer. 17:27; 21:14; 43:12; 49:27; 50:32; Amos 1:14), and this is the only time it occurs in this context." The usual phrase found in this section of Amos is וְשִׁלַּחְתִּי אֵשׁ (cf. 1:4, 7, 10, 12; 2:2, 5) [Mm 3051].

Reference source: E-S, p. 487.

בפסוקים

"In, by verses," i.e., in the number of verses. Preposition ב prefixed to פסוקים.

Examples:

a) Gen. 27:40. Mp of *BHS*: חצי הספר בפסוקים "The half way point of the book of Genesis in the number of verses." The Mp sub loco note in *BHS* indicates that the Mp note in L has been clarified in *BHS* (cf. Mynatt, pp. 71–2, #64). It is correct as now written. (Cf. also Exod. 22:27; Lev. 15:7; Num. 17:20; Deut. 17:10.)

b) Lev. 8:8. Mp of *BHS*: חצי התורה בפסוק "The halfway point of the Pentateuch in the number of verses."

c) Mic. 3:12. Mp of *BHS*: חצי הספר בפוקים "Midpoint of the Book of the Twelve (not of Micah alone) in the number of verses."

בראשית

"The book of Genesis."

Example: 1 Chr. 1:17 [Mp to בְּנֵי שֵׁם] ה בטע זקף בעינ חלוף לבראשית "One of 5 (genealogical references, 'sons of—') in this section (of Chronicles) accented with *zaqef* (*qaton*), differing from the accentuation of Genesis."

Compare the following:

1 Chr. 1:17 with Gen. 10:22	בני שם
1 Chr. 1:30 with Gen. 25:14	משמע ודומה
1 Chr. 1:38 with Gen. 36:20	ובני שעיר
1 Chr. 1:40 with Gen. 36:23	בני שובל
1 Chr. 1:42 with Gen. 36:27	בני־אצר

(Note: 1 Chr. 1:40 and Gen. 36:23 are both pointed with *zaqef*, which may account for the Mp sub loco note to 1 Chr. 1:40.)

[Mm lacking] The five references in Chronicles are easily identified by the repetition of the Mp note in chapter 1. The Genesis parallels can be located by reference to a concordance.

ברנש

"A man, male, of the masculine gender." Abbreviation for בר אנש. This word is usually preceded by שם to indicate that a given word in the text may be used as a masculine proper name (cf. שם).

Examples:

a) Gen. 26:26 [Mp to וַאֲחֻזַּת] ל̇ שום ברנש "This is the only occurrence of this word as a man's name." The same word, as the construct of אֲחֻזָּה, is frequently used in the sense of "possession of" (cf. Lev. 27:24; Num. 27:7; Gen. 23:4, 9, 20; etc.). [Mm lacking]
Reference source: BDB, p. 28.

b) 1 Sam. 1:28 [Mp to שָׁאוּל] ב̇ וכל שם ברנש דכות "The form שָׁאוּל (the passive participle of שָׁאַל) occurs twice (cf. 2 Kgs. 6:5), and elsewhere the same form is used as a man's name (Saul)." [Mm lacking]

c) Exod. 30:13 [Mp to גֵּרָה] ה̇ ג̇ כת̇ ה וב̇ בליש שם ברנש כת̇ א "One of 5 occurrences of this word, 3 of which are written with a final ה, and 2 used to mean a man's name are written with a final א" (גרה, Exod. 30:13; Lev. 11:3, 6; and גרא, Judg. 3:15; 2 Sam. 16:5) [Mm 1405]. (Note that Mm 1405 distinguishes between types of occurrences.)

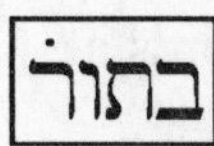

"In the Torah, Pentateuch." The preposition ב plus the abbreviation for תורה. See also אוריתא.

Examples:

a) Gen. 6:3 [Mp to לְעֹלָם] יח̇ חס̇ י̇ מנה בתור "One of 18 occurrences of this word written defectively (*plene* = עוֹלָם), 10 of which are in the Pentateuch." (Cf. Gen. 3:22; 6:3; Exod. 3:15; 15:18; 21:6; 31:17; 32:13; Lev. 25:46; Deut. 5:29; 32:40.) [Mm 25]

b) Gen. 29:31 [Mp to וַיַּרְא יהוה] ד̇ בתור "This phrase occurs 4 times in the Pentateuch." (Cf. Gen. 6:5; 29:31; Exod. 3:4; Deut. 32:19.) [Mm lacking]
Reference source: E-S, p. 1044. The more frequently occurring phrase is וַיַּרְא אֱלֹהִים (cf. Gen. 1:4, 10, 12, 18, 21, 25, etc.)

בתיבות

"In (the number of) words, according to words." The preposition ב plus תיבות.

Example: Lev. 10:16 [Mp to דָּרֹשׁ דָּרַשׁ] חצי התורה בתיבות "The midpoint of the Pentateuch according to the number of words falls between דָּרֹשׁ and דָּרַשׁ." [Mm lacking]

בתלים

"In the book of Psalms." The preposition ב plus תלים.

Example: Ps. 58:3 [Mp to עוֹלֹת] גׄ כתׄ כן בתור ובתלים "One of 3 occurrences of עוֹלֹת written thus (with *holem-vav* in the first syllable) in the Pentateuch and the book of Psalms" [Mm 297]. The references are Deut. 27:6; Ps. 58:3; 64:7. This note does not include references where both *holems* are written *plene* (cf. Ezek. 45:17; Ps. 66:13; etc.).

בתלת

"With three, with *seghol*." The preposition ב plus תלת, meaning "three," and, by analogy, "*seghol*."

Example: Gen. 26:25 [Mp to וַיֶּט־] בׄ מנוקדין בתלת "One of two occurrences of וַיֶּט־, pointed with *seghol*" (cf. 1 Chr. 15:1). [Mm lacking]

בתר

"After, behind, following, followed by, last." The alternative form is דבתר.

Examples:

a) Gen. 29:3 [Mp to וְנֶאֶסְפוּ־שָׁמָּה] יׄ מילין ר״פ ובתר שמה "One of 10 words at the beginning of a verse, each one followed (immediately) by שמה" (cf. Gen. 29:3; Exod. 29:43; Deut. 4:42; 12:6; Josh. 20:3; Judg. 18:15; 2 Kgs. 6:14; 9:2; Ezek. 11:18; Ps. 122:5) [Mm 1123].

b) Ezek. 5:11 [Mp to וְגַם] כגׄ פסוקׄ וגם ובתר תלת מילין "One of 23 verses ending in וגם followed by three words." [Mm 1629, the 23 references are given.]

בתרי לישנׄ

"With two meanings." The preposition ב plus תרי.

Examples:

a) Jer. 4:17 [Mp to מָרָתָה] בׄ בתרי לישנׄ "This word occurs twice, but with two (different) meanings." In Exod. 15:23, it means "to Marah" (with the ה directive affixed to מָרָה), while in Jer. 4:17, it is a Qal perfect 3fs from the verb מרה, translated "she has rebelled" [Mm 479].

b) Prov. 11:26 [Mp to וּבְרָכָה] בׄ ובתרי לישנׄ "This word occurs twice and with two (distinct) meanings" (cf. 1 Chr. 12:3) [Mm 3603].

"The number three."

Examples:

a) 1 Sam. 7:16 [Mp to וְסָבַב] ג֗ "One of 3 occurrences of וְסָבַב" (cf. Eccl. 9:14; 2 Chr. 33:14) [Mm 1561].

b) 1 Sam. 4:3 [Mp to וְיֹשִׁעֵנוּ] ג֗ ב֗ חס֗ וחד מל֗ "One of 3 occurrences of this form, 2 of which are written defectively (cf. 1 Sam. 4:3; 7:8), and one is written *plene*" (cf. Isa. 25:9; וְיוֹשִׁיעֵנוּ) [Mm 1550].

"Beside, close to." Alternate form is דגבי (relative pronoun ד plus גבי).

This term is normally followed by some word or phrase which gives the context for occurrences of the form marked by the Mp note. The word given in the Mp note may not literally be beside the form in question; it may not even be in the same verse. However, the word given in the Mp note will narrow the context so that the forms annotated by the Mp note can be easily found.

Example: Ps. 9:21: [Mp to מוֹרָה] ל֗ כת֗ ה וכל דגבי נזיר דכות "This word occurs once in addition to all of the occurrences close to the word נזיר which have the same form." This Mp note is calling attention to occurrences of מוֹרָה (as opposed to מוֹרָא). The note says that מוֹרָה occurs only once in addition to the occurrences which are close to the relatively rare term נזיר (cf. Judg. 16:17).

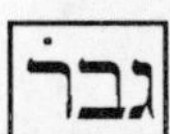

"Man, hero." Cf. אנש, ברנש. Plural גברי. This word, like ברנש, is frequently (but not always) preceded by שם, indicating that a given word in the text may be used as a masculine proper name.

Examples:

a) 1 Chr. 25:28 [Mp to הוֹתִיר] ל֗ שם גבר֗ "The only occurrence of הוֹתִיר as a man's name." Elsewhere הוֹתִיר is used as a Hif'il form of the verb יתר (cf. Exod. 10:15; Isa. 1:9; Jer. 44:7). [Mm lacking]

Reference source: BDB, p. 451; E-S, p. 515.

b) 2 Sam. 8:12 [Mp to רְחֹב] ב֗ חס֗ בגברי֗ "This word occurs twice spelled defectively as the (names of) men" [Mm 1746]. This note calls attention to the fact that רְחֹב occurs twice spelled with a defective *holem* when it refers to the personal name Rehob (cf. 2 Sam. 8:3). The personal name occurs once more spelled *plene* (Neh. 10:12). Furthermore, רְחֹב occurs spelled defectively when it is not a personal name (cf. Num. 13:21 where it is a place name).

געיא

"*ga'ya'* (*meteg*)." The absence of *ga'ya'* is called *hatef* (חטף, cf. 2 Chr. 6:42). Alternate forms are געׄי and גיעיה.

Examples:

a) Mic. 6:7 [Mp to בְּרִבְבוֹת] גׄ געיא "This form occurs 3 times with *ga'ya*'" (cf. Num. 10:36; Deut. 33:17). Note that Deut. 33:17 is marked "Mp contra textum." [Mm lacking]
Reference sources: E-S, p. 1056; on the function of *ga'ya'*, see Yeivin, pp. 240ff.

b) 2 Chr. 34:4 [Mp to וַיְנַתְּצוּ] גׄ ולא געיא "This form occurs 3 times without *ga'ya*'" (cf. 2 Chr. 31:1; 36:19). Note, however, that 2 Chr. 36:19 is written with *ga'ya'*. [Mm lacking]
Reference source: E-S, p. 798.

גריש

"The secondary accent *geresh*." Alternate form is גרש.

Example: Ps. 78:17 [Mp to לַמְרוֹת] לׄ גריש "This form is unique in that it is accented with both *ga'ya'* and *geresh*." It occurs also in Isa. 3:8, but only with *geresh*. [Mm lacking]

"The letter ד." When standing alone and without a diacritical point above it, ד represents the fourth letter of the alphabet (דלת).

Example: 2 Chr. 2:17 [Mp to לְהַעֲבִיד] לׄ כתׄ ד ושאר כתׄ ר "This is the only occurrence of this form written with final ד (Hif'il inf. cons. from עבד), and the remainder of such forms are written with final ר" (לְהַעֲבִיר, Hif'il inf. cons. from

עבר, cf. Lev. 18:21; 2 Sam. 3:10; 19:16; etc.). [Mm lacking]
Reference source: E-S, pp. 818, 827.

With the diacritical point written above it, ד̇ represents the number "four."
Examples:

a) Ezek. 28:25 [Mp to כֹּה־אָמַר אֲדֹנָי יְהוִה] ד̇ בטע ר״פ בסיפ̇ "This phrase occurs 4 times with these accents (*zarqa, munah, segolta*) at the beginning of a verse in the book of Ezekiel" (cf. Ezek. 44:9; 45:18; 46:1). [Mm lacking]
Reference source: E-S, p. 18.
b) Jer. 26:4 [Mp to וְאָמַרְתָּ אֲלֵיהֶם כֹּה אָמַר יְהוָה] ד̇ בסיפ̇ "This phrase occurs 4 times in the book of Jeremiah" (cf. Jer. 8:4; 13:13; 15:2; 26:4). [Mm 2492]

The relative pronoun "who, which, what, that," occurring only as a prefix (as illustrated below).

דאורית

"That (are) in the Pentateuch."
Example: Job 38:26 [Mp to עַל־אֶרֶץ] ט̇ וכל על ארץ מצרים דאורית דכות "This phrase occurs 9 times, and all references reading על ארץ מצרים that are in the Pentateuch are written like this" [Mm 2946]. The nine occurrences are given as Ezek. 28:17; 29:14; 38:11; Amos 9:6; Pss. 81:6; 110:6; 148:13; Job 38:26; Jer. 25:12 (וְעַל־אֶרֶץ). Pentateuchal references to על־ארץ מצרים include Gen. 41:45; Exod. 8:1, 3; 9:23; 10:6, 12, 13, 21.

דאית

"There is/are." See אית.
Example: Exod. 16:16 [Mp to וְזֶה] כ̇ו̇ פסוק דאית בהון א״ב "One of 26 verses in which are found all the letters of the alphabet." [Mm lacking]

Relative pronoun ד plus גבי. See גבי.

1) "*Dagesh.*" The opposite is רפי, "without *dagesh.*"
Examples:

a) Gen. 43:26 [Mp to וַיָּבִיאּוּ] לֹו וחד מן ד מילין דגש א בׄ מנה בליש "This is one of 36 occurrences of this word, and one of 4 words having a *dagesh* in an א, two of which are like this form" (cf. Ezra 8:18) [Mm 3916]. Note: The other two instances of *dagesh* in א are not identified, but see Yeivin, p. 285 and Mynatt, pp. 149–50, #176.

b) Gen. 2:25 [Mp to עֲרוּמִּים] דׄ מל בׄ דגש ובׄ רפי "One of 4 occurrences of this word written *plene*, two with *dagesh* (מּ) (cf. Gen. 2:25; Job 22:6) and two without *dagesh*" (cf. Job 5:12; 15:5) [Mm 18].

2) In connection with the inseparable prepositions ב, ל, and כ, the term דגש relates that the word in question should be pointed with the definite article (i.e., usually with *pathah* and *dagesh* forte). Oppositely, רפי means pointing without the article (i.e., usually *shewa*). With ו, the term דגש means that the word should be pointed with a *vav* consecutive, and רפי implies a *vav* conjunction.

Example: 1 Chr. 6:50 [Mp to בַּגּוֹרָל] וׄ דגש "One of six occurrences of בַּגּוֹרָל with *dagesh*, i.e., with ב which is pointed with the definite article" [Mm 4037]. The other five occurrences are Josh. 21:4, 5, 6, 8; 1 Chr. 6:46, 48. This note protects בַּגּוֹרָל from being harmonized with בְּגוֹרָל (cf. Num. 26:55; 33:54; etc.).

Abbreviation for דברי הימים, "the Book of Chronicles."

Example: Jer. 14:1 [Mp to עַל־דִּבְרֵי] יׄ וכל ד״ה דכות בׄ מׄ אׄ "This phrase occurs 10 times, and all occurrences in the Book of Chronicles (1 and 2) have this same form, with one exception" (cf. אֶל־דִּבְרֵי, 2 Chr. 35:22) [Mm 1718]. The ten occurrences of עַל־דִּבְרֵי (outside the Book of Chronicles) are 2 Sam. 3:8; 2 Kgs. 22:13 (2x); Jer. 7:8, 22; 14:1; 23:16; 26:5; Hag. 1:12; Ps. 7:1.

Abbreviation for דברי הימים וכל מחלה, "the Book of Chronicles is וכל מחלה."

דׄוׄםׄ is a mnemonic sign giving the correct form for the phrase כָּל־מַחֲלָה in the Book of Chronicles. Cf. תׄכׄהׄ. Cf. סימן for a discussion of mnemonic signs.

"Which is doubly defective." See חׄסׄ.

Example: Gen. 45:22 [Mp to חֲלִפֹת] בׄ חס דחס "Twice this word occurs in a doubly defective form" (with *hireq* for *hireq-yod* and *holem* for *holem-vav*) [Mm 336]. The second reference is in Judg. 14:12.

דיבור משה

"The act of Yahweh's speaking with or commanding Moses." (Cf. Hebrew דבר.)

Example: Exod. 16:34 [Mp to צִוָּה יְהוָה אֶל־מֹשֶׁה] ל̇ וכל דיבור משה ב̇ מ̇ א̇ "This phrase only occurs here in this form (with the preposition אֶל, instead of the sign of the direct object אֶת) and in all remaining references to Yahweh's addressing Moses, the phrase is צִוָּה יְהוָה אֶת־מֹשֶׁה, with one exception" (cf. Num. 3:1 דִּבֶּר יְהוָה אֶת־מֹשֶׁה). [Mm lacking] Examples of צִוָּה יְהוָה אֶת־מֹשֶׁה are found throughout the Bible (cf. Exod. 39:1, 5, 7; 40:19; Lev. 8:9; 9:10; Num. 1:19; Deut. 28:69; Josh. 11:15; 1 Chr. 22:13; etc.).

Reference sources: Mandelkern, pp. 988f; E-S, p. 980.

דין

"This, this one."

Example: Lev. 2:13 [Mp to עַל] ח̇ בטע̇ בסיפ̇ וחד מן ח̇ בטע̇ דין "One of 8 occurrences of עַל with this accentuation in Leviticus; and one of 8 occurrences of עַל with this accent (*merekha*)" [Mm 747]. This is a very complicated Mp note which has been altered from its original formulation in L. For a detailed discussion of the two text features in question, see Mynatt, pp. 176–77, #224. The first section of the note (ח̇ בטע̇ בסיפ̇) is grouping together eight occurrences of עַל in the book of Leviticus which bear any conjunctive accent as opposed to *maqqef* (cf. Mm 747, Ginsburg II:390, #356). The second section of the note (חד מן ח̇ בטע̇ דין) is drawing attention to eight occurrences of עַל or וְעַל in the Torah which actually bear the accent *merekha*. Thus, the note emphasizes the accent by use of the word דין: בטע̇ דין means "with this accent" (i.e., *merekha*).

דכות

ד prefixed to כות; דכותיה, "which is like it"; דכותיהון, "which is like them."

Examples:

a) Gen. 1:2 [Mp to וְרוּחַ אֱלֹהִים] ח̇ ב̇ מנה בליש̇ וכל שמואל דכות ב̇ מ̇ ה̇ רוח יי "One of 8 occurrences of וְרוּחַ אֱלֹהִים, two of which have this same form (i.e., with prefixed *vav*, cf. 2 Chr. 24:20) and all references in Samuel are like these (cf. 1 Sam. 10:10; 16:6; etc.), with five exceptions, where the reading is רוּחַ יְהוָה." The eight occurrences of רוח אלהים (not including those in Samuel) are Gen. 1:2; 41:38; Exod. 31:3; 35:31; Num. 24:2; Ezek. 11:24; 2 Chr. 15:1; 24:20. The five occurrences of רוּחַ יְהוָה in Samuel are 1 Sam. 10:6; 16:13, 14; 19:9; 2 Sam. 23:2 [Mm lacking].

Reference source: E-S, pp. 1064f.; Mynatt, pp. 91–92, #90.

b) 1 Sam. 1:20 [Mp to וַתִּקְרָא אֶת־שְׁמוֹ] י̇ וכל ויקרא שמו דכות ב̇ מ̇ ו̇ "This phrase (with the sign of the direct object אֶת־ prefixed to שְׁמוֹ following וַתִּקְרָא) occurs 10 times, and אֶת־ also occurs before שְׁמוֹ following וַיִּקְרָא, in all cases except 6." The ten occurrences of וַתִּקְרָא אֶת־שְׁמוֹ are Gen. 4:25; 30:11, 13, 20, 24; 38:4, 5; Judg 13:24; 1 Sam. 1:20; 2 Sam. 12:24. Some of the many references to the phrase וַיִּקְרָא אֶת־שְׁמוֹ are Gen. 4:26; 5:3, 29; 35:10; etc. The six exceptions to this way of writing this phrase are Gen. 25:26; 35:8; 38:29, 30; Exod. 17:15; Isa. 9:5, written in all instances as וַיִּקְרָא שְׁמוֹ [Mm 215, 183]. Reference sources: Mandelkern, p. 1041; E-S, p. 1028.

"The poor, a poor person."

Example: Prov. 22:22 [Mp to דַּל] י̇ב̇ וכל דל ואביון דכות "One of 12 occurrences of דַּל (written with *patah*, and including two Nif'al forms of דָּלַל, cf. Judg. 6:6 and Isa. 17:14), and in all occurrences of דַּל וְאֶבְיוֹן (cf. Ps. 72:13; 82:4), דַּל is also written with *patah*." The 12 references are Exod. 30:15; Lev. 14:21; Judg. 6:6, 15; 2 Sam. 13:4; Isa. 17:14; Ps. 141:3; Prov. 22:22; 28:11; Job 5:16; 28:4; Ruth 3:10. [Mm lacking]

Reference sources: Ginsburg, I:230, #163 (complete list given only here, and verified by the Mp notes in *BHS*); BDB, p. 195 (Nif'al forms of דָּלַל).

"Which is not." ד prefixed to לא. Cf. דלית.

דלא is simply the combination of the relative particle ד and the negative לא. The precise translation of דלא can vary as long as both aspects are retained. For an example, see מפ̇ק, example "a."

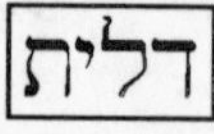

"Which is not, in which there is not." ד prefixed to לית.

Example: 1 Chr. 1:24 [Mp to שֵׁם] כ̇ב̇ פסוק דלית בהון לא ו ולא י "One of 22 verses which (do not) have in them either ו or י" [Mm 878]. The 22 references are listed.

"Which is misleading, resulting in error." ד prefixed to מ̇ט̇ע̇, abbreviation for מטעין. Applied to textual readings that might logically seem to need to be corrected, but where such correction would lead to error. See also סביר (סבירין). Many of the דמטע notes have to do with accents.

Examples:

a) Gen. 2:10 [Mp to יֵצֵא] בׄ דמטע "The form יֵצֵא occurs twice (with this accent, *munah*), which may be misleading" (but should not be emended)(cf. Ps. 19:6). (This form is misleading because it has *munah* where *pashta* might be expected.) [Mm 3227]

b) Jer. 14:4 [Mp to הָיָה] גׄ בטע דמטע "One of three occurrences of הָיָה with the accent (*merekha*, on the final instead of the next to final syllable) which, however, should not be emended since it would be incorrect to do so." [Mm lacking] The three passages (1 Kgs. 17:7; Jer. 14:4; 52:6) are listed in Ginsburg, I:305, #117, and further explained in IV:295, #117.

דמיין

"Similar, like, alike" (referring to words, phrases, etc.). From Aramaic דְּמָה (cf. Hebrew דָּמָה). See also מתאימין. In Dan. 5:19, דמין appears to be a typographical error for דמיין.

Examples:

a) Gen. 31:53 [Mp to אֱלֹהֵי] גׄ פסוק דמיין "Three verses are similar." Since the similarity is not defined in Mp, one must determine it by consulting Mm (where given). In this case, Mm 3356 in Weil's *Massorah Gedolah* gives the following notation: גׄ פסוק בקרייא דאית בהון גׄ וראשי פסוק קדמׄ ותליתׄ לא נסיבין ו תנינה נסיב ו "One of 3 verses in the Bible each having three similar words, the first of which stands as the first word of the verse. The first and third occurrences of the word are not accompanied by a (prefixed) *vav*, while the second is accompanied by (prefixed) *vav*." The three references and their words are

Gen. 31:53	אלהי	ואלהי	אלהי
Jer. 14:12	כי	וכי	כי
Ps. 92:4	עלי	ועלי	עלי

b) Ps. 73:2 [Mp to וַאֲנִי (first word in the verse)] גׄ פסוק דמיין "Three verses are alike." Since the similarity of the three verses is not specified in Mp, it must be ascertained by consulting Mm (where possible). Mm 3618 is keyed to this Mp note and gives the following data: גׄ פסוק בקרייא מן ז ז מילין וכל מילה מן ד ד אותיות "One of three verses in the Bible, each containing 7 words, and each word containing 4 letters." Mm 3618 identifies the three verses as Ps. 73:2; Prov. 12:16; 17:3.

"The book of Daniel."

Example: Ezra 5:2 [Mp to לְהוֹן] ב̇ ומל̇ וכל דניאל דכות ב̇ מ̇ א "One of 2 occurrences of this form (in Ezra) and both are written *plene*, and it is written like this (*plene*) in Daniel, with 1 exception." The two occurrences in Ezra are 4:20 and 5:2. The *plene* occurrences in Daniel include 2:35; 3:14; 6:3; 7:12. The defective form (לְהֹן) is found in Dan. 7:21. This note is designed to preserve the minority reading [Mm 3897 א].

Reference source: (for the *plene* readings in Daniel) E-S, p. 574, #59–62.

דסמי̇כ

"Which (closely) follows (ל̇)" (another word or group of words), "which is (closely) followed by (ל̇)" (another word or group of words). ד prefixed to סמי̇כ.

Examples:

a) Isa. 63:9 [Mp to וּמַלְאַךְ] ב̇ פת̇ וכל דסמי̇כ לאדכרא דכות̇ "Twice מַלְאַךְ is written with *patah* (instead of the more common מַלְאָךְ, with *qamets*), and in all four cases where it is followed by the Tetragrammaton (יהוה), it has this same form." The second occurrence of מַלְאַךְ is in Mal. 3:1. Examples of מַלְאַךְ יְהוָה are found in Gen. 16:7, 9, 10, 11; 22:11; etc." [Mm 3187]
Reference source: E-S, pp. 658f.

b) 2 Chr. 25:24 [Mp to אֱדוֹם] ל̇ מל̇ דסמי̇כ לעבד [Note: The Mp of *BHS* has to be corrected. It reads לעבר, but L has לעבד. Errors of this sort are rare.] "This is the only instance where אֱדוֹם is written *plene* (with *holem-vav*) when it follows immediately after עֹבֵד." The normal form is found in 2 Sam. 6:10, 11, 12; 1 Chr. 15:18, 21; etc. [Mm 4225] Note that Mm 4225 expands the Mp note by stating that אֱדוֹם is always written *plene* except when it stands after עֹבֵד. The Mp note protects the minority reading.

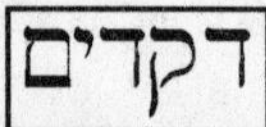

"Before, preceding." ד prefixed to קדים. See קדמ̇.

Example: Exod. 10:14 [Mp to לְפָנָיו] ד̇ דקדים אחריו "The form לְפָנָיו occurs 4 times (in the Bible) preceding the word אַחֲרָיו (in the same verse)." [Mm lacking] While a concordance search may have turned up these four verses, they were more easily located in Ginsburg, II:448, #169. They are Exod. 10:14; Josh. 10:14; Joel 2:3; 2 Kgs. 23:25.

When standing alone and without a diacritical point above it, ה represents the fifth letter of the alphabet (הא).

Examples:

a) Josh. 18:8 [Mp to וּפה] ב̇ חד כת̇ ה וחד כת̇ א "This form occurs twice, once written with (final) ה, and once written with (final) א" (cf. Job 38:11) [Mm 3556].

b) 1 Sam. 1:9 [Mp to שָׁתֹה] ג̇ כת̇ ה "One of 3 occurrences of this form written with (final) ה" [Mm 1531]. See Isa. 21:5; Jer. 49:12. The more common form is שָׁתוֹ. The Mp protects the minority reading.
Reference source: E-S, p. 1213, #4–9.

c) 1 Sam. 14:32 [Mp to שָׁלָל] חד מן י̇ג̇ חס̇ ה ר״ת בליש̇ "One of 13 cases of a missing ה at the beginning of words in this form (i.e. words that should have the definite article)." See 2 Sam. 23:9; 1 Kgs. 4:7; 7:20; 15:18; 2 Kgs. 11:20; 15:25; Jer. 10:13; 17:19; 40:3; 52:32; Ezek. 18:20; Lam. 1:18. [Mm 1856]

"Five."

Examples:

a) Gen. 28:17 [Mp to בֵּית אֱלֹהִים] ה̇ "This phrase occurs 5 times (in the Bible)" (cf. Gen. 28:22; Judg. 17:5; Ps. 42:5; 2 Chr. 34:9). The more common phrase is בֵּית הָאֱלֹהִים. The Mp note protects the minority reading. [Mm lacking]
Reference source: Mandelkern, pp. 192–95.

b) Hos. 8:9 [Mp to פֶּרֶא] ו̇ ה̇ מנה כת̇ א וחד כת̇ ה "One of 6 occurrences of this word, 5 of them written with (final) א (Gen. 16:12; Job 6:5; 11:12; 39:5) and one written with (final) ה (Jer. 2:24)" [Mm 3560].

"They, them." See בהון.

"Fifteen." This is the way that the number appears in the Masorah of the Leningrad Manuscript. One might expect it to be written as יה, but this is avoided to protect the sacredness of the Tetragrammaton (יהוה). "Fifteen" never appears in L as טו as it does in later Hebrew usage.

Examples:

a) Exod. 15:1 [Mp to וּבְנֵי יִשְׂרָאֵל] הי וכל ר״פ דכות "This phrase occurs 15 times (within a verse) and when it occurs at the beginning of a verse it has this same form" (Exod. 1:7, etc.) [Mm 470]. The other references are Exod. 14:8; 15:19; Lev. 24:23; Num. 26:4; Deut. 4:46; Josh. 10:20; 12:6, 7; Judg. 20:32; 1 Sam. 14:18; 2 Sam. 21:2; Hos. 2:2; Ezra 3:1; Neh. 7:72.

b) Jer. 2:9 [Mp to לָכֵ֗ן] הי בטע בסיפ "The form לָכֵ֗ן occurs 15 times with this accent (*revia'*) in the book of Jeremiah" [Mm 2617]. The other occurrences are 5:14; 6:21; 9:6, 14: 11:11, 21, 22; 18:13; 28:16; 35:19; 44:11; 50:18, 39; 51:36.

הכלית

"The kidneys." Also הכליות. See הכלית.

הליכה

"Walking, going." From הלך. See לשון הליכה.

Example: Gen. 27:37. [Mp to וּלְכָה] ד מל וכל לשון הליכה דכות ב מ ג "The word לְכָה is written *plene* 4 times (for לְךָ, 'to you'), and all occurrences of this form in the sense of 'walking' ('going') have this same form, with 3 exceptions (where it is written defectively as לְךְ)." This Mp note seeks to clarify the situation with reference to לְךָ and לְכָה. Each is used with two meanings. Normally, "to you" is written לְךָ; in four instances, however, it is written *plene* as לְכָה (Gen. 27:37; 2 Sam. 18:22; Isa. 3:6; Ps. 80:3). Likewise, "Go!," the imperative of הָלַךְ, is normally written לְכָה but in three instances (Num. 23:13; Judg. 19:13; 2 Chr. 25:17) it is written defectively as לְךְ [Mm 2214].

Reference sources: Ginsburg, I:722, #356; IV:495, #356.

See הון.

"To make an incense offering." This term is the Aramaic designation for Hebrew forms from the root קטר.

Example: Lev. 14:20 [Mp to הַמִּזְבֵּחָה] ה וכל הקטרה דכות ב מ ג "This word occurs 5 times, and it always occurs like this in connection with forms of the root קטר, with 3 exceptions" [Mm 4235]. The Mp is noting that הַמִּזְבֵּחָה occurs five times (Lev. 14:20; 2 Chr. 29:22 [3x], 24), and it always takes this form when it is used in connection with some form of the root קטר (e.g., Exod. 29:13; Lev. 1:9), with 3 exceptions. The three exceptions are Lev. 6:8; 9:13, 17.

ו

ו

1) When standing alone and without a diacritical point above it, ו represents the sixth letter of the alphabet.

Examples:

a) Num. 34:4 [Mp to וְהָיָה] חד מן ז בליש כת ה וקר ו ה מנה בליש "One of 7 forms having the distinction of being written with (final) ה but to be read with (final) ו (pointed as וּ), five of them from the same verb root" (היה; וְהָיוּ). The five forms of היה are found in Num. 34:4; Josh. 15:4; 18:12, 14, 19. Since the Mm list is lacking, it would involve extensive searching to find the remaining two.

Reference source: E-S, p. 290, #1456, 1464–67.

b) 1 Chr. 1:24 [Mp to שֵׁם] כב פסוק דלית בהון לא ו ולא י "One of 22 sentences in which there is not found either a ו or a י" [Mm 878]. A complete list includes the following: Exod. 20:13; Num. 7:14, 20, 26, 32, 38, 44, 50, 56, 62, 68, 74, 80; Josh. 12:13, 14, 15; Pss. 19:12; 105:11; Lam. 3:65; 1 Chr. 1:24; 16:18; 24:14.

2) When joined with other words, ו is simply the coordinating conjunction "and." This is the most frequent use of ו.

Example: Gen. 24:29 [Mp to וּלְרִבְקָה] ב חד ר״פ וחד ס״פ "This form (with וּ and לְ) occurs twice, once at the beginning of a verse and once at the end of a verse" (cf. Gen. 26:35).

3) The conjunction ו has a specific implication in notes denoting unusual spelling, position in verse, etc., such as the note ל וחס (as opposed to ל חס without ו). The note ל וחס means that the form in question occurs only once, *and* the one

occurrence is defective. The note ל̇ חס̇ means that the form in question occurs once spelled defectively, but other forms (spelled *plene*) do occur. (Users of *BHS* must realize that this distinction is not always maintained. In fact, one will find notes formulated in one way when the other meaning is actually the case: see example "d" below. A concordance must be consulted to determine the situation for the word in question. See Yeivin, p. 96.)

Examples:

a) Exod. 8:22 [Mp to יִסְקְלֻנוּ] ל̇ וחס̇ "This form occurs only once, and it is defective." The purpose of this note is not only to guard a unique form but also to guard the defective spelling of the form.

b) Gen. 27:16 [Mp to הִלְבִּישָׁה] ל̇ ומל̇ "This form occurs only once, and it is *plene.*" The purpose of this note is not only to guard a unique form but also to guard the *plene* spelling of the form.

c) Gen. 27:22 [Mp to הַקֹּל] ל̇ חס̇ "This form occurs only once spelled defectively." Although this is the only occurrence of the form with defective *holem*, other occurrences spelled *plene* do occur (e.g., Num. 7:89).

d) Gen. 24:39 [Mp to אֻלַי] ל̇ וחס̇ "This form occurs only once, and it is defective." This note implies that אֻלַי occurs only once, and the one occurrence is defective; there are no other *plene* occurrences. However, by consulting Even-Shoshan, p. 25, one will find that this is not the case. There are many occurrences of אוּלַי, spelled *plene* (cf. Gen. 16:2; 18:28, etc.).

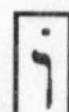

"The number six"

Examples:

a) Gen. 31:30 [Mp to הָלַךְ] ד̇ חס̇ וכל ירמיה דכות ב̇ מ̇ ו̇ "The form הָלַךְ is written defectively 4 times, in addition to its occurrences in Jeremiah, which are also defective, with 6 exceptions." The four defective occurrences outside Jeremiah are Gen. 31:30; Judg. 4:9; 1 Sam. 6:12; Isa. 20:2. The defective forms in Jeremiah are 2:2; 3:12; 17:19; etc. The six *plene* forms in Jeremiah are 13:1; 28:13; 31:2; 35:2; 39:16; 50:4 [Mm 1408].
Reference source: E-S, p. 296.

b) Gen. 31:32 [Mp to וְלֹא־יָדַע] יא̇ ו̇ מנה בתור "This phrase occurs 11 times, 6 of which are in the Pentateuch" [Mm 130]. The list of 11 includes Gen. 19:33, 35; 31:32; 39:6; Lev. 5:17; Deut. 34:6; Isa. 42:25; Job 35:15; Prov. 7:23; 9:18; Eccl. 6:5.

"And (the) needy, poor." Paired with דל in the Mp; see דל.

וכ̇ת̇

A mnemonic device giving the correct order of the abbreviated words. Cf. סימן for a discussion of this type of note.

Example: Exod. 23:28 [Mp to הַחִוִּי הַכְּנַעֲנִי הַחִתִּי] סימן ו̇ כ̇ ת̇ "The sign for the correct order of words is ו̇ (הַחִוִּי 'the Hivites'), כ̇ (הַכְּנַעֲנִי 'the Canaanites'), and ת̇ (הַחִתִּי 'the Hittites')."

וידבר

"The book of Numbers," so named because וידבר is the first word of this book. This is in agreement with the method of identifying books of the Pentateuch by their opening word(s). However, this designation for the book of Numbers seldom occurs, having been replaced by the fifth word of the first verse of the book, במדבר. Also see במדבר.

Example: Lev. 7:38 [Mp to בְּמִדְבַּר סִינָי] ל̇ וכל וידבר דכות ב̇ מ̇ ב̇ "The only occurrence of this phrase (with prefixed preposition ב), except throughout the book of Numbers, where every occurrence of the phrase has this form, with two exceptions (Num. 10:12; 33:16, which have prefixed מ)." [Mm lacking] The likely explanation of the substitution of וידבר for במדבר, the customary designation for the book of Numbers, is that the Mp is keyed to the phrase בְּמִדְבַּר סִינָי. To have repeated במדבר in the same Mp note could have been confusing.

Reference source: E-S, p. 622.

ז

Standing alone, and without a diacritical point, ז represents the seventh letter of the alphabet.

ז̇

"Seven"

Examples:

a) Gen. 1:5 [Mp to לָאוֹר] ז̇ "The word לָאוֹר occurs 7 times in the Bible" (cf. Gen. 1:5; Isa. 42:16; 59:9; Mic. 7:9; Zeph. 3:5; Job 12:22; 24:14) [Mm 3105].

b) Gen. 5:7 [Mp to וַיְחִי־שֵׁת] ז̇ בטע "There are 7 occurrences of phrases like this (in Genesis), all of which have the same accents (*maqqef/revia'*)" (cf. Gen. 5:7, 19, 30; 11:11, 15, 17, 19) [Mm 37].

c) Judg. 17:2 [Mp to וְאַתְּי] חד מן ז̇ כת כן "One of 7 occurrences of this word (2fs personal pronoun) written thus" (cf. Judg. 17:2; 1 Kgs. 14:2; 2 Kgs. 4:16, 23; 8:1; Jer. 4:30; Ezek. 36:13) [Mm 2081]. The ordinary form for 2fs is אַתְּ (Gen. 24:23; etc.). The Mp protects the minority reading.

זוגין

The plural of זוג (זוגא). "Pairs or word groups, organized on the basis of some unique feature or similarity."

The זוגין are the most esoteric of all the Masoretic collections and have doubtlessly contributed to the widespread attitude of indifference toward the Masorah itself. However, they give evidence of the consuming interest that ancient scribes had in the cataloging of even minute details about the text of the Tanakh. That which may appear to be trivia to modern minds was of immense value to them. Through the gathering of such data they were safeguarding the reliability of the transmission of their sacred scriptures. (See Chapter 4 for a discussion of זוגין notes.)

Examples:

a) Gen. 2:11, 13 [Mp to הוּא הַסֹּבֵב] יא̇ זוגין בטע "Eleven pairs of similar phrases (organized on the basis of) accents. This Mp note would be unintelligible without the accompanying Mm note (915), which gives this additional information: יא̇' זוגין מן ב̇ חד רביע וחד זקף "Eleven pairs of phrases, one accented with revia' and one with *zaqef*." The remaining pairs are given in the Mm note.

b) Gen. 18:18 [Mp to הָיוֹ יִהְיֶה] וֹ זוגין "Six groupings." The nature of these groupings is explained in Mm 2036: וֹ זוגין מטע בטעמיה וסימנהון "Six pairs of phrases which, deceptively, appear to have errors in the writing of the accents, together with their references" [Mm 2036].

c) Exod. 5:8 (17) [Mp to נִזְבְּחָה לֵאלֹהֵינוּ] גֹ זוגין "3 groupings." Note that this Mp does not clarify the nature of the groupings. This must be determined by consulting the Mm listing (3268), which has this heading: גֹ זוגין מן בֹ בֹ בחד עינין חד יְהוָה וחד אֱלֹהִים וסימנהון "3 pairs of phrases from the same (general) context, one reading יְהוָה, and the other reading אֱלֹהִים, together with their references." The other two pairs are Num. 23:16//23:4, and Pss. 40:18//70:6. [Mm 3268]

d) Exod. 12:29 [Mp to בְּבֵית הַבּוֹר] הֹ זוגין בבית בית Mm 3761 clarifies the meaning of this enigmatic note with this heading: הֹ זוגין מן בֹ בֹ מיחדין חד בְּבֵית וחד בֵּית וסימנהון "5 pairs of unusual phrases, 1 phrase (in each pair) containing בְּבֵית, and 1 containing בֵּית (without the preposition), together with their references." The five unusual pairs are Exod. 12:29//Jer. 37:16; 2 Kgs. 15:5//2 Chr. 26:21; Prov. 3:33//Mic. 6:10; Eccl. 7:4//7:2; Est. 5:1//1:9. [Mm 3761]

"Masculine gender."

Example: Num. 11:15 [Mp to אַתְּ] גֹ בלשון זכר "The word אַתְּ is used 3 times (as a pronoun) with the masculine meaning" (cf. Deut. 5:27; Ezek. 28:15) [Mm 900].

Plural of זעיר (זעירא). "Small, smaller than normal, reduced in size."

Example: Isa. 44:14 [Mp to אֹרֶן] גֹ נונין זעירין "There are 3 nuns that are reduced in size" (cf. Jer. 39:13; Prov. 16:28). [Mm lacking] See Chapter 3 for a discussion of this phenomenon.

"The accent *zaqef*."

Examples:

a) Ruth 3:13 [Mp to אָנֹכִי] חֹ בטע וכל זקף אתנח וס״פ דכות בֹ מֹ אֹ "One of 8 occurrences of this word accented on the penultima (מלעיל) syllable, and all forms of this word accented with *zaqef*, *'atnah*, or *silluq* (*sof pasuq*) are also (accented on the penultima) מלעיל, with one exception (which is accented on the ultima, מלרע, cf. Job 33:9)" [Mm 157].

b) Jer. 6:5 [Mp to בַלָּ֫יְלָה] ל̇ זקף קמ̇ "Only occurs once with *zaqef qamets*." The term זקף קמ̇ normally indicates a syllable accented by *zaqef* which elicits the vowel *qamets*. In other words, the note marks a pausal form (in which *patah* is replaced by *qamets*) brought about by *zaqef*. In this example, the note says that בַלָּ֫יְלָה is the only occurrence of this word in pausal form (with *patah* under initial ל raised to *qamets*) brought about by the accent *zaqef*. Other occurrences of this same word in pausal form are accented with *'atnah* (cf. Gen. 31:40; etc.) or *silluq* followed by *sof pasuq* (cf. Jer. 36:30; etc.).

Occasionally, the term זקף קמ̇ will be used to mark any pausal form with *qamets* for *patah* which has been brought about by an accent other than *'atnah* or *silluq*. Thus, the use of the term זקף קמ̇ does not necessarily imply that the accent *zaqef* will appear with the word in question. This is the broader sense of the term, intending to call attention to pausal forms that have been marked by an accent other than the strong accents (*'atnah* and *silluq*) which usually elicit pausal forms (e.g., see יִלְבָּ֑שׁ in Lev. 16:4; cf. Mynatt, p. 144, #170).

"The accent *zarqa* (זרקא)."

Example: Gen. 37:22 [Mp to דָּ֒ם] ב̇ דסמיכ̇ לזרקא "The form דם (accented with *segolta*) occurs twice following *zarqa*." This is Weil's revision of the Mp of L, which reads ה̇י̇ דם לזרקא "The form דם (accented with *segolta*?) occurs 15 times following *zarqa*." Scholars have been unable to make sense of the Mp of L, hence Weil's revision (*BHS*). Cf. Mynatt, p. 84, #83. [Mm lacking]

"Eight"

Examples:

a) 1 Sam. 13:20 [Mp to הַפְּלִשְׁתִּים] ח̇ "One of 8 occurrences of this word (with the article)." The other seven occurrences are Josh. 13:2; 1 Sam. 4:7; 7:13; 17:51, 52; 2 Sam. 5:19; 2 Chr. 21:16 [Mm 1315].

b) Gen. 7:10 [Mp to לְשִׁבְעַת הַיָּמִים] ח̇ ב̇ מנה בליש̇ "One of 8 occurrences of this phrase, two of which have this form (with prefixed preposition לְ)." The other prefixed form is 1 Chr. 9:25. The forms without לְ are found in Exod. 13:7; Judg. 14:17; Isa. 30:26; Ezek. 45:23, 25; 2 Chr. 30:22 [Mm 4051].

וחבי̇ר

Abbreviation for וחבירו (cf. Hebrew חבר). "And its parallel, its equal, its companion." This term is primarily employed in the Mm lists and marks a scripture reference where the identifying phrase (cf. סימן) is a repetition of the preceding entry, and therefore does not need to be written out in full. It is used much like the modern ditto sign. For examples, see Mm 130 (Gen. 19:35), Mm 136 (2 Chr. 18:23), Mm 157 (2 Chr. 18:5), Mm 158 (1 Chr. 21:24), Mm 159 (Josh. 23:1), etc. Note in these lists that, although וחבי̇ר denotes a repetition of the identifying phrase, the verse it represents (verse number) is usually different from the verse represented by the original identifying phrase. Thus, in Mm 130, the first identifying phrase represents Gen. 19:33, but וחבי̇ר represents Gen. 19:35. The context for both verses is similar but, in modern terms, the verse numbers differ.

Abbreviation for אחד. Alternate form: חדה (fem.). "One, once." When used before the preposition מן, it means "one from," or "one of."

Examples:

a) Gen. 1:20 [Mp to עַל] כ̇א̇ פסוק על על ומילה חדה ביניה̇ "One of 21 verses with two occurrences of עַל, with one word between them" [Mm 686].

b) Gen. 2:7 [Mp to וַיִּיצֶר] ב̇ חד חס̇ וחד מל̇ "One of two occurrences of this verb form (with *vav*), once written defectively (with *hireq*) and once *plene* (with *hireq-yod*)." The other reference is Gen. 2:19. [Mm lacking]
Reference source: E-S, p. 487, #35, 36.

c) Gen. 24:12 [Mp to וַיֹּאמַר] וחד מן ז̇ בטע̇ מרעימין "And one of 7 words accented with *shalshelet*." The remaining six are found in Gen. 19:16; 39:8; Lev. 8:23; Isa. 13:8; Amos 1:2; Ezra 5:15. (Note: Only the final portion of this rather extensive Mp note has been treated here.) [Mm 705]

"Ordinary, non-sacral, common, profane." חול is often preceded by לשון, "sense, meaning." (Cf. Hebrew חלל.)

Examples:

a) Gen. 19:25 [Mp to הָאֵל] ח לשון חול "One of 8 occurrences of this word with a non-sacred meaning." It is used here as an abbreviated form of the pronoun הָאֵלֶּה, "these." The form הָאֵל normally means "God" (cf. Isa. 42:5), but here it has a לשון חול, "a secular meaning." The remaining seven occurrences are found in Gen. 19:8; 26:3, 4; Lev. 18:27; Deut. 4:42; 7:22; 19:11 [Mm 119].

b) 1 Chr. 20:8 [Mp to אֵל] ב֗ לשון חול "The word אֵל is twice used in a secular sense." The second reference is in Ezra 5:15. Normally אֵל means "God," but here it is only a shortened form of אֵלֶּה, "these." [Mm 3903]

חומש

"Five." This word may refer either to the Pentateuch or to the "Five Scrolls" חומש המגילות (Song of Songs, Ruth, Lamentations, Ecclesiastes, Esther).

Example: Lev. 7:9 [Mp to נַעֲשָׂה] ח֗ קמ֗ וכל חומש המגילות דכות ב֗ מ֗ ב֗ "One of 8 occurrences of this word with a *qamets* in the final syllable (rather than the usual *seghol*), and all occurrences in the Five Megilloth are also written thus, with two exceptions." The remaining 7 occurrences (outside the Five Megilloth) are Judg. 16:11; 1 Kgs 10:20; 2 Kgs. 23:22, 23; 2 Chr. 9:19; 35:18, 19. The two exceptions in the Megilloth (written as נַעֲשֶׂה) are Song 1:11; 8:8. [Mm 692]

חטף

hatef refers to the absence of *ga'ya'* (*meteg*), usually beside the vowel of the syllable preceding the stress syllable, indicative of the fact that this vowel is short and not long.

Examples:

a) Jer. 49:28 [Mp to וְשָׁדְדוּ] ל֗ חטף "The only occurrence of this word without *meteg*" (cf. Ezek. 32:12). The form in Jeremiah is an imperative (with *qamets-hatuf*), while that in Ezekiel is a perfect (with *qamets*). [Mm lacking]
Reference sources: E-S, p. 1114, #3, 17; Gesenius, §67cc, pp. 182f.

b) 2 Chr. 6:42 [Mp to זָכְרָה] ל֗ חטף בסיפ֗ "The only occurrence of this word in the book of Chronicles lacking a *meteg* (*ga'ya'*) beside the initial vowel." This indicates that the form is an imperative (with initial *qamets-hatuf*) rather than the 3fs perfect (with *qamets*). Examples of this form outside the book of Chronicles are found in Neh. 5:19; 6:14; 13:14, 22, 29, 31, all of which are also imperatives. [Mm lacking]
Reference source: E-S, p. 331, #155–161.

חיפוי

"Covering, wrapping." This term is the Aramaic designation for the various forms of the Hebrew verb חפה "cover."

Example: 2 Chron. 3:5 [Mp to חִפָּה] חיפוי ה̇ בליש "The root חפה occurs 5 times in this and similar forms" [Mm 4160]. The Mp note indicates that the root חפה occurs five times in this and similar forms (2 Chr. 3:5 [2x], 7, 8, 9). By comparing the occurrences marked with this Mp note, one can determine that this listing is only interested in Pi'el forms. Other forms occur elsewhere (2 Sam. 15:30; Jer. 14:3, 4; etc.). Reference source: Ginsburg, I:495, #340; IV:401, #340; BDB, pp. 341–42.

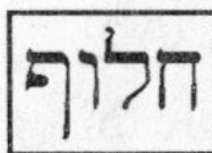

"The reverse, the opposite, reversed, different, contrary." Alternate form: חילוף. A term applied mainly to the order of words in the text.

Examples:

a) 2 Chr. 13:22 [Mp to הַנָּבִיא עִדּוֹ] ל̇ וכל קריא חילוף "The only occurrence of this phrase. Elsewhere in the Bible the order of these two words is reversed" (cf. Zech. 1:1). [Mm lacking]

b) Prov. 27:14 [Mp to בַּבֹּקֶר הַשְׁכֵּים] ל̇ וכל קרי חלוף "The only occurrence of this phrase (in this order). Elsewhere in the Bible the order of these two words is reversed" (cf. Gen. 20:8; 28:18; 1 Sam. 29:10; etc.). [Mm lacking]
Reference source: E-S, p. 1143.

c) Ruth 4:9 [Mp to לְכִלְיוֹן וּמַחְלוֹן] ל̇ וכל קריא חלוף "The only occurrence of these names in this order. Elsewhere in the Bible their order is reversed" (cf. Ruth 1:2, 5). [Mm lacking]
Reference source: E-S, p. 642.

חמדה

חֶמְדָּה is the Hebrew word for "desirable thing, precious thing."

Example: Exod. 35:22 [Mp to כְּלִי] יח̇ וכל יוצר חפץ חמדה דכות ב̇ מ̇ א̇ "One of 18 occurrences of this word in this form (with final *hireq-yod*), and all uses of the word in conjunction with יוֹצֵר, חֵפֶץ, or חֶמְדָּה have this form, with one exception" (כְּלֵי חֶמְדָּה 2 Chr. 32:27) [Mm 2781].

"Defective, lacking a letter, word, or phrase." Alternate forms: חסיר, חסי, חסירין (pl.). חס̇ is most often used to describe a word written without an expected *yod* or *vav*. חס̇ דחס̇ signals a word that is doubly defective.

Examples:

a) Gen. 17:19 [Mp to יֹלֶדֶת] ב̇ וחס̇ "There are two occurrences of this word and both are defective (simple *holem* instead of *holem-vav*)." (Cf. Jer. 15:9). [Mm

lacking]
Reference source: E-S, p. 468, #126–27.

b) 1 Sam. 10:6 [Mp to וְהִתְנַבִּיתָ] ד׳ חס א "There are 4 different forms of this verb (נבא) that are written without an א." The remaining three are found in 1 Sam. 10:13; Jer. 26:9; Ezra 5:1. [Mm 1578]

c) Gen. 24:66 [Mp to אֵת כָּל־הַדְּבָרִים] יג׳ חס האלה "One of 13 occurrences of this phrase where the demonstrative pronoun הָאֵלֶּה is lacking." The other references are Exod. 4:30; Lev. 8:36; Deut. 1:18; 1 Sam. 3:18; Jer. 26:2, 12; 30:2; 36:2, 13, 16, 20, 28 [Mm 707]. The Mm note adds that elsewhere in the Bible this phrase always occurs as אֵת כָּל־הַדְּבָרִים הָאֵלֶּה.

d) Gen. 45:22 [Mp to חֲלִפֹת] ב׳ חס דחס "One of 2 occurrences of this word written in a doubly defective form (lacking both *yod* and *vav*, cf. חֲלִיפוֹת Judg. 14:13). The second doubly defective form is found in Judg. 14:12 [Mm 336].

e) 1 Kgs. 14:16 [Mp to חַטֹּאות יָרָבְעָם] ה׳ חס בן נבט "One of 5 occurrences of this phrase without the expected words בן נבט (בְּחַטֹּאות יָרָבְעָם בֶּן־נְבָט cf. 2 Kgs. 3:3). [Mm lacking] The five occurrences are 1 Kgs. 14:16; 15:30; 2 Kgs. 10:31; 13:6; 17:22.

"Half, middle, the halfway point."
Examples:

a) Lev. 11:42 [Mp to גָּחוֹן] חצי אותיות בתור "The middle of the Pentateuch by letters." The enlarged *vav* marks it as the middle letter.

b) Lev. 10:16 [Mp to דָּרֹשׁ דָּרַשׁ] חצי התורה בתיבות "The middle of the Pentateuch by words." Apparently, the division falls between these two words.

c) Lev. 8:8 [Mp to וַיָּשֶׂם] חצי התורה בפסוק "The middle of the Pentateuch by verses." [Note: For the total number of letters, words, and verses in the Pentateuch, see the special notes (Masorah Finalis) at the end of Deuteronomy.]

"Nine"

Examples:

a) Jer. 5:24 [Mp to חֻקּוֹת] ט֗ "One of nine occurrences of this form." [Mm lacking] The remaining 8 occurrences are found in Jer. 10:3; 31:25; 33:25; Ezek. 43:18; 44:5; 46:14; Mic. 6:16; Job 38:33. Far more common than חֻקּוֹת (feminine plural) is חֻקִּים (masculine plural). The Mp note is inserted to protect the minority reading.
Reference sources: Ginsburg, I:496, #369; E-S, p. 395, #29–37.

b) Deut. 10:10 [Mp to וְאָנֹכִי] ט֗ ר״פ וכל תרי עשר דכות "One of 9 occurrences of this form at the beginning of a verse, and all similar forms found in the book of the Twelve Prophets also occur at the beginning of a verse" [Mm 1472]. The remaining eight occurrences are found in Deut. 31:18; Judg. 11:27; 2 Sam. 3:39; Isa. 51:15; 66:18; Jer. 2:21; 3:19; Ps. 22:7. Similar forms at the beginning of a verse in the Twelve Prophets occur in Hos. 11:3; 12:10; 13:4; Amos 2:9, 10.
Reference sources: Ginsburg, I:100, #978 (a list duplicating that of Mm 1472); Mandelkern, p. 1258 (forms occurring in the Twelve Prophets).

"Soiled, corrupt." (Cf. Hebrew טנף.)

Example: Isa. 30:22 [Mp to צֵא] ל֗ לשון טנוף "This is the only occurrence of this word with the meaning 'corrupt.'" The normal translation of צֵא is as the imperative of יצא, thus "Out!" "Away with you!" Here, however, it is interpreted as derived from the root צוא (BDB, p. 844), meaning "filth," as that of human excrement (cf. *New English Bible*).

"Accent, with the accent." The plural form is טעמין. It is often used with the prefixed preposition ב as בטע֗. Mp notes dealing with accents have several functions. Two of the most common uses are to indicate the position of the accent or stressed syllable within a word, and to identify a particular accent or sequence of accents within a verse.

Examples:

a) Exod. 40:4 [Mp to וְהַעֲלֵיתָ] ל וטעם באות ת "This is the only occurrence of this form, and it is accented on the letter ת, i.e., on the final syllable (מִלְרַע)." [Mm lacking]

b) Josh. 18:6 [Mp to וְאַתֶּם] ד בטע "One of 4 occurrences of this form with this accent (*garshayim*)" [Mm 1451]. The other occurrences are in Judg. 9:18; Ezek. 36:8; Neh. 13:18.

טעׄ לאחור

"(With) the accent following." Used to indicate where a specific accent follows another.

Example: Lev. 5:2 [Mp to אוֹ בְנִבְלַת] יא בטע לאחור "One of 11 combinations of accents where *pashta* stands after *yetiv* (i.e., the accent pattern is *yetiv-pashta*)." [Mm lacking] In this example, the term לאחור refers to one accent following another. Literally, the Mp note says, "one of 11 occurrences with this accent following" (i.e., one of 11 instances where *pashta* follows *yetiv*). This note safeguards these 11 occurrences from other accent patterns, such as *pashta-yetiv* (which is more common) or *mehuppak-pashta* (which is practically indistinguishable from *yetiv-pashta* because of the same signs). See Yeivin, p. 199, for a discussion of *yetiv* and the various sequences mentioned above. The list of occurrences is given in Ginsburg, I:628, #141; IV:436, #141. The references are Lev. 5:2; Deut. 1:4; Isa. 5:24; 30:32 (Mp sub loco); Jer. 14:14; 16:12; 22:30; Dan. 2:10; 7:27; Ezra 6:8; 9:4. (The reader needs to be aware of an error in *BHS*. In Jer. 14:14, the Mp note יא בטע לאחור is matched with לֹא שְׁלַחְתִּים. Instead, it should be matched with שֶׁקֶר הַנְּבִאִים, which occurs earlier in the verse. The accent pattern for the combination לֹא שְׁלַחְתִּים is *mehuppak-pashta*. The *mehuppak* and *yetiv* use the same symbol; the position of the symbol in relation to the word determines which accent is intended, but this is not always readily apparent in *BHS*, cf. *BHK* in Ezra 9:4 כֹּל חָרֵד. See Yeivin, p. 199, for a discussion of this example.)

י

י

Alone, and without a diacritical point, י represents the tenth letter of the alphabet.
Examples:

a) Lev. 25:34 [Mp to וּשְׂדֵה] ב̇ חד כת̇ י וחד כת̇ ה "One of two forms, one written with (final) י (וּשְׂדֵי 2 Sam. 1:21) and one written with (final) ה (וּשְׂדֵה Lev. 25:34)." [Mp lacking]
Reference source: E-S, p. 1116, #252, 294.

b) 2 Sam. 1:21 [Mp to וּשְׂדֵי] ב̇ חד כת̇ ה וחד מן ו̇ כת̇ י וכל רות דכות ב̇ מ̇ ב̇ [Note that this Mp note overlaps with that found in the example above, and the first part of this note is explained there.] "One of 2 occurrences of this word (with prefixed ו conjunction), one of which is written with a (final) ה (see example above), and this is one of 6 occurrences of שְׂדֵי (with or without prefixes) written with a (final) י, in addition to its occurrences in the book of Ruth, all of which end in י, with two exceptions (which end in ה)" [Mm 2329]. The Mm note lists the six occurrences of שְׂדֵי, other than those found in Ruth, as follows: 2 Sam. 1:21; Isa. 32:12; Ps. 132:6; Prov. 23:10; Neh. 12:44; 2 Chr. 31:19. It also lists the two alternate forms in Ruth as found in 1:6 and 4:3. Forms in Ruth ending in י are not listed, but with the help of a concordance may be found in 1:1, 2, 6, 22; 2:6.
Reference source: E-S, p. 1116, #293, 296, 300, 301, 302.

c) Judg. 11:6 [Mp to וְהָיִיתָה] ג̇ חד כת̇ י וב̇ כת̇ תרי י "One of 3 occurrences of this word, one written (defectively) with a (single) י, and 2 written (*plene*) with a second י" [Mm 1755]. The defective occurrence is in 2 Sam. 10:11. The *plene* occurrences are in Judg. 11:6; 2 Sam. 5:2.

י̇

"Ten."
Examples:

a) Jer. 44:13 [Mp to הַיּוֹשְׁבִים] י̇ מל̇ ב̇ מנה בליש̇ "One of 10 occurrences of this (participial form) written *plene* (with *holem-vav*), and one of 2 that have the same form (i.e., which begin with the prefixed definite article, cf. 2 Chr. 30:25)." [Mm lacking] The list of the ten occurrences must be sought elsewhere. Fortunately, it is given in Ginsburg, I:714, #678, in this order: Judg. 6:10; Jer. 36:12; Ezek. 3:15;

8:1; Isa. 10:13; 2 Chr. 18:9; Jer. 44:13; 2 Chr. 31:6; 1 Chr. 9:2; 2 Chr. 30:25. For forms of this participle prefixed with the *vav* conjunction, see the final Mp note in Jer. 24:8, with the accompanying explanation in Mm 2592.

b) Lev. 2:4 [Mp to תַקְרִב] י חס בליש "One of 10 occurrences of this and similar forms of the verb קרב written with a defective *hireq-yod*" [Mm 667]. The defective forms are found in Lev. 2:4; 9:9; Num. 3:4; 7:19; Deut. 1:17; Josh. 8:23; Ezek. 46:4; Dan. 3:8; 6:13 (*contra textum*); Ezra 6:17.

יהושע

"The book of Joshua."

Examples:

a) Num. 22:33 [Mp to וְאוֹתָה] יב מל ב מנה בתור וכל יהושע שפטים ויחזק דכות ב מ ג "One of 12 occurrences of אוֹתָה written *plene* (with *holem-vav*), 2 of which are in the Pentateuch (Num. 22:33; 30:9), in addition to occurrences in the books of Joshua, Judges, and Ezekiel, all of which are also *plene*, with 3 exceptions (which are written defectively, i.e., with a simple *holem*)" [Mm 1009]. This Mm note lists the twelve *plene* occurrences (not including those in Joshua, Judges, and Ezekiel) as Num. 22:33; 30:9; 1 Sam. 14:27; 2 Sam. 13:18; Isa. 27:11; 28:4; 37:26; Jer. 32:31; 33:2; Hos. 4:19; Mal. 1:13; Ps. 27:4. The three defective occurrences (אֹתָה) are found in Josh. 8:24; 18:5; Ezek. 21:16.

b) 1 Sam. 15:28 [Mp to מַמְלְכוּת] ד וכל יהושע דכות "One of 4 occurrences of this word, in addition to the occurrences in Joshua, all of which are like these" [Mm 1612]. The four occurrences (outside Joshua) are given as 1 Sam. 15:28; 2 Sam. 16:3; Jer. 26:1; Hos. 1:4. There are no occurrences given for Joshua, but the concordance lists these as 13:12, 21, 27, 30, 31. This word does not occur elsewhere in the Hebrew Bible.

Reference source: E-S, p. 675, #1–5.

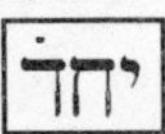

"Unusual" (used of a word or combination of words). See מיחד (מיח).

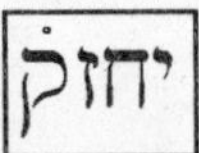

"The book of Ezekiel." Abbreviation for יחזקאל.

Example: 1 Sam. 12:7 [Mp to אֲבוֹתֵיכֶם] ז מל וכל יהושע שפטים מלכים ירמיה יחזק וכתיב דכות ב מ ח "One of 7 occurrences written *plene* (with *holem-vav*), besides the occurrences in Joshua, Judges, Kings, Jeremiah, Ezekiel, and the Writings, all of which are written *plene*, with 8 exceptions" [Mm 1586]. Note that some of the forms included here also have prefixes. The seven *plene* forms referred to in the Mp

note are listed as Exod. 3:13; 1 Sam. 12:7, 8; Isa. 65:7; Hos. 9:10; Zech. 1:2, 5. *Plene* forms in Joshua, Judges, Kings, Jeremiah, Ezekiel, and the Writings are not listed, nor is the number of their occurrences given. However, the eight defective forms found in this additional list of books are located in Judg. 2:1; 2 Kgs. 17:13; Jer. 35:15; 44:3; Ezek. 36:28; 47:14; 2 Chr. 13:12; 29:5. Mm 1586 supplies the additional information that all occurrences of this form in the book of Ezra are written defectively. Two such forms are found in Ezra 8:28 and 10:11.
Reference source: E-S, p. 4, #1001–1002.

יי

Abbreviation for "יְהוָה."
Example: Gen. 1:2 [Mp to וְרוּחַ אֱלֹהִים] חׄ בׄ מנהׄ בלישׄ וכל שמואל דכותׄ בׄ מׄ הׄ רוח יי "One of 8 occurrences of וְרוּחַ אֱלֹהִים, 2 of which have this form (with prefixed *vav*), and all references (to the divine Spirit) in Samuel read רוּחַ אֱלֹהִים, with 5 exceptions, which read רוּחַ יְהוָה." [Mm lacking] The only clarification *BHS* gives for this rather extensive Mp note is to cite (at the bottom of page) 2 Chr. 24:20 as the only other reference to וְרוּחַ אֱלֹהִים (prefixed *vav*). To find the remaining references to רוּחַ אֱלֹהִים one must look at other Masoretic lists or search out the references in a concordance. Fortunately, Ginsburg gives most of the data called for in lists he collected from various sources. In one list (II:572, #240), the eight occurrences of וְרוּחַ אֱלֹהִים are located in Gen. 1:2; 41:38; Exod. 31:3; 35:31; Num. 24:2; Ezek. 11:24; 2 Chr. 15:1; 24:20. The second part of this list gives the Samuel occurrences as 1 Sam. 10:6; 16:13,14; 19:9; 2 Sam. 23:2. Ginsburg's list throws no new light on instances of רוּחַ אֱלֹהִים in Samuel. Even-Shoshan lists these occurrences as 1 Sam. 10:10; 11:6; 16:15, 16, 23; 19:20, 23 (p. 1065, #175–181). Ginsburg also gives the two occurrences of וְרוּחַ אֱלֹהִים in list #244 on p. 572, which concurs with the information given in *BHS* in the note to Gen. 1:2. Cf. Mynatt, pp. 91–92, #90.

ירמיה

"The book of Jeremiah."
Example: Gen. 43:19 [Mp to עַל־בֵּית] יׄגׄ וכל מלכים ישעיה וירמיה דכותׄ בׄ מׄ יׄאׄ "One of 13 occurrences of עַל־בֵּית (or וְעַל־בֵּית) and this phrase always has this form in Kings, Isaiah, and Jeremiah, with 11 exceptions (אֶל־בֵּית or וְאֶל־בֵּית)" [Mm 324]. The other 12 passages are listed as Num. 2:34; Judg. 9:18; 2 Sam. 1:12; 2:4, 11; 14:9; Ezek. 13:5; 39:29; Est. 8:2; 1 Chr. 17:17; 2 Chr. 23:18; 26:21. The 11 exceptions (with אֶל־בֵּית) found in Kings, Isaiah, and Jeremiah (plus the Book of the Twelve Prophets, as indicated in Ginsburg, I:66, #544) are listed as 1 Kgs. 14:10; Isa. 2:3; Mic.

4:2; Isa. 29:22; Jer. 33:14; 35:2; 37:16, 18; Zech. 5:4 (2x); Mal. 3:10.

ישעיה

"The book of Isaiah."

Example: 2 Sam. 13:39 [Mp to נִחַם] ו̇ פת̇ וכל ישעיה דכות "One of 6 occurrences of נִחַם with *patah* in the final syllable, and all occurrences of this word in Isaiah are like this" [Mm 1775]. The other five occurrences are listed as Ezek. 32:31; Amos 7:3, 6; Jon. 3:9; Zech. 1:17. No indication is given of occurrences of this word in Isaiah. A concordance search yields these passages: Isa. 49:13; 51:3 (2x); 52:9.

Reference sources: E-S, p. 754, #63–66; Ginsburg, II:278, #187.

י̇ ש̇ ת̇

Abbreviation for "יהושע ושפטים ותהלים" (Joshua, Judges, Psalms).

Example: Gen. 47:3 [Mp to אֲבוֹתֵינוּ] ח̇ מל̇ וכל̇ י̇ ש̇ ת̇ דכות̇ ב̇ מ̇ א̇ "One of 8 occurrences of this word written *plene* (with *holem-vav*) and all occurrences in Joshua, Judges, and Psalms are also written *plene*, with one exception." Note that some of the forms included here also have prefixes [Mm 346]. The other seven occurrences are listed here as being found in Jer. 3:24, 25; 14:20; 16:19; 1 Chr. 12:18; 2 Chr. 29:9; 34:21. The exception to the *plene* writing in Psalms is found in Ps. 22:5 (אֲבֹתֵינוּ).

Reference source: For a parallel Mm list, see Ginsburg, I:20, #44, and IV:18, #44.

יתיר

"Superfluous, extra," usually applied to letters of the alphabet. Cf. Hebrew יתר.

Examples:

a) 2 Sam. 10:9 [Mp to בִּישְׂרָאֵל] חד מן ד̇ יתיר ב לא קר̇ "One of 4 occurrences of a superfluous ב which is not to be read" (i.e., not to be pointed) [Mm 1754]. The four occurrences are as follows:

(1)	בִּישְׂרָאֵל	2 Sam. 10:9
(2)	בבֵית יְהוָה	2 Kgs. 22:5
(3)	בבֵית הַפְּקֻדֹּת	Jer. 52:11
(4)	וּבתַרְבִּית	Prov. 28:8

b) 2 Sam. 16:2 [Mp to וְלהַלֶּחֶם] חד מן ד̇ יתיר ל "One of 4 occurrences of a superfluous ל" [Mm 1794]. The four occurrences are as follows:

(1)	וְלהַלֶּחֶם	2 Sam. 16:2
(2)	עָלַּיִן	Dan. 4:4
(3)	עָלַּיִן	Dan. 5:8

(4) עַלַּלְת Dan. 5:10

c) Num. 13:9 [Mp to רָפוּא] יב̇ יתיר א ס״ת "One of 12 occurrences of a superfluous א at the end of a word" [Mm 907]. The other eleven occurrences are as follows:

(1)	הָהָלְכוּא	Josh. 10:24
(2)	הַקָּלִיא	1 Sam. 17:17
(3)	אָבוּא	Isa. 28:12
(4)	רָצוֹא	Ezek. 1:14
(5)	וְאַתּוּקֶיהָא (ק̇ = ואתיקיהא)	Ezek. 41:15
(6)	דָּם־נָקִיא	Joel 4:19
(7)	דָּם־נָקִיא	Jon. 1:14
(8)	אֲרַעא	Dan. 2:39
(9)	נְגוֹא	Dan. 3:29
(10)	יָפוֹא	Ezra 3:7
(11)	וְשֵׁיצִיא	Ezra 6:15

"20."

Examples:

a) Gen. 29:22 [Mp to וַיֶּאֱסֹף] כ̇ ה̇ מנה בתור "There are 20 occurrences of this form, 5 of them in the Pentateuch" [Mm 4234]. The references are Gen. 29:22; 42:17; 49:33; Num. 11:24; 21:23; Josh. 24:1; Judg. 3:13; 11:20; 2 Sam. 10:17; 12:29; 1 Kgs. 10:26; Hab. 1:9; 2:5; 1 Chr. 15:4; 19:17; 23:2; 2 Chr. 1:14; 28:24; 29:20; 34:29. Cf. the interesting variation on the Mp notes in Gen. 29:22; Josh. 24:1; Judg. 3:13; 2 Sam. 10:17; 1 Kgs. 10:26; Hab. 1:9; and 1 Chr. 15:4.

b) Exod. 19:11 [Mp to לַיּוֹם] כ̇ "There are 20 occurrences of this form" [Mm 875]. The references are Exod. 19:11; 29:36, 38; Num. 7:11 (2x); 28:3, 24; Jer. 37:21; Ezek. 4:10; 30:2; 43:25; 45:23 (2x); 46:13; Joel 1:15; Mal. 3:17; Est. 3:14; 8:13; 1 Chr. 26:17 (2x). The more commonly used form is בַּיּוֹם (cf. Gen. 1:18; 2:2; etc.). The purpose of this Mp note is to safeguard the minority reading.

"21." The number letter כ֗, "twenty," followed by the first nine number letters to make the numbers 21 (כ֗א) through 29 (כ֗ט).

"Here." See מכה.

Example: 1 Sam. 13:19 [Mp to אָמַר] ז֗ חד מן ז֗ פסוק֗ מן ה֗י מילין ז֗ (*Qere*) אמרו מכה וז֗ מכה "The form אָמַר is written with a defective *shureq*, but should be read with a *plene shureq* (אָמְרוּ). This is one of seven verses of fifteen words each, seven words from here (i.e., before the *Ketiv/Qere* word), and seven words from here (i.e., after the *Ketiv/Qere* word)" [Mm 1594]. The 7 verses are given as 1 Sam. 13:19; 30:24; Jer. 33:8; Ezek. 45:5; Ps. 17:14; Job 42:16; Dan. 11:39.

"The same as, like, equal to." See דכות֗. This word is frequently prefixed with the inseparable relative pronoun ד (דכות֗), as in the examples given below. Common compounds and phrases using the word are כותיה "like it," כותיהין "like them," and ולית כותה "and there is no other like it."

Examples:

a) Gen. 31:32 [Mp to יִחְיֶה] י֗ח וכל חיו יחיה דכות֗ "This form occurs 18 times (as a *plene* form with final ה, and standing alone) and in combination with the infinitive absolute חָיוֹ (or חָיֹה), it also has the *plene* form" [Mm 107]. The 18 occurrences of יִחְיֶה (standing alone) are Gen. 17:18; 31:32; Exod. 19:13; Num. 24:23; Deut. 8:3 (2x); 2 Sam. 1:10; 2 Kgs. 10:19; Ezek. 18:13, 22; 33:19; 47:9; Hab. 2:4; Ps. 89:49; Prov. 15:27; Eccl. 6:3; 11:8; Neh. 2:3. (A slightly different list is given in Ginsburg, I:485, #173.) Ginsburg (IV:384f., #173) suggested that the purpose of this Mp note was to exclude the two instances where the textual reading (*Ketiv*) is also יִחְיֶה, while the Masoretic correction (*Qere*) is וְחָיָה (cf. Jer. 21:9; 38:2). The combination of the infinitive absolute followed by the Qal imperfect of חָיָה occurs in Ezek. 3:21; 18:9, 17, 19, 21; 33:15, 16.
Reference source: E-S, p. 362, #3–11.

b) Gen. 3:10 [Mp to אָנֹכִי] ח֗ בטע וכל זקף אתנח וס״פ דכות֗ ב֗ מ֗ א֗ "One of 8 occurrences of אָנֹכִי, accented on the next to last syllable (מלעיל), and all occurrences of this word accented with *zaqef*, *'atnah*, or *sof pasuq* are also accented מלעיל, with one exception (Job 33:9, where the accentuation with *'atnah* is מלרע, i.e., on the final syllable)" [Mm 1571]. The remaining seven occurrences of אָנֹכִי accented מלעיל (besides those marked by *zaqef*, *'atnah*, or *sof pasuq*) are found in Exod. 4:10; Judg. 17:9; 1 Sam. 9:21; 30:13; Amos 7:14; Ruth 3:13; 2 Sam. 3:8.

"Thirty." ל, the regular symbol for a hapax legomenon, is not employed by *BHS* to represent "thirty." However, 31–39 are represented by לא, לב, לג, etc.

Examples:

a) Gen. 8:10 [Mp to וַיֹּסֶף] כֹּ֗י "This form occurs 30 times (in the Bible)." [Mm lacking] Since the Leningrad Codex provides no list for this Mp note, the 30 references must be ascertained from other sources. Ginsburg is not helpful, since this is not one of the lists he collected. Only Frensdorff (p. 85) offers assistance, with this terse entry: וַיֹּסֶף וַיּוֹסֶף ז מלא וחד ויאסף כתיב ושארא "The word וַיּוֹסֶף occurs 7 times with full *holem-vav*, and וַיֹּאסֶף is written once, and the rest are written (with the defective *holem*) as וַיֹּסֶף." Even-Shoshan lists the seven occurrences of וַיּוֹסֶף, the one occurrence of וַיֹּאסֶף, and twenty-two occurrences of וַיֹּסֶף (p. 475, #141–70). The sum total of all of these is thirty, the number indicated by the Mp note. This shows clearly that the Mp note was intended to encompass all occurrences of these three forms.

b) Deut. 32:51 [Mp to אוֹתִי] כֹּ֗י מל ול֗ בתור "The form אוֹתִי occurs 30 times with a full *holem-vav* (rather than אֹתִי), and this is the only such occurrence in the Pentateuch" [Mm 1238א]. The full list is given, along with the additional information that all occurrences in Joshua and Judges are also written *plene*, with two exceptions (Josh. 14:7; Judg. 9:15). The forms written defectively (אֹתִי) are far more frequent in the Bible than those written *plene*. The Mp note safeguards the minority reading.

See כנוי.

"Every, all, each, always."

Examples:

a) Deut. 32:13 [Mp to אָרֶץ] י֗ד קמ֗ וכל אתנח וס״פ דכות ב֗ מ֗ ד֗ "One of 14 occurrences of אָ֫רֶץ (accented either with *zaqef*, *segholta*, or *revia'*, none of which normally functions as a pausal accent), a pausal form with *qamets* in the tone syllable. All occurrences of this word accented with the pausal *'atnah* or *sof pasuq* (*silluq*) also have *qamets* in the tone syllable, with 4 exceptions (where the vowel in the tone syllable remains *seghol*)" [Mm 1234]. The remaining 13 forms are found in Isa. 14:9, 21; 33:9; 44:23; 49:13; 51:13, 16; 52:10; Jer. 9:18; 16:19; 31:8; Zech. 12:1; Ps. 44:4. There are 48 instances where the pausal form אָֽרֶץ is accented with *'atnah* and 49 where it is accented with *sof pasuq* (*silluq*). Mm 1234 lists the four exceptions (where even with *'atnah* or *sof pasuq* the vowel in the tone syllable remains *seghol*) as Pss. 35:20; 48:11; Prov. 30:14, 21. Reference sources: Ginsburg, IV:129, #1097; E–S, p. 113, #127ff.

b) Num. 4:48 [Mp to שְׁמֹנַת] כל אורית חס וכל קריא דכות ב̇ מ̇ א̇ "This word is always written with a defective *holem* in the Pentateuch, and all other occurrences in the Bible are likewise defective, with one exception." [Mm lacking] The one exception (וּשְׁמוֹנַת) is found in 1 Chr. 29:7.

כלייה

"The act or state of being completed, finished, spent, vanquished (from the verb כָּלָה)." In essence, the term calls attention to the verb כָּלָה in some form, as in the following example.

Example: Deut. 28:32 [Mp to וְכָלוֹת אֲלֵיהֶם] ג̇ כלייה אל "There are 3 occurrences of some form of the verb כלה, followed by the preposition אל." [Mm lacking] While the Leningrad Codex lacks a listing of these three occurrences, such a list can be found in Frensdorff (p. 100), and in Ginsburg, II:45, #321. The references are Deut. 28:32; 1 Sam. 25:17; Est. 7:7. This can be verified by checking the Mp notes in *BHS* for each of these references.

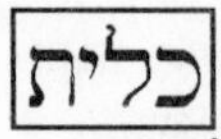

Also הכליות and הכלית. "Kidneys," pointed הַכְּלָיֹת.

Examples:

a) Gen. 18:17 [Mp to הַֽמְכַסֶּה] ב̇ וכל הכליות דכות "One of two occurrences of this verb form (though with a slightly different meaning, the ה of the first being the sign of the interrogative, and the second the definite article, cf. Ps. 147:8). (In addition to this), all references to covering the kidneys involves the same verb form." [Mm lacking] The two references can be found in Ginsburg, II:49, #397. A concordance is necessary for locating the other references to covering the kidneys (cf. E-S, p. 554, #66–72, 74).

b) Gen. 19:15 [Mp to וְאֶת־שְׁתֵּי] ו̇ וכל ואת שתי הכלית דכות "One of 6 occurrences of this combination (standing before a noun other than הַכְּלָיֹת), and in all instances where ואת שתי stands before הַכְּלָיֹת, it has this same form" [Mm 124]. The six occurrences of וְאֵת שְׁתֵּי (or וְאֶת־שְׁתֵּי) before a noun other than הַכְּלָיֹת are Gen. 19:15; 32:23; Exod. 28:25; 39:18; 1 Sam. 30:18; Ezek. 35:10.

Ginsburg (IV:159, #1413) lists nine instances where ואת שתי is followed by הכלית: Exod. 29:13, 22; Lev. 3:4, 10, 15; 4:9; 7:4; 8:16, 25. Ginsburg observes that the purpose of this Masoretic note was to safeguard the minority, i.e., the six passages where this combination is followed by a noun other than הכלית. An additional purpose was to distinguish this combination from occurrences of שְׁתֵּי אֵת (without ו), which is more common. [Cf. also Mm 669.]

כמתפוס

A mnemonic device giving the correct order of the abbreviated words. Cf. סימן for a discussion of this type of note.

Example: Exod. 33:2 [Mp to הַכְּנַעֲנִי...וְהַיְבוּסִי] סימן כמתפוס "The sign for the correct order of words is כ (הַכְּנַעֲנִי 'the Canaanites'), מ (הָאֱמֹרִי 'the Amorites'), ת (הַחִתִּי 'the Hittites'), פ (הַפְּרִזִּי 'the Perizzites'), ו (הַחִוִּי 'the Hivites'), ס (הַיְבוּסִי 'the Jebusites')."

כמתפסו

A mnemonic device giving the correct order of the abbreviated words. Cf. סימן for a discussion of this type of note.

Example: Josh. 11:3 [Mp to הַכְּנַעֲנִי...הַחִוִּי] וסימן כמתפסו "The sign for the correct order of words is כ (הַכְּנַעֲנִי 'the Canaanites'), מ (הָאֱמֹרִי 'the Amorites'), ת (הַחִתִּי 'the Hittites'), פ (הַפְּרִזִּי 'the Perizzites'), ס (הַיְבוּסִי 'the Jebusites'), ו (הַחִוִּי 'the Hivites')."

כן

"Thus, so, in this form, after this manner." Often appears in the combination כת כן (כ״כ), "written thus." This term is frequently used with reference to words with two *plene*/defective issues, calling attention to the spelling in both cases, as in example "a" below.

Examples:

a) Judg. 21:21 [Mp to שִׁילוֹ] ג כת כן "One of 3 instances of this form written thus, i.e., with *hireq-yod* and *holem-vav*" [Mm 2489]. The three references are Judg. 21:21 (2x); Jer. 7:12. The same list is found in Ginsburg, II:619, #360. The most common form this word takes is שִׁלֹה (cf. Josh. 18:1). The Mp note safeguards the minority reading.

b) Isa. 9:2 [Mp to לֹא] חד מן יז כת כן בליש (*Qere*) לו "One of 17 instances where לא, written thus, has the meaning of לו" [Mm 1795]. The references are Exod. 21:8; Lev. 11:21; 25:30; 1 Sam. 2:3; 2 Sam. 16:18; 2 Kgs. 8:10; Isa. 9:2; 49:5;

63:9; Pss. 100:3; 139:16; Job 13:15; 41:4; Prov. 19:7; 26:2; Ezra 4:2; 1 Chr. 11:20.

כנגד

"Matching" or "corresponding." Prefixed preposition כ, plus נגד (cf. Gen. 2:18, 20).

Example: Ps. 136:1 [Mp applies to the entire verse] אילן כו פסוק כנגד "These 26 verses (are divided into) corresponding halves."

כנוי

"Nickname, surname, descriptive name, patronymic name." Also, כינוי (Ps. 105:9; Jer. 33:26).

Example: Jer. 33:26 [Mp to יִשְׂחָק] ד כינוי ליצחק "There are 4 occurrences of יִשְׂחָק, written as a nickname (surname, patronymic name) for יצחק" [Mm 2659]. The other three references are Amos 7:9, 16; Ps. 105:9. It is possible that the substitution of שׂ for צ in these four passages is a cryptic reference to יִשְׂרָאֵל (יַעֲקֹב), the one who succeeded יִצְחָק (cf. the LXX rendering of these four passages).

כף

"The letter *kaf*, כ."

Example: Dan. 10:19 [Mp to וּכְדַבְּרוֹ] ל כף "Occurs once spelled with *kaf*." This word occurs three more times spelled with ב (cf. וּבְדַבְּרוֹ in 10:15), and all of them are, coincidentally, in the book of Daniel (8:18; 10:11; 10:15). The three occurrences spelled with ב have the Mp note ג, and thus, the minority occurrence with כ is protected by its own note.

כפתוי דשמשון

"The subduing (cf. Hebrew כפה) of Samson." (Most authorities prefer "The binding of Samson.")

Example: Gen. 42:24 [Mp to וַיֶּאֱסֹר] ל וכל כפתוי דשמשון דכות "This is the only time (in the Pentateuch) that a form of the verb אסר appears with *hatef-seghol* written beneath the א; but throughout the record of the binding of Samson (Judg. 15:10, 12, 13) the א is pointed with *hatef-seghol*." [Mm lacking] Ginsburg (IV:121, #1020) explains the meaning of this Mp note. Otherwise, it would be difficult to decipher. Even-Shoshan lists all the forms of אסר written with a *hatef-seghol* under the א (p. 99, #1, 3, 7, 46, 55, 62, 63).

"Written," i.e., in a certain manner. Abbreviation for כתיב, but not to be confused with כתי̇ב, "the Writings," the designation for the third division of the Hebrew Canon. The Masorah Parva of *BHS* avoids confusion by using only the abbreviated form (כת̇) for "written," and the full form (כתי̇ב) for "the Writings" (cf. כתי̇ב below).

1) Written with (or without) a certain letter or word.
   Examples:
   a) Lev. 11:43 [Mp to וְנִטְמֵתֶם] ט̇ כת̇ חס̇ א ול̇ בליש "One of 9 words (in the Pentateuch) written without an (expected) א (i.e., וְנִטְמֵאתֶם, cf. Ezek. 20:43), and this is the only occurrence of this particular form" [Mm 922]. The nine references are Gen. 20:6; Lev. 11:43; Num. 11:11; 15:24; Deut. 11:12; 28:57, 59; 32:32; 34:6.
   b) 1 Sam. 19:22 [Mp to אֵיפֹה] י̇ כת̇ ה "One of 10 occurrences of this word written with a final ה (instead of the more frequent אֵפוֹא or אֵפוֹ)" [Mm 1750]. The references are Gen. 37:16; Judg. 8:18; 1 Sam. 19:22; 2 Sam. 9:4; Isa. 49:21; Jer. 3:2; 36:19; Job 4:7; 38:4; Ruth 2:19.
   Reference source: E-S, p. 49 (אֵיפֹה), #1–10; p. 101 (אֵפוֹא or אֵפוֹ), #1–15.
2) כת̇ כן, "written thus," cf. כן.
3) כת̇ ולא קר, "written but not read," i.e., not pointed (supplied with vowels).
   Example: Ezek. 48:16 [Mp to חמש] חמש חד מן ח̇ כת̇ ולא קר "The word חמש is one of 8 words which are written but not to be read" [Mm 2752]. The references are 2 Sam. 13:33; 15:21; 2 Kgs. 5:18; Jer. 38:16; 39:12; 51:3; Ezek. 48:16; Ruth 3:12. See Chapter 3 for a discussion of this phenomenon.
4) ------- כת̇ ------- וקר, "written (thus), but read (thus)." This formula indicates places where a consonantal form in the text has been judged to be incorrectly written and has been corrected on the adjacent margin, in which case the intended pronunciation of the form on the margin has been indicated by the vowels supplied to the form in the text. In critical terminology, the supposedly corrupt form appearing in the text is called the *Ketiv*, while the proposed marginal emendation is known as the *Qere*, indicated by ק̣ placed beneath the emendation. The *Ketiv/Qere* combination is referred to often in the critical apparatus at the bottom of the page in *BHS* (cf. Gen. 33:4a; Exod. 16:2a; Num. 1:16a; Isa. 29:11a; Job 41:4a; 42:2a, 10a). Note that in the critical apparatus in Isaiah, Q is written differently when it is the abbreviation for קרי (Q, *Qere*) and when it refers to the Qumran scroll of Isaiah ($\mathfrak{Q}^{a}$), (cf. Isa. 10:32a; 25:10a; 28:15b; 55:13a; 56:10a).
   Examples:
   a) Gen. 30:11 [Mp to בָּגָד] חד מן ה̇ כת̇ מילה חדה וקר תרי̇ (*Qere*) בא גד

The *Ketiv*, בָּגָד, is here emended to the *Qere*, בא גד, which should be pointed with the vowels of the *Ketiv*, i.e., as בָּא גָד, meaning "Fortune has come!" The accompanying Mp note reads: "One of 15 textual forms written as one word but to be read as two." [Mp 214] The 15 references are Gen. 30:11; Exod. 4:2; Deut. 33:2; Isa. 3:15; Jer. 6:29; 18:3; Ezek. 8:6; Pss. 10:10; 55:16; 123:4; Job 38:1; 40:6; Neh. 2:13; 1 Chr. 9:4; 27:12.

b) Exod. 21:8 [Mp to לֹא] חד מן יז כת כן לא (*Qere*) לו The *Ketiv*, לֹא, is emended to the *Qere*, לוֹ, "to him, his." The accompanying Mp note reads: "One of 17 forms written as לֹא, (but to be read as לוֹ)" [Mm 1795]. This group of emendations has special significance for interpretation. The 17 references are Exod. 21:8; Lev. 11:21; 25:30; 1 Sam. 2:3; 2 Sam. 16:18; 2 Kgs. 8:10; Isa. 9:2; 49:5; 63:9; Pss. 100:3; 139:16; Job 13:15; 41:4; Prov. 19:7; 26:2; Ezra 4:2; 1 Chr. 11:20.

כֹּתֹּפֹּגֹּמֹּסֹּ

A mnemonic device giving the correct order of the abbreviated words. Cf. סימן for a discussion of this type of note.

Example: Josh. 3:10 [Mp to הַכְּנַעֲנִי...וְהַיְבוּסִי] סימן כֹּתֹּוֹפֹּגֹּמֹּסֹּ "The sign for the correct order of words is כֹּ (הַכְּנַעֲנִי 'the Canaanites'), תֹּ (חַחִתִּי 'the Hittites'), וֹ (הַחִוִּי 'the Hivites'), פֹּ (הַפְּרִזִּי 'the Perizzites'), גֹּ (הַגִּרְגָּשִׁי 'the Girgashites'), מֹּ (הָאֱמֹרִי 'the Amorites'), סֹּ (הַיְבוּסִי 'The Jebusites')."

כתיֹב

Abbreviation for כתובין (cf. Hebrew כתובים). "The Writings," the third division of the Hebrew Canon (Ps., Job, Prov., Ruth, Song of Songs, Eccl., Lam., Est., Dan., Ezra, Neh., 1–2 Chr.).

Examples:

a) Ps. 139:21 [Mp to הֲלוֹא] טֹ מל בכתיֹב "There are 9 occurrences of this word pointed with a full *holem-vav* in the Writings" [Mm 3664]. The references are Ps. 139:21; Prov. 14:22; Ruth 2:8, 9; Est. 10:2; Ezra 9:14; Neh. 5:9; 13:18, 26. The more common form in the Writings is הֲלֹא, which is found 46 times (cf. E-S, p. 581, #5003–49). The Mp note protects the minority reading.

b) Exod. 25:18 [Mp to כְּרֻבִים] כל אורית חסֹ וכל נביאֹ וכתיֹב מל בֹ מֹ יבֹ "All occurrences of this word in the Pentateuch are written defectively (*qibbuts* instead of *shureq*), while all occurrences in the Prophets and Writings are written *plene* (*shureq* instead of *qibbuts*), with 12 exceptions (which are written defectively)" [Mm 543]. Only the 12 exceptions (written defectively) are listed. They are 1 Sam. 4:4; 2 Sam. 6:2; 1 Kgs. 6:25, 27; 8:7; 2 Kgs. 19:15; Isa. 37:16;

Ezek. 10:1, 2, 3, 7, 8. All these references are in the Prophets.
Reference source: E-S, p. 561, # 28–91.

c) Deut. 31:30 [Mp to אֶת־דִּבְרֵי הַשִּׁירָה] ג׳ חד באור חד בנביא וחד בכתיב "There are three occurrences of this phrase, one in the Pentateuch, one in the Prophets, and one in the Writings" [Mm 4256]. The other occurrences are 2 Sam. 22:1 (Prophets), and Ps. 18:1 (Writings).

כֹּתֹמֹוֹסֹ

A mnemonic device giving the correct order of the abbreviated words. Cf. סימן for a discussion of this type of note.

Example: Exod. 13:5 [Mp to הַכְּנַעֲנִי... הַיְבוּסִי] סימן כֹּתֹמֹוֹסֹ "The sign for the correct order of words is כֹּ (הַכְּנַעֲנִי 'the Canaanites'), תֹ (הַחִתִּי 'the Hittites'), מֹ (הָאֱמֹרִי 'the Amorites'), וֹ (הַחִוִּי 'the Hivites'), סֹ (הַיְבוּסִי 'the Jebusites')."

כֹּתֹמֹפֹוֹסֹ

A mnemonic device giving the correct order of the abbreviated words. Cf. סימן for a discussion of this type of note.

Example: Judg. 3:5 [Mp to הַכְּנַעֲנִי... הַיְבוּסִי] סימן כֹּתֹמֹפֹוֹסֹ "The sign for the correct order of words is כֹּ (הַכְּנַעֲנִי 'the Canaanites'), תֹ (הַחִתִּי 'the Hittites'), מֹ (הָאֱמֹרִי 'the Amorites'), פֹּ (הַפְּרִזִּי 'the Perizzites'), וֹ (הַחִוִּי 'the Hivites'), סֹ (הַיְבוּסִי 'the Jebusites')."

כֹּתֹמֹפֹסֹגֹ

A mnemonic device giving the correct order of the abbreviated words. Cf. סימן for a discussion of this type of note.

Example: Neh. 9:8 [Mp to הַכְּנַעֲנִי...הַגִּרְגָּשִׁי] סימן כֹּתֹמֹפֹסֹגֹ "The sign for the correct order of words is כֹּ (הַכְּנַעֲנִי 'the Canaanites'), תֹ (הַחִתִּי 'the Hittites'), מֹ (הָאֱמֹרִי 'the Amorites'), פֹּ (הַפְּרִזִּי 'the Perizzites'), סֹ (הַיְבוּסִי 'the Jebusites'), גֹ (הַגִּרְגָּשִׁי 'the Girgashites')."

כֹּתֹפֹסֹעֹאֹצֹמֹ

A mnemonic device giving the correct order of the abbreviated words. Cf. סימן for a discussion of this type of note.

Example: Ezra 9:1 [Mp to הַכְּנַעֲנִי...הָאֱמֹרִי] סימן כֹּתֹפֹסֹעֹאֹצֹמֹ "The sign for the correct order of words is כֹּ (הַכְּנַעֲנִי 'the Canaanites'), תֹ (הַחִתִּי 'the Hittites'), פֹּ (הַפְּרִזִּי 'the Perizzites'), סֹ (הַיְבוּסִי 'the Jebusites'), עֹ (הָעַמֹּנִי 'the Ammonites'), אֹ (הַמֹּאָבִי 'the Moabites'), צֹ (הַמִּצְרִי 'the Egyptians'), מֹ (הָאֱמֹרִי 'the Amorites')."

Inseparable preposition, meaning "to, for, by, before, according to."

Examples:

a) Isa. 63:9 [Mp וּמַלְאַ֣ךְ] ב֗ פת֗ וכל דסמיכ֗ לאדכרא דכות֗ "One of 2 occurrences of this form written with final *patah* (instead of the ordinary מַלְאָךְ, with *qamets*), but all occurrences which are followed by the Tetragrammaton (יהוה) are also like these (with final *patah*)" [Mm 3187]. The other occurrence with final *patah* is found in Mal. 3:1. Similar occurrences followed by יהוה are too numerous to list (cf. E-S, pp. 658f., #50ff.). This Mp note safeguards the minority reading, since the instances of מַלְאָךְ are also quite numerous.

b) Gen. 8:18 [Mp to וַיֵּֽצֵא־נֹ֑חַ] י֗ בטע֗ "10 occurrences of this combination of accents." Mm 3661 identifies the note as referring to מאילא לאתנחתא, "*ma'yela* before *'atnah.*" The references are Gen. 8:18; Num. 28:26; 2 Kgs. 9:2; Jer. 2:31; Ezek. 7:25; 11:18; Ruth 1:10; 2 Chr. 20:8; Dan. 4:9, 18.

c) Job 3:5 [Mp to תִּשְׁכָּן־] כן לבן אשר "This form is pointed with *qamets-hatuf* in the final syllable, according to the Ben Asher tradition" [Mm 3302]. The Ben Naphtali tradition reads תִּשְׁכֹּן. Cf. Ps. 62:4.

"Unique, occurs only once." Abbreviation for לית (לא אית).

Examples:

a) Lev. 11:43 [Mp to וְנִטְמֵתֶם] ט֗ כת֗ חס֗ א ול֗ בליש "One of 9 words (in the Pentateuch) written without an (expected) א (instead of וְנִטְמֵאתֶם, as in Ezek. 20:43), and the only occurrence of this particular form" [Mm 922]. The other eight forms are found in Gen. 20:6; Num. 11:11; 15:24; Deut. 11:12; 28:57, 59; 32:32; 34:6.

b) Gen. 19:2 [Mp to אֲדֹנַי] ל֗ "This is a unique form, occurring only once (with *patah-yod* ending)." [Mm lacking] The *patah-yod* ending indicates the one instance where this word has a non-sacred usage. Elsewhere, it is pointed with a *qamets-yod* ending (אֲדֹנָי), and always refers to God. The latter form is found some 425 times. The Mp note safeguards the minority reading.

c) Lev. 19:3 [Mp to אִמּוֹ וְאָבִיו] ל̇ וכל קר̇יא אביו ואמו "This is the only time this phrase occurs in this order; elsewhere in the Bible the order is always אביו before ואמו." [Mm lacking] For the ubiquitous phrase אביו ואמו, see Gen. 2:24; Exod. 21:15; Lev. 20:9; etc.
Reference source: E-S, pp. 2f.

"No, Not." This is the particle of negation, לֹא in Hebrew. In Masoretic notes, it is used much like it is used in the Hebrew text. Thus, in example "a," לא simply negates an element of the note. At other times, as in example "b," לא is cited as an element from the text, much like any other word cited by a Masoretic note.

Examples:

a) Num. 35:15 [Mp to לִבְנֵי יִשְׂרָאֵל] ו̇ ד̇ פסוק דאית בהון ד̇ מילין ר״פ ב̇ קדמ̇ לא נסבין ו̇ וב̇ בתר נסבין "Four verses in which there are 4 words at the beginning of a verse, the first 2 not including ו and the last two including ו" [Mm lacking, Mp sub loco]. See Mynatt, p. 175, #223.
b) Deut. 11:2 [Mp to לֹא] מ̇ז̇ פסוק לא לא לא "Forty-seven verses in which there are three occurrences of לֹא." [Mm lacking]

"31." Because ל̇ is widely used to mark phenomena that occur only once, it is never used in the Masorah of *BHS* to represent the number 30. However, 31 is written as ל̇א̇, 32 as ל̇ב̇, 33 as ל̇ג̇; etc. The designation for 30 is כ̇י̇ (i.e., 20 + 10).

Example: 1 Kgs. 13:12 [Mp to אֵי־] ל̇א̇ "The word אֵי occurs 31 times (in the Bible)." [Mm lacking] A list of occurrences can be found in E-S, p. 44.
Reference source: Mynatt, pp. 36–37, #12.

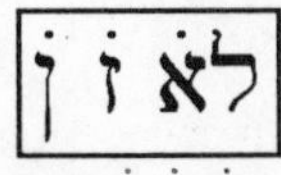

See א̇ ז̇ ן̇.

"At the end, last, following" (as one accent following another). The preposition ל prefixed to אחור.

Example: Lev. 5:2 [Mp to אוֹ בְּנִבְלַת] י̇א̇ בטע לאחור "One of 11 combinations of accents where *pashta* stands after *yetiv* (i.e., the accent pattern is *yetiv-pashta*)." [Mm lacking] In this example, the term לאחור refers to one accent following another. Literally, the Mp note says, "one of 11 occurrences with this accent following" (i.e., one of 11 instances where *pashta* follows *yetiv*). This note safeguards these 11 occurrences from other accent patterns, such as *pashta-yetiv* (which is more common) or *mehuppak-pashta* (which is practically indistinguishable from *yetiv-pashta* because of the same signs). See Yeivin, p. 199, for a discussion of *yetiv* and the various sequences mentioned above. The list of occurrences is given in Ginsburg, I:628, #141; IV:436, #141. The references are Lev. 5:2; Deut. 1:4; Isa. 5:24; 30:32 (Mp sub loco); Jer. 14:14; 16:12; 22:30; Dan. 2:10; 7:27; Ezra 6:8; 9:4. (The reader needs to be aware of an error in *BHS*. In Jer. 14:14, the Mp note יא׳ בטע לאחור is matched with לֹא שְׁלַחְתִּים. Instead, it should be matched with שֶׁקֶר הַנְּבִאִים, which occurs earlier in the verse. The accent pattern for the combination לֹא שְׁלַחְתִּים is *mehuppak-pashta*. The *mehuppak* and *yetiv* use the same symbol; the position of the symbol in relation to the word determines which accent is intended, but this is not always readily apparent in *BHS*, cf. *BHK* in Ezra 9:4 כֹּל חָרֵד. See Yeivin, p. 199, for a discussion of this example.)

Abbreviation for לגרמיה. "The accent *legarmeh*, consisting of *munah* (placed on the stressed syllable of the word) and *paseq* (placed after the word)."

Example: Dan. 3:2 [Mp to לְמִכְנַשׁ ׀ לַאֲחַשְׁדַּרְפְּנַיָּא] ב בטע לגר "One of 2 occurrences of a word accented with *legarmeh*, where *legarmeh* is followed by and subordinate to the disjunctive accent *pazer*, placed on the following word." This interpretation of the intention behind this Mp note is based on the information supplied by Yeivin (pp. 214ff., #279). While Mm 2801 cites Ezek. 9:2 as one of the two passages accented by *legarmeh*, the *pazer* in this case occurs on the word preceding the *legarmeh*. Yeivin cites as an alternative to this Neh. 8:7, where *legarmeh* precedes *pazer*, as is the case also with Dan. 3:2. Yeivin's view, therefore, is to be preferred. The reader of *BHS* should be warned: in *BHS* there is an additional circule joining שְׁלַח לְמִכְנַשׁ and thus implying that the Mp note applies to the three-word phrase; this appears to be an error. (Cf. Yeivin, p. 215.)

Abbreviation for לישנא, לישן, לשון. Alternate form: לישׁ̇. Often used with the prefixed preposition ב, as בליש, בלישנא.

1) "Language," literally, "tongue."

   Examples:

   a) 2 Kgs. 20:3 [Mp to אָנָּה] ו כת ה וכל ר״פ וכל לשון ארמית דכות "One of six cases where אָנָּה is written with final ה (instead of the more frequent אָנָּא, cf. Gen. 50:17; etc.) and all occurrences of this word at the beginning of a verse, as well as all forms in the Aramaic language, are written likewise (i.e., with a final ה, cf. Dan. 2:8; etc.)" [Mm 2169].

b) Ps. 61:8 [Mp to מַן] ל לשון קדש "The only occurrence of מַן in the holy language (i.e., Hebrew)."

2) "Form."

Examples:

a) Num. 13:22 [Mp to וַיָּבֹא] ח סביר לשון רבים "One of 8 cases where it is wrongly suggested that a plural form should be substituted for the singular" (וַיָּבֹאוּ for וַיָּבֹא, to be in agreement with the plural subject). The Mp was placed here to protect the more difficult reading. Cf. Yeivin, pp. 62ff. [Mm lacking]

b) Jer. 17:17 [Mp to מַחֲסִי] ח רפי ב מנה בליש וכל אחסה דכות ב מ א "One of 8 cases where a form of the verb חסה occurs with composite sheva (ֲ) under the guttural ח, two of which have this form (i.e., מַחֲסִי, cf. Ps. 71:7), and all occurrences of אחסה have a composite sheva (ֱ) under ח, with one exception" (אֶחְסֶה, Ps. 57:2) [Mm 3046, 3278].

3) "Meaning."

Examples:

a) Gen. 46:21 [Mp to וָרֹאשׁ] ב בתרי לישנ "The form וָרֹאשׁ appears (only) twice, (and) with two (different) meanings" (in Gen. 46:21, it is the personal name "Rosh"; in Lam. 3:19, it means "wormwood") [Mm 343].

b) Exod. 15:23 [Mp to מָרָתָה] ב בתרי לישנ "The word מָרָתָה occurs twice, with two meanings" (in Exod. 15:23, it means "to Marah"; in Jer. 4:17, it means "she has rebelled") [Mm 479].

Abbreviation for לא אית. Cf. ל. "There is not, there is none."

Example: Exod. 20:13 [Mp to לֹא] ח פסוק לא לא לא לא וחד מן כב פסוק דלית בהון לא ו ולא י "One of 8 verses where לא appears 4 times (in this case, in verses 13, 14, 15, and 16, which are treated as if they were only one verse); and this is one of 22 verses in which there is neither a *vav* nor a *yod*" [Mm 3132; Mm 878]. The eight verses with the fourfold לא are listed in Mm 3132 (Exod. 20:13; Lev. 19:20; Jer. 42:14; Ezek. 16:4; 18:6; 31:8; Zeph. 3:2; Zech. 11:16); the 22 verses lacking both *vav* and *yod* are given in Mm 878. Regarding the verse divisions in Exod. 20, see Mynatt, p. 252.

According to, in accordance with." Preposition ל prefixed to פי.

Example: Zeph. 1:1 [Mp to חִזְקִיָּה] ג לפי מֹג וחד מן יב לפי מֹק "One of 3 occurrences of חִזְקִיָּה (instead of חִזְקִיָּהוּ), according to Masorah gedolah (Mm), and one of twelve occurrences, according to the Masorah qetanah (Mp)." This is a rather convoluted entry which is nowhere found in L itself. Weil has used this Mp note in order to draw attention to different data found throughout L. The note tells us that the word חִזְקִיָּה occurs 12 times according to the Mp. Nine of the occurrences have no prefixes: 2 Kgs. 18:1, 14 (2x), 15, 16 (2x); Zeph. 1:1; Prov. 25:1; Neh. 10:18. Three of the occurrences have prefixes: 1 Chr. 3:23 (with *vav*) and 2 Kgs. 18:10 and Neh. 7:21 (with *lamed*). Each of these occurrences has either the Mp note cited above or the shorter note יב matched with it in *BHS*.

Mm 3125 gives the occurrences in a different formulation. It lists three occurrences (Zeph. 1:1; Prov. 25:1; Neh. 7:21) and then draws attention to most of the rest by stating that all of the occurrences of this name from 2 Kgs. 18:1–17 are spelled in the same way (חִזְקִיָּה) with the exception of one time, חִזְקִיָּהוּ in 2 Kgs. 18:9. The only occurrence not included by the formulation in Mm 3125 is 1 Chr. 3:23. Mm 3983 also gives three of the occurrences of חִזְקִיָּה outside of the 2 Kgs. passage (Zeph. 1:1; Prov. 25:1; Neh. 7:21), but omits 1 Chr. 3:23.

Thus, in summary, the Mp note in Zeph. 1:1 is demonstrating the two ways that the Masorah of L calls attention to the name Hezekiah spelled חִזְקִיָּה. The Mp simply notes the number of occurrences, יב (this note is found in 2 Kgs. 18:1, 14, 16). The Mm (3125 and 3983) elaborates the same occurrences (except 1 Chr. 3:23) by numbering the three instances outside of 2 Kgs. 18:1–17 and noting that the rest of the occurrences in 2 Kgs. 18:1–17 are spelled the same (except 2 Kgs. 18:9). Note also that a thirteenth occurrence of חִזְקִיָּה in Neh. 10:18 has been excluded by both the Mp and the Mm (it has no Mp in *BHS*). This is presumably due to the fact that in this case, Hezekiah is another person and not the famous king of Judah.

See שמיעה.

See בליש.

"Forty." As is the usual pattern in Masoretic numerical notation: מֹא = "41," מֹב = "42," מֹג = "43" (מֹג can also stand for "Masorah gedolah," see מג below), etc.

Examples:

a) Gen. 25:14 [Mp to וּמַשָּׂא] מֹא "One of 41 occurrences of מַשָּׂא (only 2 of which have *vav* conjunction prefixes, cf. Jer. 23:36)." [Mm lacking] The 41 references can be discovered by consulting Even-Shoshan and verifying the list by making certain that each reference has the same Mp note (מֹא). The search yielded the following references: Gen. 25:14; Num. 4:15, 47; 11:11; 2 Kgs. 5:17; 8:9; Isa. 13:1; 15:1; 17:1; 19:1; 21:1, 11, 13; 22:1; 23:1; 30:6; 46:1, 2; Jer. 17:21, 22, 24, 27; 23:33 (2x), 34 (2x), 36, 38 (3x); Ezek. 24:25; Nah. 1:1; Zech. 9:1; 12:1; Mal. 1:1; Prov. 31:1; Neh. 13:15, 19; 1 Chr. 1:30; 2 Chr. 17:11; 20:25; 35:3.
Reference sources: E-S, pp. 713f.; Mandelkern, p. 772.

b) Deut. 6:11 [Mp to לֹא־מִלֵּאתָ] מֹז פסוק לא לא לא "One of 47 verses (in the Bible) with a threefold repetition of לֹא." [Mm lacking] This type of entry is very common in the Masorah. Early Masoretes were essentially "counters." The 47 verses are not listed in Weil's *Massorah Gedolah*, but can be found in Ginsburg, II:122f., #64.

c) Josh. 9:7 [Mp to יוֹשֵׁב] מֹט מל̇ בנביא ול̇ בסיפ̇ "One of 49 occurrences in the Prophets of יוֹשֵׁב written *plene* (with *holem-vav*), and this is the only occurrence of this *plene* form in the book of Joshua." [Mm lacking] In L the Mp note to יוֹשֵׁב in Josh. 9:7 incorrectly reports that this *plene* form occurs only 16 times in the Prophets (יֹו מל̇ בנב̇). Weil has corrected this error here and elsewhere in the *BHS* edition of L. In the absence of an Mm listing, the 49 occurrences of יוֹשֵׁב in the section of the canon known as the Prophets can be determined by consulting Mandelkern, pp. 515f. Ginsburg has no comparable listing. Even-Shoshan is more cumbersome to use in such cases.

See מוקדם ומאוחר.

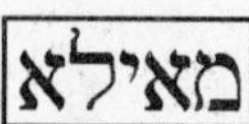

"The conjunctive accent *ma'yela*." This accent is used to indicate the secondary tone in words accented with *'atnah* or *silluq*, or joined by *maqqef* to words so accented.

Examples:

a) Gen. 8:18 [Mp to וַיֵּצֵא־נֹחַ] י בטע "One of 10 occurrences of the accent *ma'yela* (before *'atnah*)" [Mm 3661]. The ten occurrences include some examples where *ma'yela* and *'atnah* are found in the same word, and other examples where two words joined by a *maqqef* have *ma'yela* in the first and *'atnah* in the second. The ten references are given in Mm 3661 as: Gen. 8:18; Num. 28:26; 2 Kgs. 9:2; Jer. 2:31; Ezek. 7:25; 11:18; Ruth 1:10; 2 Chr. 20:8; Dan. 4:9, 18. Ginsburg cites another list with 11 references, including all those listed here, plus Ezek. 10:13 (Ginsburg, I:644, #177; IV:438, #177). Ginsburg attributed the different lists to two different schools of textual redactors.

b) Lev. 21:4 [Mp to לְהֵחַלּוֹ] ד בטע ס״פ "One of 4 occurrences of the accent *ma'yela* before *silluq* (both in the same word at the end of the verse)" [Mm 4015]. (The abbreviation ס״פ literally means "the end of the verse," but since the accent *silluq* always occurs at this position, *silluq* is implied in the note.) The four references are given as: Lev. 21:4; Num. 15:21; Hos. 11:6; 1 Chr. 2:53.

This term has two meanings. It normally indicates the accent *merekha*, but may be used occasionally to indicate a *meteg* (*ga'ya'*).

Examples:

a) Lev. 23:21 [Mp to מוֹשְׁבֹתֵיכֶם] ח בטע This brief Mp note is amplified in Mm 796: [ח מלין בב טעמ מרכא טפחא] "One of 8 words (in the Bible) with two accents (on each word), *merekha* and *tifha*" [Mm 796]. These eight words are longer than most Hebrew words. The eight words are found in: Lev. 23:21; 2 Kgs. 15:16; Jer. 8:18; Ezek. 36:25; 44:6; Song 6:5; Dan. 5:17; 1 Chr. 15:13.

b) 2 Kgs. 1:2 [Mp to אֶחְיֶה] ד מאריך "One of 4 occurrences of אֶחְיֶה with *meteg* in the initial syllable" [Mm 2039]. What is unusual about these forms is that the initial syllable is closed and stands immediately before the tone syllable. The four references are 2 Kgs. 1:2; Pss. 118:17; 119:17; Job 7:16. These are the only occurrences of אֶחְיֶה in the Bible and the Mp and Mm notes specify that all four occurrences should have *meteg*. Notice, however, that the occurrence in 2 Kgs. 1:2 lacks the *meteg* in spite of its own Mp note to the contrary. Either the Mp note derives from a different text tradition or the scribe of L omitted the *meteg* by accident.

מאשי

"From the offerings made by fire (to the Lord)." אִשֵּׁי (plural construct of אִשֶּׁה, "an offering made by fire") plus the prefixed preposition מִן ("from").

Example: Lev. 4:35 [Mp to אִשֵּׁי] ט כת י וכל מאשי דכות "One of 9 occurrences of אִשֵּׁי written with a (final) י (instead of final ה), and the ending is the same whenever the preposition מִן is prefixed to this form." [Mm lacking] The nine occurrences of אִשֵּׁי can be located, by use of a concordance, in Lev. 4:35; 5:12; 7:30; 10:15; 21:6, 21; Deut. 18:1; Josh. 13:14; 1 Sam. 2:28. (The same list can be found in Ginsburg, I:109, #1139; IV:133, #1139.) There are seven examples of אִשֵּׁי prefixed with the preposition מִן: Lev. 2:3, 10; 6:11; 7:35; 10:12, 13; 24:9. There is a Mp sub loco note to אִשֵּׁי in Lev. 4:35. It indicates that the Mp note in L (יו כת י וכל מאשי דכות) is in error and has been corrected in *BHS*. The number sixteen indicated in L would be correct if all the occurrences of אִשֵּׁי and מֵאִשֵּׁי were combined. Some scribe apparently made the error by combining all plural construct forms, both with and without prefixed מִן.

Reference sources: Mynatt, pp. 137–38, #159; E-S, p. 122, #48–63.

מג̇

"Masorah Gedolah," also called "Masorah Magna" (Mm). This refers to the longer lists placed above and below the text. The Masorah Gedolah of L has been edited and published by Gérard E. Weil in a volume entitled *Massorah Gedolah*. (Cf. מק̇.)

Example: Zeph. 1:1 [Mp to חִזְקִיָּה] ג לפי מג̇ וחד מן יב̇ לפי מק̇ "One of 3 occurrences of חִזְקִיָּה (instead of חִזְקִיָּהוּ), according to Masorah gedolah (Mm), and one of twelve occurrences, according to the Masorah qetanah (Mp)." This is a rather convoluted entry which is nowhere found in L itself. Weil has used this Mp note in order to draw attention to different data found throughout L. The note tells us that the word חִזְקִיָּה occurs 12 times according to the Mp. Nine of the occurrences have no prefixes: 2 Kgs. 18:1, 14 (2x), 15, 16 (2x); Zeph. 1:1; Prov. 25:1; Neh. 10:18. Three of the occurrences have prefixes: 1 Chr. 3:23 (with *vav*) and 2 Kgs. 18:10 and Neh. 7:21 (with *lamed*). Each of these occurrences has either the Mp note cited above or the shorter note יב̇ matched with it in *BHS*.

Mm 3125 gives the occurrences in a different formulation. It lists three occurrences (Zeph. 1:1; Prov. 25:1; Neh. 7:21) and then draws attention to most of the rest by stating that all of the occurrences of this name from 2 Kgs. 18:1–17 are spelled in the same way (חִזְקִיָּה) with the exception of one time, חִזְקִיָּהוּ in 2 Kgs. 18:9. The only occurrence not included by the formulation in Mm 3125 is 1 Chr. 3:23. Mm 3983 also gives three of the occurrences of חִזְקִיָּה outside of the 2 Kgs.

passage (Zeph. 1:1; Prov. 25:1; Neh. 7:21), but omits 1 Chr. 3:23.

Thus, in summary, the Mp note in Zeph. 1:1 is demonstrating the two ways that the Masorah of L calls attention to the name Hezekiah spelled חִזְקִיָּה. The Mp simply notes the number of occurrences, יב֯ (this note is found in 2 Kgs. 18:1, 14, 16). The Mm (3125 and 3983) elaborates the same occurrences (except 1 Chr. 3:23) by numbering the three instances outside of 2 Kgs. 18:1–17 and noting that the rest of the occurrences in 2 Kgs. 18:1–17 are spelled the same (except 2 Kgs. 18:9). Note also that a thirteenth occurrence of חִזְקִיָּה in Neh. 10:18 has been excluded by both the Mp and the Mm (it has no Mp in *BHS*). This is presumably due to the fact that in this case, Hezekiah is another person and not the famous king of Judah.

מגלה

Plural: מגילות. "Roll, or Scroll of Scripture." In its plural form, this word designates the "Five Scrolls" (חומש המגילות), i.e., Ruth, Song of Songs, Ecclesiastes, Lamentations, and Esther). In its singular form, the word designates only the book of Esther.

Examples:

a) 1 Sam. 4:13 [Mp to וַיָּבוֹא] הׄי מל וכל מגלה דכות בׄ מׄ בׄ "One of fifteen occurrences of וַיָּבוֹא written *plene* (with *holem-vav*) besides its occurrences in the book of Esther, where it is always *plene* (4 times), with 2 exceptions (5:5; 7:1)" [Mm 1552]. A full list is given here, as well as in Ginsburg, I:170, #118; IV:185, #118. This word is written defectively (וַיָּבֹא) over 200 times in the Bible. The Mp note safeguards the minority reading.

b) Lev. 7:9 [Mp to נַעֲשָׂה] חׄ קׄמׄ וכל חומש המגילות דכות בׄ מׄ בׄ "One of 8 occurrences of נַעֲשָׂה (*qamets* after שׂ), besides the occurrences in the Five Scrolls, which always have this form, with 2 exceptions (where it is נַעֲשֶׂה)" [Mm 692]. The 8 occurrences outside the Five Scrolls are Lev. 7:9; Judg. 16:11; 1 Kgs. 10:20; 2 Kgs. 23:22, 23; 2 Chr. 9:19; 35:18, 19. The Five Scrolls exhibit נַעֲשָׂה some 12 times and נַעֲשֶׂה twice (Song of Songs 1:11; 8:8). This Mp note seeks to prevent the interchange of these two similar forms. נַעֲשֶׂה (Qal imperfect, 1cp, from עָשָׂה) is the more common of the two, occurring some 37 times. נַעֲשָׂה (Nif'al participle, ms, from עָשָׂה) occurs 20 times. נַעֲשָׂה is the minority reading outside the Five Scrolls, while נַעֲשֶׂה is the minority reading within the Five Scrolls. The Mp note is designed to protect each where it is the minority reading.

Reference sources: Ginsburg, II:424f., #873; E-S, p. 923, #2186–2217; pp. 924f., #2529–48.

מדי̇נ̇

Abbreviation for מדנחאי. Often used with prefixed ל, as in למדי̇נ̇. (Cf. מערב̇.) "The Madinha'e, or Babylonian Masoretes, as opposed to the Ma'arba'e, or Palestinian Masoretes." למדי̇נ̇ (cf. Ps. 8:4) means "according to the Babylonian school of Masoretes." Yeivin (#153, pp. 139f.) notes that a list at the end of L gives about 250 differences between the Eastern (Babylonian) and Western (Palestinian) Masoretes. The Mp notes in *BHS* comment on many of these differences.

Examples:

a) Ps. 8:4 [Mp to מַעֲשֵׂי] כן למדי̇נ̇ "This word should be pointed thus (with a final *yod*) according to the Babylonian (Eastern) Masoretes" [Mm 3206]. The Mm notation further clarifies the differing opinions of the two schools of Masoretic tradition regarding Ps. 8:4.

למדנחאי : מעשי אצבעתיך כתיב י
למערבאי : [מעשה] כתיב ה

"According to the Babylonian Masoretes this form is written with a final י; according to the Palestinian Masoretes it should be written with a final ה." The issue here is whether 8:4 should be read "the *works* of your fingers," or "the *work* of your fingers."

b) Ezra 10:29 [Mp to וּשְׁאָל] כת̇ כן למערב "According to the Palestinian Masoretes, this form should be written thus" [Mm 3932]. The meaning is clarified as follows:

למערבאי : יָשׁוּב וּשְׁאָל כת̇ וכן קרי
למדינחאי : יָשׁוּב יְשְׁאָל כת̇ וּשְׁאָל קרי

"According to the Palestinian Masoretes, וּשְׁאָל, 'and Sheal,' is both written and read; according to the Babylonian Masoretes, יְשְׁאָל is written but וּשְׁאָל is to be read."

מוגה

"A carefully corrected text or codex." This word is found in the phrase סי̇פ̇ מוגה. Yeivin (#152, pp. 138f.): "These are no doubt texts which were well known and renowned in their day for their accuracy and their authoritative Masorah, but we know nothing about them today."

Example: Eccl. 9:15 [Mp to מִסְכֵּן חָכָם] ל̇ בסי̇פ̇ מוגה "A unique combination, (but one) attested by a carefully corrected codex." The issue here is why מִסְכֵּן חָכָם should occur without a connecting *vav* conjunction between the two words. The same combination occurs in Eccl. 4:3 as מִסְכֵּן וְחָכָם, "poor and wise." וְחָכָם is also found in three other references in the Bible (Gen. 41:33, 39; Prov. 29:11). The Mp note in Eccl. 9:15 states that חָכָם should be allowed to stand as it is written (without *vav* conjunction), since it has this form in a reliable and authoritative codex.

מ̇ו̇ח̇מ̇ו̇

A mnemonic device giving the correct order of the abbreviated words. Cf. סימן for a discussion of this type of note.

Example: Num. 26:33 [Mp to מַחְלָה...וְתִרְצָה] סימן מ̇ו̇ח̇מ̇ו̇ "The sign for the correct order of words מ̇ (מַחְלָה 'Mahlah'), ו̇ (וְנֹעָה 'and Noah'), ח̇ (חָגְלָה 'Hoglah'), מ̇ (מִלְכָּה 'Milcah'), ו̇ (וְתִרְצָה 'and Tirzah')" [Mm 983]. Notice that in this example, the abbreviation ו̇ denotes that the word begins with a *vav* conjunction. Thus, the correct order of the words is given and whether or not each begins with the conjunction. Cf. מ̇נ̇ו̇ו̇.

מוקדם ומאוחר

"That coming before and that coming after. The former and the latter." The combination of these two terms means that two consonants in a word have been transposed (metathesis), so that the first should be placed second, and the second should be placed first. One of the consonants will be a vowel letter, either *vav* or *yod*. This notation always appears in combination with a *Ketiv/Qere*.

Example: Dan. 4:9 [Mp to יְדָרוֹן] חד מן ד̇ מוקדם ומאוחר בסיפ̇ ידורן (*Qere*) The *Ketiv* (יְדָרוֹן) is emended to the *Qere* (ידורן) which should be pointed with the vowels of the *Ketiv*, i.e., as יְדוּרָן (from Aramaic דּוּר). The accompanying Mp note reads: "One of 4 words in the book of Daniel that have two of their consonants transposed" [Mm 3854]. This Mp note is unique in that it refers to *words* and not to *verses*. The four words and the places in Daniel where they occur are as follows: a) K: ידרון, Q: ידורן (Dan. 4:9); b) K: תוכל, Q: תכול (Dan. 5:16, 2x); c) K: והמונכא, Q: והמניכא (Dan. 5:7, 16, 29) (Note: L has a final א in all three *Qere* forms of this word, but *BHS* incorrectly changes this to a final ה in Dan. 5:7 and 16. Errors of this sort are rare.); d) K: הרים, Q: הורם (Dan. 8:11).

מחלפ̇

Alternate form מחליפ̇. Abbreviation for מחליפין. "A contrasting form or tradition, a variant, a word or phrase that is opposite to or different from another word or phrase."

Examples:

a) Exod. 30:23 [Mp to וְקִנְּמָן] ל̇ מחליפין "The word וְקִנְּמָן ('and cinnamon') occurs only once (with this vocalization), but there is a variant form." [Mm lacking] The note is saying that וְקִנְּמָן occurs only once spelled this way, but there is a variant tradition with a different spelling here (וְקִנָּמוֹן; cf. Prov. 7:17 and Song 4:14). The occurrences of this word in both its forms are listed in E-S, p. 1022, #1–3. Cf. Yeivin, p. 100.

b) Gen. 14:1 [Mp to אַמְרָפֶל] ח̇ זוגין מחליפין "One of 8 pairs of contrasting phrases (the first word in each pair stands without a *vav* conjunction, the second with a *vav* conjunction)" [Mm 3964].

(Gen. 14:1)	אמרפל	(Gen. 14:9)	ואמרפל	
(Exod. 25:6)	שמן	(Exod. 35:8)	ושמן	
(Exod. 25:7)	אבני	(Exod. 35:9)	ואבני	Etc.

c) Dan. 2:16 [Mp to זְמָן] ל̇ ומחליפין פת̇ "This is the only occurrence of this word written with a *qamets*, but there is a variant form written with *patah* (cf. Dan. 7:12)." The note is saying that זְמָן occurs only once, but there is a variant tradition in which the word is spelled with *patah* here, זְמַן. See Dan. 7:12 for a similar situation (where the word is זְמַן but the variant is זְמָן). Although not specified, the note in Dan. 2:16 is restricted to the Aramaic sections of the Bible. The word זְמָן actually occurs twice more in Hebrew (Eccl. 3:1 and Neh. 2:6). Reference source: E-S, p. 334, #1–2 (זְמָן); Yeivin, p. 100.

d) Dan. 4:22 [Mp to וְעִשְׂבָּא כְתוֹרִין] ד̇ פסוק מחליפין "One of 4 contrasting verses (in Daniel), (each of which contains this same combination of words but in the first and the third a *vav* conjunction is added[וְעִשְׂבָּא]; in the second and the fourth there is no *vav* [עִשְׂבָּא])" [Mm 3823]. The four references in the order in which they stand are Dan. 4:22; Dan. 4:29; Dan. 4:30; and Dan. 5:21.

מטע̇

Abbreviation for מטעין. It may be prefixed with ד (דמטע̇). (Cf. סביר.) "That which may be deceptive in appearance, but whose alteration could lead to error." This may be applied to consonants, words, combinations of words, verses, or accents.

Examples:

a) Lev. 17:11 [Mp to verse beginning with כִּי] ב̇ פסוק דמטע "One of 2 verses in which there is the possibility of confusion due to their similarity" [Mm 765]. The second reference is given as Lev. 17:14. The longer reading in the Mm clarifies the meaning of the Mp note. It reads: ב̇ פסוק בענינ̇ מטע קדמיה אית בה הִוא הוּא ותינ̇ אית בה הוּא הִוא "Two verses in the same context that may be confusing since the first has הִוא followed later by הוּא, and the second has הוּא followed later by הִוא."

b) Gen. 19:25 [Mp to וְאֵת] ז̇ דמטע בטע "There are 7 occurrences of וְאֵת (or אֵת) accented with *tifha*, which may seem to be in error, but which should not be corrected" [Mm 2139]. The seven occurrences are Gen. 19:25; Num. 32:28; 2 Kgs. 15:37; Isa. 36:22; Ezek. 3:2; Zech. 8:9; Neh. 5:6. Ginsburg suggested that in these seven instances of וְאֵת (אֵת), being accented with a disjunctive (and thus retaining its long vowel), there were ancient sources that exhibited a different form, i.e., וְאֶת־ (אֶת־) with *maqqef* and without any accent (Ginsburg, I:124, #1289; IV:148, #1289). This Mp note warns against any attempt to adopt this variant method of accentuation in the these seven instances.

"Unusual (applied to a word or a combination of words)." (Cf. יחיד.)

Examples:

a) Deut. 9:5 [Mp to וּלְמַעַן] ט מיחד "One of 9 unusual occurrences of וּלְמַעַן" [Mm 1113]. The unusual nature of these occurrences is that each stands alone in a verse where there is no preceding occurrence of לְמַעַן (cf. Deut. 6:2). This Mm list contains only two of the unusual forms, the two standing at the beginning of a verse (Exod. 10:2 and Deut. 11:9). Weil has placed an "Mp sub loco" note to Deut. 9:5, since the Mp note to this verse in L reads ו מיח, "six unusual occurrences," and Weil has corrected it to the form listed above. The nine occurrences are listed in Ginsburg, II:239, #635. The remaining seven are found in Exod. 9:16; Deut. 4:40; 9:5; 2 Kgs. 19:34; 20:6; Isa. 37:35; Ps. 31:4. There is an explanation for the reference to six occurrences in L's Mp to Deut. 9:5. This reduced number is arrived at by eliminating 2 Kgs. 19:34; 20:6; and Isa. 37:35. Their elimination is due to the use of לְמַעֲנִי before וּלְמַעַן in each of the three. An alternate list of these six occurrences is also given in Ginsburg (II:239, #634). Reference sources: Mynatt, pp. 192–93, #246; Frensdorff, p. 252.

b) Isa. 30:7 [Mp to וָרִיק] ג מילין מיחד דמיין "Three unusual words that are similar in form (but different in meaning)" [Mm 3953]. The three words are וָרִיק (Isa. 30:7), וָרֹק (Isa. 50:6), וָרֵק (Neh. 5:13).

c) Gen. 34:21 [Mp to הָאֲנָשִׁים] הי ר״פ מיחד "There are 15 unusual words at the beginning of verses (in the Bible)." The 15 words involved are unusual in that each occurs only once in the Bible in this form (without *vav* conjunction) and in this position (at the beginning of the verse). There are other occurrences of these words with *vav* conjunctions at the beginning of verses. And there are other occurrences within verses both with and without *vav* conjunctions. The Mp notes to these fifteen words have a different form in L, where they read: ל רא(ש) פסו(ק), "unique at the beginning of a verse" [Mm 944]. The fifteen unusual words stand at the beginning of the following verses: Gen. 34:21; 48:16; Lev. 6:19; Num. 7:19; 19:11; 32:4; Deut. 28:54; 1 Sam. 20:41; 2 Sam. 16:8; 1 Kgs. 6:12; Ezek. 7:27; 18:20; Zeph. 3:15; Lam. 2:5 (no Mp in L); 3:13.

מילה

"Word, words." Plural מילין.

Examples:

a) Exod. 15:26 [Mp to כָּל־] י׳ פסוק כל כל ומילה חדה ביניה "One of 10 verses where כל is followed by כל with one word between them" [Mm 3316]. The references are Exod. 15:26; Judg. 20:2; 1 Kgs. 8:38; 2 Kgs. 17:13; Ezek. 17:23; Pss. 39:6; 72:11; Lam. 3:60; Neh. 10:36; 2 Chr. 32:15. This list is also found in Ginsburg, II:34, #191.

b) Ps. 119:15 [Mp to בְּפִקֻּדֶיךָ] ד̇ פסוק מן ד̇ מילין בא״ב "One of 4 verses in Ps. 119 consisting of 4 words each [Mm 3403]." (Cf. א״ב above.) The four verses are 15, 47, 113, and 146.

c) Gen. 42:22 [Mp to וְגַם־] כ̇ג̇ פסוק וגם ובתר תלת מילין "One of 23 verses where וְגַם occurs with 3 words after it" [Mm 1629]. All 23 references are given. The only Mp note out of these that occurs in L is found in 1 Sam. 18:5, and it reads "21 verses" כ̇א̇ פסוק) instead of "23." *BHS* not only corrects this Mp note but also adds the corrected note to all the passages listed in Mm 1629. This list is not found in Ginsburg or Frensdorff.

מינינא

"Number."

Example: 2 Chr. 3:3 [Mp to אַמּוֹת] כן כתיב קדים למנינא "Thus written before the number" [Mm 4159]. The word אַמּוֹת is written before the number rather than after it. Mm 4159 indicates that אַמּוֹת is written before the number in 2 Chr. 3:3–15.

מיתא

"Death." Usually with prefixed ל (למיתא).

Example: Gen. 47:29 [Mp to וַיִּקְרְבוּ יְמֵי־יִשְׂרָאֵל לָמוּת] ג̇ קריבה למיתא "One of 3 references to the time of someone's death drawing near" [Mm 1874]. The references are Gen. 47:29; Deut. 31:14; 1 Kgs. 2:1 (cf. Gen. 27:41). The Mp note in L reads as ב̇ in Gen. 47:29, and as ג̇ in Deut. 31:14 and 1 Kgs. 2:1. *BHS* corrects the ב̇ and clarifies the ג̇.

"Here, from here." See כה.

מ̇כ̇ם̇

Abbreviation for מלכים כל מחלה, "the Book of Kings is כל מחלה." מ̇כ̇ם̇ is a mnemonic sign giving the correct form for the phrase כָּל־מַחֲלָה in the book of Kings. Cf. ת̇כ̇ה̇. Cf. סימן for a discussion of mnemonic signs.

מ̇כ̇ת̇פ̇ו̇ס̇

A mnemonic sequence giving the correct order of the abbreviated words. Cf. סימן for a discussion of this type of note.

Example: Exod. 34:11 [Mp to הָאֱמֹרִי...הַיְבוּסִי] סימן מ̇כ̇ת̇פ̇ו̇ס̇ "The sign for the correct order of words is מ̇ (הָאֱמֹרִי 'the Amorites'), כ̇ (הַכְּנַעֲנִי 'the Canaanites'), ת̇ (הַחִתִּי 'the Hittites'), פ̇ (הַפְּרִזִּי 'the Perizzites'), ו̇ (הַחִוִּי 'the Hivites'), ס̇ (הַיְבוּסִי 'the Jebusites')."

מל

Abbreviation for מלא. "Full, *plene*." See מל דמל. This usually refers to the presence of the vowel letters *yod* or *vav*. The opposite of מל is חס, translated "defective," and is usually used to refer to the absence of the vowel letters *yod* or *vav* in the spelling of a word.

Examples:

a) Judg. 19:10 [Mp to חֲמוֹרִים] ו̇ מל "Occurs 6 times written *plene* (with *holem-vav*)" [Mm 1507]. The references are Judg. 19:10, 21; 2 Sam. 16:2; Ezek. 23:20; 1 Chr. 5:21; 12:41. This list includes plurals with the definite article and other prefixes. Forms written defectively (with defective *holem*) outnumber those written *plene*. The Mp note safeguards the minority reading.

b) Gen. 27:8 [Mp to בְּקֹלִי] כל אורית חס ב̇ מ̇ א̇ מל "All occurrences of this form in the Pentateuch are written defectively (as here), with one exception, which is written *plene* (בְּקוֹלִי)" [Mm 153]. This list includes nine references where בְּקֹלִי is found (Gen. 22:18; 26:5; 27:8, 13, 43; 30:6; Exod. 4:1; 18:19; 19:5). The only *plene* form in the Pentateuch is in Num. 14:22. The minority reading is protected.

c) Judg. 18:16 [Mp to חֲגוּרִים] ג̇ חד מל וב̇ חס "This form occurs 3 times (in the Bible), once written *plene* (with *shureq*) and twice written defectively (with *qibbus*)." [Mm lacking] These three forms (Qal passive participle, mp) can easily be located in a concordance. The list is also given in Ginsburg, I:478, #41; IV:370, #41. The *plene* form is found in Judg. 18:16, and the two defective forms are found in Exod. 12:11 and Dan. 10:5.

מל דמל

"Doubly *plene*, i.e., written with two vowel letters." See מל.

Example: Neh. 6:17 [Mp to הוֹלְכוֹת] ל מל דמל "This word occurs only once (in the Bible) doubly *plene*." [Mm lacking]

מלאכי

"The book of Malachi."

Example: Isa. 45:13 [Mp to אָמַר יְהוָה צְבָאוֹת] ז וכל מלאכי דכות ב מ ג "This phrase occurs 7 times, and it is always this way in the book of Malachi with 3 exceptions" [Mm 2379]. This note is calling attention to occurrences (Isa. 45:13; Hag. 2:7, 9; Zech. 1:3; 4:6; 7:13; 8:14) of אָמַר יְהוָה צְבָאוֹת without the word כֹּה preceding and without the words אֱלֹהֵי יִשְׂרָאֵל following. (The identical phrase occurs several times in Malachi.) Mm 2379 notes that the three exceptions are 1:13 (end of verse); 2:16; and 3:13 (in these the phrase does not include צְבָאוֹת) and that they occur between 1:6 and the end of the book. Note that there is a typographical error in Zech. 1:3: the Mp incorrectly marks כֹּה אָמַר יְהוָה צְבָאוֹת earlier in the verse; אָמַר יְהוָה צְבָאוֹת at the end of the verse should be marked.

מלכים

"The book of Kings."

Example: Exod. 15:11 [Mp to עֹשֵׂה] ח קמ קטן וכל דברים מלכים תרי עשר תלים קהלת עזרא ד״ה דכות ב מ כב "One of 8 occurrences of עֹשֵׂה written with *sere* (*qamets qatan*) in the final syllable. And this same form occurs throughout Deuteronomy, Kings, the Book of the Twelve, Psalms, Ecclesiastes, Ezra, and Chronicles, except in 22 instances (where it is written as עֹשֶׂה)" [Mm 475]. The eight occurrences of עֹשֵׂה (besides those found in the other books listed in the Mp) are given as Exod. 15:11; 35:35; Isa. 19:10; 64:4; Jer. 10:12; 51:15; Prov. 12:22; 22:2. The 22 exceptions are also listed as a part of Mm 475, beginning with Deut. 5:10 and concluding with 1 Chr. 18:14.

מלעיל מלרע

"מִלְעֵיל ('from above') is used in contrast to מִלְרַע ('from below')." These terms are used in two ways: 1) They define two different positions that major accents may take in Hebrew words. Those accented on the next to the last syllable (the penultimate syllable) are said to be מִלְעֵיל, i.e., closer to the beginning of the word. When the tone (stressed) syllable is the final syllable of the word, the word is said to be accented מִלְרַע, i.e., at the end of the word. The terms may also be used to distinguish between accents placed above words (מִלְעֵיל) and those placed below words (מִלְרַע). 2) Vowels may also be categorized as either מִלְעֵיל or מִלְרַע, the longer vowels מִלְעֵיל, and the shorter vowels מִלְרַע. This distinction may be made if two words have the same consonants but a different vocalization. The same distinction is sometimes made between the prefixed particles ב, כ, or ל. When they are pointed with the article, they are said to be מִלְעֵיל; pointed without the article they are said to be מִלְרַע. Likewise the *vav* pointed as *vav* consecutive will normally be מִלְעֵיל, but as *vav* conjunction will normally be מִלְרַע. In 2 Sam. 24:3, the form מלעי, which appears in the Mp, is a misprint: the final ל has been left off.

Examples:

a) Gen. 25:8 [Mp to וַיֵּאָסֶף] ז̇ ה̇ מלעיל וב̇ מלרע "One of 7 occurrences of this verb form (Nif'al imperfect 3ms) with *vav* consecutive, 5 of them accented מִלְעֵיל, and 2 acccented מִלְרַע." [Mm lacking] The seven must be located with a concordance. The five accented מִלְעֵיל (וַיֵּאָסֶף) are Gen. 25:8, 17; 35:29; 49:33; Deut. 32:50. The two accented מִלְרַע (וַיֵּאָסֵף) are Num. 11:30 and Judg. 20:11. Reference sources: Ginsburg, I:102, #1008 (for a variant listing); Frensdorff, p. 23 (partial listing); E-S, p. 98, #152–58; Mynatt, p. 163, #200.

b) 1 Sam. 1:11 [Mp to וַתִּאמַר] ה̇ ד̇ מלרע וחד מלעיל "This form occurs 5 times (with *vav* consecutive), 4 times accented מִלְרַע, and once מִלְעֵיל" [Mm 3587]. The four forms accented מִלְרַע are found in 1 Sam. 1:11; 2:1; Est. 5:7; 7:3. The only form accented מִלְעֵיל is found in Prov. 7:13. There are 187 occurrences of וַתֹּאמֶר (with final *seghol*) accented מִלְעֵיל and ten occurrences accented מִלְרַע. The Mp note to וַתֹּאמַר is designed to protect the minority reading. References source: E-S, p. 88, #2403–13; pp. 89f., #4567–4744.

c) Ps. 27:13 [Mp to לוּלֵא] ד̇ כת̇ א ול̇ נקוד מלעיל ומלרע ב̇ מ̇ אות ו וחד מן ה̇י נקוד "One of 4 occurrences written with a final א (instead of the more common לוּלֵי), and the only occurrence in the Bible of a word with special diacritical points both above (מִלְעֵיל) and below (מִלְרַע) all consonants, except the consonant *vav*, and this is one of 15 words in the Bible with special diacritical points" [Mm 1714]. (Cf. נקוד.) This Mm note lists only the four references where לוּלֵא (with final א) instead of לוּלֵי (with final י) occurs: Gen. 43:10; Judg. 14:18; 2 Sam. 2:27; Ps. 27:13. See Chapter 3 regarding the special diacritical points.

מן

"From, of." Cf. מ̇נ̇ה̇.

Examples:

a) Judg. 20:13 [Mp to ‸ ‥] בני חד מן י׳ קר ולא כת "The consonants בני are to be read with the unaccompanied vowels (‥ ‸) in the text (as בְּנֵי). This is one of 10 places in the Bible where consonants are to be read with unaccompanied vowels in the text, although the consonants are not written" [Mm 2745]. The ten passages where these words are found are listed as Judg. 20:13; 2 Sam. 8:3; 16:23; 18:20; 2 Kgs. 19:31, 37; Jer. 31:38; 50:29; Ruth 3:5, 17. See Chapter 3 regarding this phenomenon.

b) 1 Sam. 9:1 [Mp to מִבִּן־יָמִין] חד מן ח׳ כת ב׳ מילין וקר (*Qere*) מבנימין חדה וחד מן יז׳ מל "This is one of 8 instances where what is written as two words is read as one. And this is one of 17 occurrences of בִּנְיָמִין written *plene* (instead of the more frequently occurring בִּנְיָמִן)" [Mm 214]. The second part of this Mm note lists the verses where two words written in the text are read as one. They are Judg. 16:25; 1 Sam. 9:1; 24:9; Isa. 9:6; 44:24; Lam. 1:6; 4:3; 2 Chr. 34:6 [Mm 262]. This is a list of occurrences of בִּנְיָמִין written *plene*. It extends from Gen. 35:18 to Neh. 11:36.
Reference source: E-S, pp. 192f., #1–112 (בִּנְיָמִין).

מנה

Abbreviation for מנהון. "Of them, from them."
Examples:

a) 1 Kgs. 9:9 [Mp to אֲבֹתָם] ה׳ חס ג׳ מנה בנביא וכל תורה דכות ב׳ מ׳ ב׳
"Occurs 5 times written defectively (instead of אֲבוֹתָם), 3 of them in the Prophets, and all occurrences in the Pentateuch are written defectively, with 2 exceptions" [Mm 3967]. The five defective forms (besides those found in the Pentateuch) are listed as 1 Kgs. 9:9; 14:22; 2 Kgs. 17:41; Ezra 10:16; Neh. 7:61. The two *plene* forms in the Pentateuch are found in Num. 1:16 and 17:18 (cf. Mm 833). The three defective forms occurring in the Prophets are listed again in Mm 1973 as 1 Kgs. 9:9; 14:22; and 2 Kgs. 17:41.

b) Exod. 5:16 [Mp to נִתָּן] כא׳ ד׳ מנה קמ׳ "There are 21 occurrences of this word in the Bible, 4 of them written with *qamets* in the final syllable (instead of the more common *patah*)" [Mm 2838]. All 21 occurrences are given, extending from Exod. 5:16 to 2 Chr. 34:16 [Mm 403]. Here the four forms with *qamets* are listed as occurring in Exod. 5:16; Isa. 33:16; Ezek. 32:25; 2 Chr. 28:5.

מ̇נ̇ו̇ו̇ו̇

Example: Num. 27:1 [Mp to מַחְלָה...וְתִרְצָה] סימן מ̇נ̇ו̇ו̇ו̇ "The sign for the correct order of words מ̇ (מַחְלָה 'Mahlah'), נ̇ (נֹעָה 'Noah'), ו̇ (וְחָגְלָה 'and Hoglah'), ו̇ (וּמִלְכָּה 'and Milcah'), ו̇ (וְתִרְצָה 'and Tirzah')" [Mm 983]. Notice that in this example, the abbreviation וֹ denotes that the word begins with a *vav* conjunction. Thus, the correct order of the words is given and whether or not each begins with the conjunction. Cf. מוחמו.

מנוקדין

"Pointed, punctuated." Also מנוקד. Cf. נקוד.

Examples:

a) 1 Chr. 15:1 [Mp to וַיֵּט־] בֹ מנוקדין בתלת "One of 2 occurrences of וַיֵּט־ (from נטה) pointed with *seghol* (instead of the more frequently occurring וַיֵּט)." [Mm lacking] The second occurrence is in Gen. 26:25.
Reference source: E-S, p. 757, #88–89.

b) 2 Chr. 9:24 [Mp to נֵשֶׁק] ג מנוקדין כן בליש "Pointed thus 3 times in this and similar forms" [Mm 4174]. The three passages where this word occurs with *sere* (instead of *seghol*) as the initial vowel are 1 Kgs. 10:25; Job 20:24; 2 Chr. 9:24. Note that the prefixes vary in each of the occurrences. The purpose of this note is to protect נֵשֶׁק (in any form) from harmonization to נֶשֶׁק, which occurs more frequently.
Reference source: E-S, p. 787, #1–10 (נֶשֶׁק).

מנין

"A (cardinal) number, a numerical adjective."

Example: Gen. 30:30 [Mp to לְרַגְלִי] חֹ בֹ מנה בליש וכל מנין איש רגלי דכות "There are 8 occurrences of רַגְלִי, 2 of which have this same form (with a prefixed ל), and when רַגְלִי (or אִישׁ רַגְלִי) refers to "foot soldiers," and is preceded by numerical adjectives, it has this same form (רַגְלִי)" [Mm 3533]. The eight occurrences of רַגְלִי that do not refer to foot-soldiers are found in Gen. 30:30; Pss. 26:12; 38:17; 94:18; 116:8; 119:105; Job 23:11; 31:5. References to foot soldiers (רַגְלִי or אִישׁ רַגְלִי) occur in Exod. 12:37; Num. 11:21; Judg. 20:2; 1 Sam. 4:10; 15:4; 2 Sam. 8:4; 10:6; 1 Kgs. 20:29; 2 Kgs. 13:7; 1 Chr. 18:4; 19:18.
Reference source: E-S, p. 1060, #27–34; p. 1061, #1–11 (רַגְלִי).

מסכינו

"Poor, poverty." Cf. סכן.

Example: Deut. 1:21 [Mp to רֵשׁ] גֹ בֹ חס וחד מל וכל לשון מסכינו דכות "This word occurs 3 times, twice written defectively (רֵשׁ) and once *plene* (רֵאשׁ), and all occurrences of the word signifying 'poor' or 'poverty' are likewise written *plene* (רֵישׁ or רֵאשׁ)" [Mm 2032]. The two defective forms (רֵשׁ) are in Deut. 1:21 and 1

Kgs. 21:15 (where רֵשׁ is the 2ms imperative of יָרַשׁ); the *plene* form (רֵאשׁ) occurs in Dan. 7:1, and is the Aramaic word for "beginning" (cf. רֵאשִׁית). Examples of *plene* forms (רֵישׁ or רֵאשׁ) referring to the poor or to a state of poverty are found in Prov. 13:18 and 30:8 (cf. Mm 3608). The Mp note to Deut. 1:21 is concerned with words that are similar in form but different in meaning.

מערבׄ

Usually written with prefixed ל (למערבׄ). Abbreviation for למערבאי. Cf. מדינׄ. "Westerners, i.e., Masoretes from Syria/Israel," as opposed to Easterners (מדנחאי), i.e., Masoretes from Babylonia.

Examples:

a) Dan. 11:6 [Mp to כּוֹחַ] לׄ מלׄ למערבׄ "The only occurrence (in the Bible) of כּוֹחַ written *plene* (כּוֹחַ instead of the regular כֹּחַ, as in Deut. 8:18), according to the Western tradition." [Mm lacking] For occurrences of כֹּחַ, see E-S, p. 528, #1ff.

b) Ps. 29:1 [Mp to אֵלִים] וׄ חסׄ בכתיבׄ למערבׄ "One of 6 occurrences written defectively (אֵלִים instead of אֵילִים, cf. Gen. 32:15) in the Writings, according to the Western tradition" [Mm 879]. The occurrences are found in Pss. 29:1; 89:7; Job 41:17; Dan. 11:36; 1 Chr. 29:21; 2 Chr. 29:22.

מעשה בראשית

"The work (of creation) in the beginning." This is the name used to identify the creation account in Gen. 1:1ff.

Example: Gen. 6:12 [Mp to וַיַּרְא אֱלֹהִים] בׄ בתורׄ וכל מעשה בראשית דכותׄ "This phrase occurs twice in the Pentateuch, in addition to its occurrences in the Creation Story (Gen. 1:1ff.), all of which have this same form." [Mm lacking] The other Pentateuchal occurrence is in Exod. 2:25. Its occurrences in the Creation Story are in Gen. 1:4, 10, 12, 18, 21, 25, 31. (Cf. Mynatt, pp. 38–39, #16).

מ״פ

"Within the verse." See אמצ, מצע.

מׄפׄכׄתׄגׄוׄסׄ

A mnemonic sequence giving the correct order of the abbreviated words. Cf. סימן for a discussion of this type of note.

Example: Josh. 24:11 [Mp to הָאֱמֹרִי...הַיְבוּסִי] סימן מׄפׄכׄתׄגׄוׄסׄ "The sign for the correct order of words is מׄ (הָאֱמֹרִי 'the Amorites'), פׄ (הַפְּרִזִּי 'the Perizzites'), כׄ (הַכְּנַעֲנִי 'the Canaanites'), תׄ (הַחִתִּי 'the Hittites'), גׄ (הַגִּרְגָּשִׁי 'the Girgashites'), וׄ

(הַחִוִּי 'the Hivites'), ס֗ (הַיְבוּסִי 'the Jebusites')" [Okhl 274].

Abbreviation for מַפִּיק. "Read, pronounced, audible." The term describes weak letters like א, ה, ו, or י when they have consonantal value, instead of being silent or quiescent. It applies most often to final ה, which without *mappiq* is silent (not pronounced), but with *mappiq* is audible (pronounced). By analogy, א, ו, and י are said to be מפק֗ (pronounced) when they initiate a syllable, and thus function as consonants, but are said to be "not מפק֗" (not pronounced) when they function as vowel letters in a diphthongal construction. When the term מפק֗ is combined with a negative particle like לא or דלא, it can indicate that the letter in question does not even appear in the word, as in example "a" below.

Examples:

a) 1 Sam. 1:17 [Mp to שֵׁלָתֵךְ] יא֗ מילין דלא מפק֗ א ול֗ בליש֗ "One of 11 words in which א is not pronounced, and this word is unique in its form" [Mm 4069]. The 11 references are 1 Sam. 1:17; 2 Sam. 22:40; 1 Kgs. 11:39; 2 Kgs. 16:7; 19:25; Pss. 99:6; 119:101; Job 41:17; Neh. 3:13; 1 Chr. 5:26; 12:39. The interesting thing to observe is that in most of these passages the quiescent א has dropped out of the word with the Mp note, whereas in other occurrences of similar words the א is present and is pronounced as a regular consonant: 1 Sam. 1:17 (cf. Est. 5:6); 2 Sam. 22:40 (cf. Ps. 18:40); 1 Kgs. 11:39 (cf. Ps. 119:42); 2 Kgs. 16:7 (cf. 2 Kgs. 15:29); 2 Kgs. 19:25 (cf. Isa. 37:26); Ps. 99:6 (cf. 2 Sam. 15:11); Job 41:17 (cf. Ps. 62:5); Neh. 3:13 (cf. Neh. 3:14); 1 Chr. 5:26 (cf. 1 Chr. 5:6); 1 Chr. 12:39 (cf. Gen. 45:7).
Reference source: For an alternate list containing many of these same references, see Ginsburg, I:11, #15; IV:6ff., #15.

b) Gen. 42:38 [Mp to וּקְרָאָהוּ] ל֗ מפק֗ א "This is the only occurrence of this form, and א is pronounced (functions as a consonant)" [Mm 331]. This Mm note informs us that this word is included in one of the זוגין. The first part of the note reads: ד֗ זוג֗ מן תרי֗ קדמ֗ מפק֗ א ותנ֗ לא מפק֗ א "One of 4 word groups, with two words each, the first word having an א that is pronounced and the second word having an unpronounced א (in which case א drops out entirely)."

Gen. 42:38	וּקְרָאָהוּ;	Gen. 44:29	וְקָרָהוּ
Josh. 21:30	מִשְׁאָל;	1 Chr. 6:59	מָשָׁל
2 Sam. 23:37	הַבְּאֵרֹתִי;	1 Chr. 11:39	הַבֵּרֹתִי
Jer. 6:14	וַיְרַפְּאוּ;	Jer. 8:11	וַיְרַפּוּ

Reference source: E-S, p. 1029, #2 (קרא[2]); p. 1034, #4 (קרה[1]). See Mm 922 for an alternative way of indicating words that have lost a quiescent א.

c) Zech. 5:11 [Mp to הָלָה] ג לא מפק ה "One of 3 instances where ה (representing the 3fs pronominal suffix) occurs without *mappiq* (and therefore is not pronounced)" [Mm 3154]. The three references are Num. 32:42; Zech. 5:11; Ruth 2:14.

Abbreviation for מצעא. "Within, in the middle." (Cf. אמצֹ, מ״פ, and מ״ת.) When used with reference to a word within a verse (any word other than the first or last word of a verse), it is abbreviated as מ״פ. A consonant's location within a word may be indicated by the abbreviation מ״ת.

Examples:

a) Gen. 25:21 [Mp to וַיֶּעְתַּר] ד ב ר״פ וב מ״פ "This form occurs 4 times, twice at the beginning of the verse, and twice within the verse" [Mm 180]. The occurrences at the beginning of the verse are Gen. 25:21 and Judg. 13:8; those within the verse are found in Exod. 8:26 and 10:18.

b) Lev. 7:9 [Mp to וְכָל־] י ר״פ וכל ומ״פ וכל "There are 10 instances where וְכָל־ (or וְכֹל) occurs at the beginning of a verse and is repeated in the middle of the same verse." [Mm lacking] A listing is supplied, however, by Ginsburg (II:37f., #224). It includes Gen. 2:5; Exod. 13:13; Lev. 7:9; 15:17, 20; Josh. 13:21; 1 Kgs. 10:21; 2 Chr. 9:20; Jer. 31:40; Ezek. 12:14.

"Egypt." See משיחה.

"Masorah qetanah," also called "Masorah Parva" (Mp), consisting of the abbreviated notes placed in the margin beside the text. (Cf. מֹגֹ.)

Example: Zeph. 1:1 [Mp to חִזְקִיָּה] ג לפי מג וחד מן יב לפי מק "One of 3 occurrences of חִזְקִיָּה (instead of חִזְקִיָּהוּ), according to Masorah gedolah (Mm), and one of 12 occurrences, according to the Masorah qetanah (Mp)" [Mm 3125, 3983]. This is a rather convoluted entry which is nowhere found in L itself. Weil has used this Mp note in order to draw attention to different data found throughout L. The note tells us that the word חִזְקִיָּה occurs 12 times according to the Mp. Nine of the occurrences have no prefixes: 2 Kgs. 18:1, 14 (2x), 15, 16 (2x); Zeph. 1:1; Prov. 25:1; Neh. 10:18. Three of the occurrences have prefixes: 1 Chr. 3:23 (with *vav*) and 2 Kgs 18:10 and Neh. 7:21 (with lamed). Each of these occurrences has either the Mp note cited above or the shorter note יֹבֹ matched with it in *BHS*.

Mm 3125 gives the occurrences in a different formulation. It lists three occurrences (Zeph. 1:1; Prov. 25:1; Neh. 7:21) and then draws attention to most of the rest by stating that all of the occurrences of this name from 2 Kgs. 18:1–17 are spelled in the same way (חִזְקִיָּה) with the exception of one time, חִזְקִיָּהוּ in 2 Kgs. 18:9. The only occurrence not included by the formulation in Mm 3125 is 1 Chr. 3:23. Mm 3983 also gives three of the occurrences of חִזְקִיָּה outside of the 2 Kgs passage (Zeph. 1:1; Prov. 25:1; Neh. 7:21), but omits 1 Chr. 3:23.

Thus, in summary, the Mp note in Zeph. 1:1 is demonstrating the two ways that the Masorah of L calls attention to the name Hezekiah spelled חִזְקִיָּה. The Mp simply notes the number of occurrences, יֹבֹ (this note is found in 2 Kgs. 18:1, 14, 16). The Mm (3125 and 3983) elaborates the same occurrences (except 1 Chr. 3:23) by numbering the three instances outside of 2 Kgs. 18:1–17 and noting that the rest of the occurrences in 2 Kgs. 18:1–17 are spelled the same (except 2 Kgs. 18:9). Note also that a thirteenth occurrence of חִזְקִיָּה in Neh. 10:18 has been excluded by both the Mp and the Mm (it has no Mp in *BHS*). This is presumably due to the fact that in this case, Hezekiah is another person and not the famous king of Judah.

"*Maqqef.*"

Example: Gen. 30:19 [Mp to בֵּן־] דֹ מקף "One of 4 occurrences of בֵּן followed by *maqqef* (בֵּן־)." [Mm lacking] The reason for the Mp note is that בֵּן־ is in the construct state to שִׁשִּׁי ("a sixth son"), and the construct form for בֵּן should be בֶּן־ (with *seghol*, cf. Gen. 12:5; 15:3; etc.). The note protects the minority reading. The four occurrences can be located with the aid of a concordance. They are Gen. 30:19; 1 Sam. 22:20; 2 Sam. 9:12; Ezek. 18:10.

See קרי״א. "The Bible." Cf. Mm 3557.

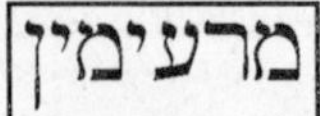

"Accented with *shalshelet.*"

Example: Gen. 24:12 [Mp to וַיֹּאמַר] צֹאֹ יֹטֹ מנהֹ ר״פ י מנהֹ בתורֹ וחד מן ז בטע מרעימין This Mp note makes several statements about וַיֹּאמַר: 1) It occurs 91 times in the Bible (but see Mynatt, pp. 52–3, #38 where it is demonstrated that it actually occurs 123 times; cf. Gen. 14:19 [Mp to וַיֹּאמַר] צֹאֹ וכל ויען ויסף דאיוב דכותֹ, which provides the clue to the "missing" occurrences); 2) of these, 19 stand at the beginning of the verse; 3) of these 19, ten occur in the Pentateuch; 4) this (Gen. 24:12) is one of seven words in the Bible which are accented with *shalshelet* (all standing at the beginning of their verse; the accent *shalshelet* can only be placed on the first word of a verse; cf. Yeivin, pp. 188–89) [Mm 705]. The only information supplied by Mm 705 is a list of the seven occurrences in the Bible of a word (at the beginning of the sentence) accented with *shalshelet*. They are Gen. 19:16; 24:12; 39:8; Lev. 8:23; Isa. 13:8; Amos 1:2; Ezra 5:15. The same listing can be found in Ginsburg, I:653, #236; IV:449, #236. The 91 occurrences of וַיֹּאמַר must also be sought in Ginsburg, I:89, #839; II:102, #839. The 19 occurrences of וַיֹּאמַר at the beginning of the verse could be determined by consulting each of the 91 references listed by Ginsburg. Though all 19 are not listed here, the ten verses in the Pentateuch which begin with וַיֹּאמַר are Gen. 15:8; 16:8; 18:3; 19:7; 24:12 (with *shalshelet*); 24:34; 30:28; Exod. 33:14, 18; Deut. 33:2.

משיחה

The act of anointing to office, used here specifically as applying to kings." Cf. משח.

Example: Num. 21:29 [Mp to לְמֶלֶךְ] כט וכל משיחה מצרים אשור ישראל דכות "The form לְמֶלֶךְ (instead of the more frequently occurring לַמֶּלֶךְ) occurs 29 times, in addition to its always being used with reference to the anointing of the kings of Egypt, Assyria (Aram), or Israel" [Mm 958]. The 29 occurrences of לְמֶלֶךְ (which do not follow the word משח) are listed here. However, a concordance must be used to find occurrences of the form with reference to the anointing of the kings of Egypt, Assyria, and Israel.

Reference sources: Ginsburg, II:230f., #490 (for a list of 29 occurrences of לְמֶלֶךְ, slightly different from the list given in Mm 958); E-S, p. 668, #1213–49 (including all references to לְמֶלֶךְ in the Bible).

משכן

"The tabernacle," and by extension, "the passages of the Bible that deal with the building of the tabernacle in the wilderness, i.e., Exod. 25–31, 36–40."

Example: Judg. 7:5 [Mp to לְבָד] ל וכל משכן ותרי עשר דכות "The form לְבָד (with *qamets* rather than *patah*) is always used in the Twelve Prophets and in the 'tabernacle' passages, and elsewhere it occurs only once (i.e., Judg. 7:5)." [Mm lacking] A concordance offers numerous examples of לְבַד (with *patah*, cf. Exod. 12:37; Deut. 3:5; etc.). The references with לְבָד include Exod. 26:9 (2x); 36:16 (2x); Zech. 12:12 (5x), 13 (4x), 14 (2x).

Reference source: E-S, p. 150, #3–35.

משלי

"The Book of Proverbs."

Example: Gen. 25:32 [Mp to הוֹלֵךְ] כז מל ט מנה בתור וכל משלי וקהלת דכות ב מ ה "Occurs 27 times (written *plene*, i.e., with *holem-vav*), 9 of the 27 in the Pentateuch. (This is in addition to) the occurrences in Proverbs and Ecclesiates, which are also written *plene*, with 5 exceptions" [Mm 1788]. The information given here includes the 27 occurrences of הוֹלֵךְ found outside Proverbs and Ecclesiastes. It also lists the 5 forms written defectively (הֹלֵךְ) in Proverbs and Ecclesiastes (Prov. 13:20; Eccl. 1:4; 9:10; 10:3; 12:5). [Mm 935] This is a list of the 9 *plene* forms occurring in the Pentateuch (Gen. 15:2; 25:32; 28:20; Exod. 19:19; Lev. 11:27, 42 (2x); Num. 22:22; 24:14). The *plene* forms in Proverbs and Ecclesiastes could be found with the aid of a concordance, as could the defective forms outside Proverbs and Ecclesiastes.

משנה תורה

"Another designation for the book of Deuteronomy, based on Deut. 17:18."

Examples:

a) Exod. 20:24 [Mp to עֹלֹתֶיךָ] ג וכל משנה תורה דכות "Occurs 3 times, in addition to its occurrences in Deuteronomy, which are all like this" [Mm 3285]. עֹלֹתֶיךָ occurs twice (Exod. 20:24; Isa. 43:23), and וְעוֹלֹתֶיךָ occurs once (Ps. 50:8). The references in Deuteronomy must be located with the aid of a concordance (cf. Deut. 12:13, 14, 27).

b) Josh. 11:11 [Mp to הַחֲרֵם] ל וכל משנה תורה דכות "The only occurrence outside the book of Deuteronomy, and all occurrences in Deuteronomy are like this." [Mm lacking] The references in Deuteronomy are indicated in E-S, p. 400, #1–3 (חרם) as 3:6; 7:2; 20:17.

משני

Abbreviation for משנין. "Different, distinct, not the same, not like."

Example: Gen. 41:26 [Mp to שֶׁבַע] ל ר״פ בתור וחד מן ח פסוק מן ד מילין דמיין ותלת משני "The form שֶׁבַע occurs only once at the beginning of a verse in the Pentateuch. This verse is one of 8 (in the Bible) in which the same word occurs 4 times, except that the third occurrence differs from the others." [Mm lacking] Three of the eight verses are Gen. 41:26; Deut. 1:31; Ezra 8:16. These are all noted in the margin of *BHS* and a careful search would likely turn up the others. The repeated words in these verses are as follows:

Gen. 41:26	Deut. 1:31	Ezra 8:16
שֶׁבַע	אֲשֶׁר	וּלְאֶלְנָתָן
שֶׁבַע	אֲשֶׁר	וּלְאֶלְנָתָן
וְשֶׁבַע	כַּאֲשֶׁר	וּלְנָתָן
שֶׁבַע	אֲשֶׁר	וּלְאֶלְנָתָן

Cf. Mm 456 for a similar rubric which also uses the term משני. See also 1 Sam. 9:4; Isa. 30:16; 31:1; Ezek. 48:16.

מ״ת

Abbreviation for מצעא תיבותא. "Within a word." This may apply to any consonant except the first or last in a word. Cf. אמצ̇, מצע̇.

Example: 1 Sam. 18:1 [Mp to וַיֶּאֱהָבֵו] ויאהבהו (*Qere*) חד מן ג̇ חס ה מ״ת וחד מן ב̇ בליש "The *Qere* is וַיֶּאֱהָבֵהוּ. This is one of 3 words lacking ה within the word and one of 2 occurrences of וַיֶּאֱהָבֵהוּ (spelled according to the form given in the *Qere*)" [Mm 2090]. (Cf. 1 Sam. 16:21.) The three words lacking an internal ה are found in 1 Sam. 18:1; 2 Kgs. 9:15; Isa. 32:15.

Reference source: E-S, p. 20, #179–80.

מתא̇

"Similar, the same, identical." Abbreviation for מתאימין.

Examples:

a) Gen. 5:32 [Mp to נֹחַ] ה̇ פסוק דאית בהון ה̇ מילין מתאימין "One of 5 verses each of which has within it 5 similar words" [Mm 1890]. The Mm note suggests that there may be six verses with similar words. They are Gen. 5:32; 35:17; 1 Sam. 20:29; 1 Kgs. 3:26; Neh. 2:2; and perhaps Exod. 17:16. The similarity can only be discovered by a close examination of the word marked with the circule and the four succeeding words in each verse. The similarity is that each word has only two consonants. Cf. Mynatt, pp. 118–20, #132.

b) Gen. 46:2 [Mp to יַעֲקֹב יַעֲקֹב] ד̇ שמואתא מתאימין "The same name is repeated in 4 instances." [Mm lacking] Note that an "Mp sub loco" note appears in the footnote to Gen. 46:2. This is apparently because there are two passages where Abraham's name is repeated (Gen. 22:11; 25:19). Other names repeated in succession in the Bible are Jacob (Gen. 46:2), Moses (Exod. 3:4), and Samuel (1 Sam. 3:10). The Mp note to Gen. 46:2 apparently counts the repetition of Abraham's name only once, thus arriving at a total of four repetitions.

Reference source: Mynatt, p. 94, #95 (cf. pp. 59–60, #47).

מתחלפׄ

"Varied, placed in reverse order, changed." Abbreviation for מתחלפין. See חלוף.

מׄתׄפׄוׄסׄ

A mnemonic sequence giving the correct order of the abbreviated words. Cf. סימן for a discussion of this type of note.

Example: 1 Kgs. 9:20 [Mp to הָאֱמֹרִי...הַיְבוּסִי] סימן מׄתׄפׄוׄסׄ "The sign for the correct order of words is מׄ (הָאֱמֹרִי 'the Amorites'), תׄ (הַחִתִּי 'the Hittites'), פׄ (הַפְּרִזִּי 'the Perizzites'), וׄ (הַחִוִּי 'the Hivites'), סׄ (הַיְבוּסִי 'the Jebusites')" [Okhl 274 and Mp sub loco].

מׄתׄפׄכׄוׄסׄ

A mnemonic sequence giving the correct order of the abbreviated words. Cf. סימן for a discussion of this type of note.

Example: Exod. 23:23 [Mp to הָאֱמֹרִי...הַיְבוּסִי] סימן מׄתׄפׄכׄוׄסׄ "The sign for the correct order of words is מׄ (הָאֱמֹרִי 'the Amorites'), תׄ (הַחִתִּי 'the Hittites'), פׄ (הַפְּרִזִּי 'the Perizzites'), כׄ (הַכְּנַעֲנִי 'the Canaanites'), וׄ (הַחִוִּי 'the Hivites'), סׄ (הַיְבוּסִי 'the Jebusites')" [Okhl 274 and Mp sub loco].

נ

"The letter נ."

Example: 1 Chr. 12:2 [Mp to נֹשְׁקֵי קֶשֶׁת] יא ר״פ וס״פ נ וחד מן ב "This is one of 11 verses which both begin and end with a נ, and one of 2 occurrences of the phrase נֹשְׁקֵי קֶשֶׁת" [Mm 729 & 4199]. Mm 729 lists the 11 verses beginning and ending with נ: Lev. 13:9; Num. 32:32; Deut. 18:15; Jer. 50:8; Pss. 46:5; 77:21; 78:12; Prov. 7:17; 20:27; Song 4:11; 1 Chr. 12:2. Mm 4199 lists the other occurrence of the phrase נֹשְׁקֵי קֶשֶׁת, 2 Chr. 17:17.

נ̇

"Fifty." נ̇א̇ = "51," נ̇ב̇ = "52," נ̇ג̇ = "53," etc.

Example: Deut. 7:17 [Mp to מִמֶּנִּי] נ̇ז̇ וכל תל̇ים דכות̇ ב̇ מ̇ י̇א̇ "This form occurs 47 times in the Bible (instead of מִנִּי), besides its occurrences in the book of Psalms, which are all written like this, with 11 exceptions (מִנִּי)." [Mm lacking] A list of 47 occurrences of מִמֶּנִּי can be found in Ginsburg, II:233f., #545. The 11 occurrences of מִנִּי in the Psalms (e.g., Ps. 44:10, 18) can be found in E-S, p. 677, #736–43, 770–72.

See ן ז א.

"The Prophets, the second division of the Bible."

Examples:

a) Mic. 4:10 [Mp to כִּי־עַתָּה] י̇ב̇ י̇א̇ מנה̇ בנביא̇ "This phrase occurs 12 times (outside the Pentateuch and Job), 11 of which are in the Prophets" [Mm 230]. This Mm listing makes it clear that the 12 occurrences of כִּי־עַתָּה are exclusive of those that occur in the Pentateuch and Job. The 12 are 1 Sam. 2:16; 13:13; 14:30; 2 Sam. 16:11; 18:3; Isa. 49:19; Hos. 5:3; 10:3; Mic. 4:10; 5:3; Zech. 9:8; Dan. 10:11. (Cf. Ginsburg, II:31, #145; p. 32, #155.) There are several more occurrences of כִּי־עַתָּה in the Pentateuch and Job (cf. Gen. 43:10 and Job 3:13).

b) Jon. 2:8 [Mp to וַתָּבוֹא] י̇ מל̇ בנביא̇ "Occurs 10 times in the Prophets written *plene* (instead of וַתָּבֹא)." [Mm lacking] A list is given in Ginsburg, I:171, #123 (Judg. 4:21; 1 Sam. 28:21; 2 Sam. 11:4; 20:22; 2 Kgs. 11:16; Ezek. 22:4; 33:4, 6; 37:10; Jon. 2:8). The defective spelling occurs 26 times in the Prophets, as listed in Ginsburg, IV:186, #123. As is customary, the Mp protects the minority reading.

"Vows, or votive offerings," and, by extension, the section in the book of Numbers (30:1ff.) dealing with these matters.

Example: Jer. 6:24 [Mp to שָׁמְעוֹ] ד̇ וכל נדרים דכות̇ "The form שָׁמְעוֹ occurs 4 times, in addition to its occurrences in the section on vows from Num. 30:1ff., where it has this same form." [Mm lacking] A concordance identifies the four occurrences (outside Num. 30) as Josh. 6:27; 9:9; Jer. 6:24; Est. 9:4. It also occurs five times in Num. 30 (vv. 6, 8, 13, 15, 16). The four occurrences are based on the noun שֵׁמַע, and the five occurrences on the verb שָׁמַע.

Reference source: E-S, p. 1181, #1–4 (שְׁמַע); p. 1176, #122–26 (five occurrences in Num. 30).

"The letter נ." Plural: נונין. See נונין זעירין and נון רבתי.

נון הפוכה

"An inverted נ." See Num. 10:34, 36; Ps. 107:21–26, 40. The inverted nuns occur nine times, standing before the verses noted in Ps. 107 and before Num. 10:34 and after 10:36. The reason for their appearance is unknown. (See chapter 3 on phenomena of the Proto-Masoretic Text. Cf. Yeivin, pp. 46–47, #81.)

נונין זעירין

"Small נs."

Example: Isa. 44:14 [Mp to אֹרֶן] ג̇ נונין זעירין "There are 3 nuns that are reduced in size." [Mm lacking] (Cf. Jer. 39:13; Prov. 16:28.) (See chapter 3 on phenomena of the Proto-Masoretic Text.)

נון רבתי

"A large נ."

Example: Num. 27:5 [Mp to מִשְׁפָּטָן] ל̇ נון רבתי "There is one occurrence of large nun." The reason for the enlargement of the nun is unknown. (See chapter 3 on phenomena of the Proto-Masoretic Text. Cf. Yeivin, pp. 47–48, #84.)

ניחח

"Soothing, pleasing, tranquillizing," referring to sacrifices that are acceptable to God.

Example: Gen. 8:21 [Mp to רֵיחַ הַנִּיחֹחַ] ח̇ וכל אשה ריח ניחח דכות "This phrase ('a pleasing odor') occurs 8 times, besides its occurrences in conjunction with אשה ('an offering by fire'), where it also has this form." [Mm lacking] A concordance locates the eight references to רֵיחַ הַנִּיחֹחַ (when not preceded by אשה): Lev. 6:8, 14; Num. 15:3, 7; 28:13; 29:8; Ezek. 6:13. Examples of this phrase used in conjunction with אשה are Exod. 29:18; Lev. 1:9, 13, 17; etc.

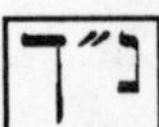

Abbreviation for נביאים and כתובים. "The Prophets and the Writings." Sometimes written with the prefixed preposition ב, as בנ״ך (cf. Exod. 6:6 "in the Prophets and the Writings").

Example: Gen. 41:51 [Mp to הַבְּכוֹר] ד מל בתור וכל נ״ך דכות ב מ א "This form occurs 4 times in the Pentateuch (with *holem-vav* in the final syllable), and all occurrences in the Prophets and Writings are like it (with *holem-vav*), with one exception" [Mm 1146]. (Cf. הַבְּכֹר in 1 Chr. 6:13.) The four occurrences in the Pentateuch are Gen. 41:51; 48:14; Deut. 15:19; 25:6. For a fuller treatment, see Ginsburg, I:182, #297; IV:207, #297.

נסיב

"Accompanied by, added to, included with." Plural: נסיבין or נסבין. Alternate form נסבא. This usually refers to *vav* added to the beginning of a word.

Examples:

a) Gen. 24:35 [Mp to וּבָקָר] ד פסוק דאית בהון ח מילין נסיב ו "There are 4 verses (in the Bible) in each of which there are 8 words, each accompanied by (prefixed with) *vav*" [Mm 4156]. The heading in Mm 4156 clarifies the meaning of the Mp note: ד פסוק בקריא דאית בהון ח ח מילין קדמית לא נסבא ו ושבעה נסבין ו "There are 4 verses in the Bible in each of which 8 words occur in a series, the first of which is not accompanied by a (prefixed) ו, but the seven (following) words are accompanied by (prefixed) ו." The four verses are Gen. 24:35; Deut. 28:22; Isa. 11:11; 2 Chr. 2:6.

b) Num. 35:15 [Mp to לִבְנֵי יִשְׂרָאֵל וְלַגֵּר וְלַתּוֹשָׁב] ד פסוק דאית בהון ד מילין ר״פ ב קדמ לא נסבין ו וב בתר נסבין ו "One of 4 verses, each having 4 words at the beginning, the first two without a prefixed ו, and the last two with a prefixed ו." [Mm lacking] Mynatt, p. 175, #223, lists the four verses as Num. 35:15; Josh. 15:55; 19:7; 1 Chr. 22:16.

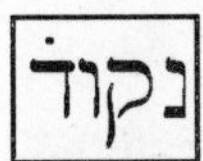

נקוד

"Points (dots) placed above or below a word or a group of words in the text of the Bible." Abbreviation for נקודות. See מנוקדין. The origin and purpose of these extra points are obscure. They may have originated in the pre-Masoretic period to indicate letters of words that were considered questionable but left in the text. Similar points are used in this manner in the Dead Sea manuscripts and in early Samaritan manuscripts. It is striking that many of the letters and words thus marked are lacking in the Septuagint and Syriac translations of the Bible, and also from the Samaritan Pentateuch. (See Chapter 3 on phenomena of the Proto-Masoretic Text.)

Examples:

a) Num. 29:15 [Mp to וְעִשָּׂרוֹן] ה ג מל וב חס וחד מן הי נקוד י מנה בתור

"This form occurs 5 times, 3 times written *plene* (with *holem-vav*) and 2 times written defectively (with *holem*). And this occurrence is one of 15 instances in the Bible where (special diacritical) points occur with letters or words, 10 of which are in the Pentateuch" [Mm 999]. This listing refers only to the five occurrences of this form, which include *plene* forms in Lev. 14:21; Num. 29:4, 15; and defective forms in Exod. 29:40 and Num. 28:13. The verses where special dots are found are distributed as follows: ten in the Pentateuch, four in the Prophets, and one in the Writings. The references are as follows: Gen. 16:5; 18:9; 19:33; 33:4; 37:12; Num. 3:39; 9:10; 21:30; 29:15; Deut. 29:28; 2 Sam. 19:20; Isa. 44:9; Ezek. 41:20; 46:22; Ps. 27:13.
Reference source: Mynatt, p. 54 #40.

b) Ps. 27:13 [Mp to לוּלֵא] ד̇ כת̇ א ול̇ נקוד מלעיל ומלרע ב̇ מ̇ אות ו וחד מן ה̇י̇ נקוד "One of 4 occurrences written with a (final) א (instead of the more common לוּלֵי), and the only occurrence in the Bible of a word with special diacritical points both above (מִלְעֵיל) and below (מִלְרַע) all consonants, except the consonant ו, and this is one of 15 words in the Bible with special diacritical points" [Mm 1714]. (Cf. נקוד.) This Mm note lists only the four references where לוּלֵא (with final א) instead of לוּלֵי (with final י) occurs: Gen. 43:10; Judg. 14:10; 2 Sam. 2:27; Ps. 27:13. The remainder of the Mp note to לוּלֵא in Ps. 27:13 deals with the extraordinary points that occur above and below all the consonants in the word לוּלֵא except the ו.

"Feminine gender."
Examples:

a) Gen. 39:9 [Mp to אוֹתָךְ] י̇ז̇ מל̇ בלשון נקיבה "This word occurs 17 times written *plene* (with *holem-vav*) in its feminine (2fs) form" [Mm 287]. This has to do with את (sign of the direct object) and the second feminine singular pronominal suffix (ָךְ). The *plene* form (אוֹתָךְ) is less common than the defective form (אֹתָךְ). The Mp note safeguards the minority reading. The *plene* forms of the (2s) feminine gender are found in Gen. 39:9; Num. 5:21; Judg. 14:15; Jer. 2:35; 11:17; 30:14; Ezek. 16:4 (contra textum; for a treatment of such notes see Chapter 4 "Working with Masoretic Notes"), 39(2x), 40, 57, 59, 60; 22:14, 15; 23:25, 29. A slightly different list of 13 occurrences is cited by Ginsburg, I:136, #1426.

b) Num. 27:7 [Mp to אֲבִיהֶם] ג̇ נקיבה "The pronominal suffix הֶם, which is normally masculine, is read feminine when attached to אֲבִי in three instances (אֲבִיהֶם instead of אֲבִיהֶן)." [Mm lacking] However, Ginsburg (I:19, #34) gives the references as Num. 27:7; 36:6; Job 42:15.

Abbreviation for סדר. Plural: סדרים. Literally: "order, sequence." This was the name assigned to the sections into which the Torah was divided for the Sabbath readings in the synagogues. In Palestine, where the custom was to complete the reading in three to three and a half years, the Torah was divided into 154 or 167 סדרים (*sedarim*). *BHS* has 167 Torah *sedarim* (Gen. has 45; Exod. has 33; Lev. has 25; Num. has 33; Deut. has 31). The beginning of each is marked by ס̇ printed in the center margin on each page (in the same column as the verse numbers), so as not to interfere with Mp notes on the outer margin (cf. Gen. 1:1; 2:4; 3:22; etc.). In Babylonia, the custom was to complete the reading of the Torah in one year, which led to the Torah's being divided into 54 larger sections, known as פָּרָשׁוֹת (see פרשׁ). The beginning of these sections in *BHS* is indicated by פרשׁ printed in the center margin of the page (cf. Gen. 6:9; 12:1; 18:1; 23:1; etc.). The number of the *sedarim* is indicated in notes placed at the end of each of the books of the Torah, but the number of the *parashot* is not so indicated. The Babylonian custom of reading the Torah in one year eventually became the norm in Palestine, even though the *sedarim* divisions continued to be indicated in the margins of manuscripts like L.

Abbreviation for סתומא. (See פתוחא.) Long before the introduction of chapter divisions, the entire Bible (except the Psalter) was divided on the basis of content into short paragraphs, also known as פרשיות (*parashiyyot*). A paragraph could be either "open" (פתוחא) or "closed" (סתומא). An open paragraph had to commence at the beginning of a new line. Furthermore, the preceding line had to be left partially or wholly blank. Closed paragraphs, on the other hand, had to commence at a point other than the beginning of a line. It could begin on the same line with the concluding word of the previous paragraph (separated by a brief space), or written after an indentation on the next line. A ס in the body of the text indicates that the following paragraph is closed; a פ indicates that it is open. The first paragraph in a book is assumed to be open without a written פ, since it begins on the first line of the manuscript. These distinctions are no longer valid for printed Bibles, since their line and paragraph divisions are of necessity different from those of ancient manuscripts.

However, the original format of L is indicated in *BHS* by the printing of either ס or פ in the space before the beginning of a new paragraph. These symbols have more relevance in the context of a manuscript than in a printed edition.

Standing alone, and without a diacritical point, ס represents the letter ס.

Example: Hab. 3:14 [Mp to יִסְעֲרוּ] ב׳ חד כת ש וחד כת ס "The word יִסְעֲרוּ occurs twice, once written with ש and once written with ס" [Mm 2919].

"Sixty." The number letter ס׳, "sixty," followed by the first nine number letters makes the numbers 61 (סא׳) through 69 (סט׳).

Examples:

a) Gen. 26:1 [Mp to הָרִאשׁוֹן] סד׳ "This form (with ה prefix, including ה interrogative in Job 15:7) occurs 64 times in the Bible." [Mm lacking] Even-Shoshan shows 63 occurrences of הָרִאשׁוֹן (p. 1051, #9–71) and one occurrence of הֲרִאישׁוֹן (p. 1051, #72). Ginsburg omits the latter form (from Job 15:7) and cites a list of only 63 occurrences (II:565f., #131). It is interesting to note that the original entries in L, whenever they occurred, also read 63 (סג׳). Weil altered these to read 64 (except in the case of Dan. 10:4). Thus a seemingly simple entry becomes somewhat complicated.

b) Gen. 18:3 [Mp to בְּעֵינֶיךָ] סו׳ "This form (with preposition ב and pronominal suffix, 2 ms) occurs 66 times in the Bible." [Mm lacking] The 66 occurrences can be found in E-S (p. 855, #544–609). Ginsburg cites a shorter list containing only occurrences in the Pentateuch (II:386f., #311).

Abbreviation for סבירין. Cf. מטע׳. סְבִיר is the passive participle of the Aramaic סְבַר, meaning "supposed." It cites a possible emendation for a problem text, but warns that the emendation, which might be "supposed" to be superior, should nevertheless be avoided. It insists that the text be left as it is, problems notwithstanding.

Examples:

a) Gen. 19:23 [Mp to יָצָא] ג׳ סביר׳ יצאה "One of 3 cases where it is wrongly supposed that יָצְאָה would be superior to יָצָא" [Mm 127]. This is because the subject of the verb is שֶׁמֶשׁ, which is normally feminine in gender, and normally would be expected to take a feminine form of the verb. The three occurrences are Gen. 19:23; Jer. 48:45; Dan. 8:9. See also Ginsburg, I:731, #472.

b) Num. 13:22 [Mp to וַיָּבֹא] ח׳ סביר׳ לשון רבים "One of 8 cases where the plural form (וַיָּבֹאוּ) is wrongly supposed (by some) to be superior to (the singular) וַיָּבֹא." [Mm lacking] These are cases where the subject after the verb is plural. Ginsburg (I:170, #119a) lists 12 cases where וַיָּבֹאוּ is wrongly suggested as a correction for וַיָּבֹא, but the last four references in his listing are problematic. The first eight, however, are verifiable when compared with the Mp notes in *BHS*. They are Num. 13:22; 2 Sam. 3:22; Isa. 45:24; Jer. 51:48; Ezek. 14:1; 20:38; 23:44; 36:20.

סדרים

"*Sedarim*." Mf to Gen., Exod., etc. See ס̊.

סוֹף פָּסוּק

Abbreviated as ס״פ. This may be used in two ways: 1) It may indicate the "end of the verse." 2) It may stand for the last accent in the verse (also known as "*silluq*").

Examples:

a) Deut. 31:3 [Mp to יְהוָה] ג̇ ר״פ וס״פ "One of 3 verses where יְהוָה stands at the beginning of the verse and at the end of the verse" [Mm 1226]. The references are Deut. 31:3; 1 Sam. 26:23; Isa. 38:20.

b) Gen. 3:10 [Mp to אָנֹכִי] ח̇ בטע̇ וכל זקף אתנח וס״פ דכות ב̇ מ̇ א̇ "The form אָנֹכִי occurs 8 times with the accent in this position (מלעיל), in addition to its occurrences with *zaqef*, *'atnah*, and *sof pasuq* (*silluq*), which are also accented מלעיל, with one exception (which is מלרע)" [Mm 1571]. The eight occurrences (not including those involving *zaqef*, *'atnah*, or *sof pasuq*) are listed as Gen. 3:10; Exod. 4:10; Judg. 17:9; 1 Sam. 9:21; 30:13; 2 Sam. 3:8; Amos 7:14; Ruth 3:13. The one instance where אָנֹכִי is מלרע with *'atnah* is in Job 33:9. A slightly different list reflecting another school of tradition is given in Ginsburg (I:100, #966).

סימן

"Mnemonic devices, excerpts, or signs used for referring to such things as the location of words, phrases, or verses; the order of familiar nouns commonly occurring in series; or the differences in two similar passages." Plural: סימנים "signs"; סימנהון "their signs." Plural abbreviation סימנ̇. The term סימן is flexible and has several different meanings and nuances. For those who use *BHS* and *Massorah Gedolah* as primary tools in studying the Masorah, there are three distinct meanings of סימן which need to be distinguished and illustrated.

1) Mnemonic Excerpts

During the period in which the Masoretes worked, the contemporary system of chapter and verse divisions had not yet been developed. The verses were divided, but they were not numbered. There was no standard system of reference. Thus, the usual system of marking a verse reference was by citing a short excerpt from the verse. It was expected that this short quote would be sufficient to jog the reader's memory so that the reader could then locate the specific passage.

This is the standard method of citing references for occurrences in Mm lists. The note giving the pertinent information for the textual item under consideration is followed by a list of excerpts. Usually, the list of excerpts is preceded by the term וסימנהון, "and their signs" (see the example below). This term indicates that what follows is the list of excerpts for the note. Fortunately, in *Massorah Gedolah*, the editor, G.E. Weil, has supplied the chapter and verse reference for us with each excerpt.

Example: 2 Kgs. 18:18 [Mp to וְשֶׁבְנָה] ב̇ כת̇ ה "One of 2 occurrences of this word written with a final ה (cf. 2 Kgs. 18:26)" [Mm 2161]. The heading to this Mm note, like most other headings, refers to the "signs" for recalling the two verses where שֶׁבְנָה (instead of the more common שֶׁבְנָא) occurs. In *Massorah Gedolah*, Mm 2161 reads:

וְשֶׁבְנָה ב̇ כת̇ ה וסימנהון:
2 R. 18,18 ויקראו אל המלך
2 R. 18,26 ויאמר אליקים בן חלקיהו

2) Mnemonic Sequences

Similar lists of words sometimes appear in the Hebrew Bible, with the order of the words varying in different versions of the list. Especially where the list was more than two or three words long, there was always a danger that the order in a particular text might be corrupted in the copying process. If the copyist did not follow the order precisely in the text he was copying, but instead relied on memory or a more familiar parallel text, an error could easily creep in.

In order to prevent this kind of error, the Masoretes developed Mp notes attached to these sequences which give the correct order of the words in abbreviated form. These abbreviated words are always introduced or followed by the term סימן in *BHS*. The term alerted the copyist (and the reader) that the order of the abbreviations that followed was the prescribed order for the words in the corresponding text.

For example, the lists of the nations inhabiting Canaan differ from one another. The number of nations occurring in separate versions of the lists varies, as does their order. If one considers only those lists where six nations are named, no fewer than six different sequences will be found (cf. Exod. 23:23; 33:2; 34:11; Josh. 11:3; 12:8; Judg. 3:5), complicated by the fact that other versions of six included different nations (Neh. 9:8).

Thus, Mp notes are attached to the sequence of words in each of these texts giving the correct order. For example, in Josh. 12:8, the Mp note is סימן מׄתׄכׄפׄוׄסׄ, and in Exod. 23:23, the Mp note is סימן מׄתׄכׄפׄוׄסׄ. In both cases, the abbreviated letters function as a mnemonic sign, giving the correct order of the six words. They are introduced by the term סימן, "sign," which announces that a mnemonic sequence follows.

All of the mnemonic sequences in *BHS* are given elsewhere in the glossary, alphabetized according to the letters in the sequence. For another discussion of this same type of Mp note, see Chapter 4, "Working with Masoretic Notes," under the subheading "Mnemonic Notes."

3) Aramaic Mnemonics

The Masoretes would sometimes construct artificial sentences as a means of remembering the location of the occcurrences constituting the topic of a Masoretic note. These mnemonic sentences were almost always in Aramaic, and they were written in the Masorah Magna where there was sufficient space. Each word in the sentence represented a biblical verse in which an occurrence was found. Similar devices are used in music where, for example, the sentence "Every good boy does fine" is used to remember the lines in the treble clef: E, G, B, D, F. Each word in the sentence begins with the corresponding letter of the treble clef. In the Aramaic mnemonics, each word from the mnemonic sentence is similar in some way to a Hebrew word from a verse in which an occurrence is found.

It is important to remember that a word from the Aramaic mnemonic sentence represents the *verse* in which an occurrence is found, not the occurrence itself. Thus, the words in the mnemonic sentence usually do not remotely resemble the occurrences themselves. Furthermore, since the mnemonic sentence is in Aramaic, the Hebrew verses it represents may be based on Aramaic equivalents or synonyms. Thus, a strong command of Aramaic is essential to deciphering these mnemonic sentences and identifying the targeted Hebrew verses.

Example: Gen. 22:20 [Mp to וַיְהִי אַחֲרֵי הַדְּבָרִים הָאֵלֶּה] גׄ "This combination occurs 3 times" [Mm 154]. The Mm note elaborates further: ויהי אחרי הדברים האלה גׄ וסימנהון אתילד ואתבאש ומית. "וַיְהִי אַחֲרֵי הַדְּבָרִים הָאֵלֶּה occurs 3 times and their signs are אתילד ואתבאש ומית." These three words are the Aramaic mnemonic sentence. In English, they are translated "he was born, and he became ill, and he died." Each one of the Aramaic words in the sentence corresponds to a Hebrew word from a verse in which an occurrence of וַיְהִי אַחֲרֵי הַדְּבָרִים הָאֵלֶּה can be found. The word אתילד ("he was born") represents Gen. 22:20 which contains יָלְדָה. The word ואתבאש ("and he became ill") represents Gen. 48:1 which contains חֹלֶה. The word ומית ("and he died") represents Josh. 24:29 which contains וַיָּמָת. Thus, the location of all three occurrences of וַיְהִי אַחֲרֵי הַדְּבָרִים הָאֵלֶּה are accounted for, and the Aramaic mnemonic sentence serves as a reminder.

There are 38 Aramaic mnemonics in L. Most of these are three to five words in length, although some are considerably longer. The longest Aramaic mnemonic in L is 22 words (Mm 1444). Some of these Aramaic mnemonics are problematic even for scholars of the Masorah. The Aramaic sentence may lack the correct number of words for the rubric, or a word in the Aramaic sentence may not correspond to an appropriate Hebrew verse. For a thorough discussion of these problems as well as other issues involved in understanding the Aramaic mnemonics, consult "Aramaic Mnemonics in Codex Leningradensis," by David Marcus.[1]

Abbreviation for סיפרא. Usually prefixed with ב. (Cf. בסיפ.) For סיפ מוגה, see מוגה. "Book, in this book." This refers to a specific book of the Bible. It must not be forgotten, however, that the two books of Samuel are regarded as one book. The same is true for the two books of Kings, the two books of Chronicles, the books of Ezra and Nehemiah, and the Twelve Prophets.

Examples:

a) Ezra 2:40 [Mp to הַלְוִיִּם] ג ר״פ בסיפ "Occurs 3 times at the beginning of the verse in this book." [Mm lacking] Ginsburg (II:142, #316) lists the three references as Ezra 2:40; Neh. 7:43; 12:22. ("Ezra-Nehemiah" were reckoned as one book, see עזרא below.)

b) Amos 6:10 [Mp to וְאָמַר] ז בסיפ ג מנה בפסוק "This form (with *vav*) occurs 7 times in this book, 3 of them in this verse." [Mm lacking] Ginsburg (I:88, #812) gives a list of eight occurrences, seven of which are included in *BHS*. They are Amos 6:10(3x); Nah. 3:7; Zech. 13:5, 6(2x).

"Sum, total number."

Examples: (See Masorah finalis [Mf] at the end of Deuteronomy [*BHS*, p. 353].)

a) ----- סכום הפסוקים של ספר "The total number of verses of (של = abbreviation for אֲשֶׁר לְ) this book (Deut.) is -----."

b) ----- סכום הפסוקים של תורה "The sum of the verses in the Torah is -----."

[1]David Marcus, "Aramaic Mnemonics in Codex Leningradensis," (publication forthcoming). The example cited above is elaborated further in this very helpful article. Marcus provides a comprehensive survey of the Aramaic mnemonics in L, as well as a discussion of their problematic elements. This article is crucial for anyone who wishes to understand the dynamics involved in the Aramaic mnemonics. See also Yeivin, pp. 74–77, #126–27 and Dotan, pp. 1424–25.

c) -----סכום התיבות של תורה "The sum of the words in the Torah is -----."

d) -----סכום האותיות של תורה "The sum of the letters of the alphabet in the Torah is -----."

סמיׄכׄ

"Close, near, either closely preceding or closely following." This term may refer to a word or a combination of words. It is usually preceded by ד (e.g., דסמיׄכׄ).

Examples:

a) Gen. 31:32 [Mp to מָה] הׄ קמׄ דסימכׄ "The form מָה occurs 5 times with *qamets* (instead of מֶה) when it is followed by (ע or ח)" [Mm 592]. The translation of the Mp given above is based on the fuller heading in the Mm 592 entry. Exodus 32:1 is the primary focus here. Its Mp note states that מֶה occurs as the form for this interrogative pronoun 24 times. Mm 592 first lists these 24 occurrences, which are scattered throughout the Bible. Then it has a supplementary note as follows: וכל דסמיך לע ולח דכות בׄ מׄ הׄ [מָה] "And all occurrences of this form when it is followed by (a word beginning in) ע or ח are like this (מֶה), with 5 exceptions (where it is מָה)." The five exceptions where the form is מָה before words beginning in ע or ח are Gen. 31:32; 2 Kgs. 8:13; Mal. 2:14; Dan. 4:32; Ezra 6:9.

b) 1 Sam. 28:15 [Mp to לָמָּה] הׄ דגש דסמיכׄ "The form לָמָּה occurs 5 times with *dagesh* in the consonant מ when it is followed by (certain consonants)" [Mm 3274]. The fuller heading informs that לָמָה (without *dagesh*) occurs only twice (Pss. 42:10; 43:2) outside those passages where it is followed by ע,א,ה, or the Tetragrammaton (יהוה), where it always occurs as לָמָה (without *dagesh*), except in five instances. They are 1 Sam. 28:15; 2 Sam. 2:22; 14:31; Jer. 15:18; Ps. 49:6. References source: E-S, pp. 601f.

ס״פ

Abbreviation for סוֹף פָּסוּק. It may indicate the end of the verse or the final accent in the verse (*silluq*).

Examples:

a) Exod. 11:10 [Mp to וּמֹשֶׁה וְאַהֲרֹן] בׄ חד ר״פ וחד ס״פ "This combination (with *vav* conjunction on each word) occurs twice, once at the beginning of the verse (Exod. 11:10) and once at the end of the verse (Num. 16:18)" [Mm 442].

b) Exod. 26:5 [Mp to הָאֶחָת] גׄ קמׄ וכל אתנח זקף וס״פ דכות בׄ מׄ בׄ "There are 3 occurrences of הָאֶחָת (instead of the more common הָאַחַת) with final *qamets*, in addition to the instances where the form is accented with *'atnah*, *zaqef*, or *sof pasuq* (*silluq*), in which case it will always be written as הָאֶחָת, with 2 exceptions." [Mm lacking] Frensdorff (p. 9) lists the three occurrences of הָאֶחָת

as Exod. 26:5; 36:9; and 1 Kgs. 7:18 (not including occurrences accented with *'atnah, sof passuq*, or *zaqef*). Ginsburg (I:42, #291) has a similar list, except that he correctly lists Exod. 36:12 instead of 36:9 (36:9 is accented with *'atnah*, 36:12 with *segholta*). Ginsburg's lists can be verified by comparing each of its references with the Mp notes in *BHS*. The many occurrences of הָאֶחָת accented with *'atnah, zaqef*, or *sof pasuq* can be examined in E-S, p. 43, #199–229. The two exceptions mentioned in the Mp note to Exod. 26:5 are not given in any of the Mm lists. A careful search of the concordance (E-S, p. 43, #194, 198) shows them to be 1 Kgs. 7:38 and 1 Chr. 27:1, both accented with *zaqef*, and yet written not with *qamets* but with *patah* (הָאַחַת). Incidentally, the Mp note to 1 Kgs. 7:38 in *BHS* is incorrectly written. It reads בׄ זקף קמׄ, "twice written with *zaqef* and *qamets*," but should instead read בׄ זקף פתׄ, "twice with *zaqef* and *patah*" (cf. L and 1 Chr. 27:1).

ס״ת

Abbreviation for סוף תיבותא. "The end of the word."

Examples:

a) Gen. 32:15 [Mp to עִזִּים, as first word of the verse] בׄ פסוקׄ בתורׄ כל ס״ת ם "One of 2 verses in the Pentateuch in which the end of every word is ם (*mem*)" [Mm 1005]. The second verse is Num. 29:33.

b) Exod. 7:29 [Mp to וּבְכָה] כׄ מילין כתׄ ה ס״ת גׄ מנהׄ בליש "There are 20 words (in the Bible) written with (an extra) ה at the end of the word, 3 of which have this same form (בְּכָה)" [Mm 964]. The list of 20 includes Exod. 7:29; 13:16; 15:11(2x); Num. 22:33; 1 Sam. 1:26; 2 Sam. 22:30; 1 Kgs. 18:10, 44; 2 Kgs. 7:2; Jer. 7:27; 29:25; Ezek. 40:4; Pss. 10:8, 14; 139:5; 141:8; 145:10; Prov. 2:11; 24:10. בְּכָה (for בְּךָ) occurs in Exod. 7:29; 2 Sam. 22:30; Ps. 141:8.

סתומה

See ס; cf. פ (פתוחא).

"Seventy." עׄא = "71," עׄב = "72," עׄג = "73," etc.

Example: Josh. 21:1 [Mp to רָאשֵׁי] עׄה בׄ מנה בפסוק "There are 75 occurrences of רָאשֵׁי, two of which are in this verse." [Mm lacking] The 75 occurrences are easily located in Even-Shoshan, p. 1050, #473–547. They include only those forms occurring without prefixes.

עזרא

"The book of Ezra-Nehemiah."

Examples:

a) Gen. 1:28 [Mp to וַיֹּאמֶר לָהֶם] כׄב וכל ד״ה ועזרא דכות בׄ מׄ הׄ חס בליש "This combination occurs 22 times, besides its occurrences throughout Chronicles and Ezra-Nehemiah, where it is written likewise, with 5 exceptions, where it is written defectively as וַיֹּאמֶר עֲלֵהֶם (instead of וַיֹּאמֶר עֲלֵיהֶם)" [Mm 11–12]. The 22 references extend from Gen. 1:28 to Jer. 36:18. The five exceptions are all found in the book of Chronicles: 2 Chr. 10:5, 9, 10; 18:5; 23:14. Ginsburg calls this an "artificial and complicated Massorah." He gives 23 occurrences of וַיֹּאמֶר לָהֶם, and states that this number can be maintained only by reckoning the seven instances found in the account of the exploits of Samson (Judg. 14:12, 14, 18; 15:3, 7, 11, 12) as one (cf. Ginsburg, I:93, #874; IV:106, #874). Along similar lines, Mm 11–12 lists 23 occurrences; however, after Judg. 14:12, the notation "pass" is given indicating that the combination actually occurs several times in this section.

b) Exod. 15:11 [Mp to עֹשֵׂה] חׄ קמׄ קטן וכל דברים מלכים תרי עשר תלים קהלת עזרא ד״ה דכות בׄ מׄ כׄב "This form appears 8 times written with *sere* (*qamets qatan* = *sere*), in addition to its occurrences in Deuteronomy, Kings, the Twelve Prophets, Psalms, Ecclesiates, Ezra-Nehemiah, and Chronicles, where it is written like this form, with 22 exceptions (where it is עֹשֶׂה)" [Mm 475]. This list consists of two parts, the first giving the location of the eight occurrences of עֹשֵׂה (Exod. 15:11; 35:35; Isa. 19:10; 64:4; Jer. 10:12; 51:15; Prov. 12:22; 22:2). The second part consists of the 22 occurences of עֹשֶׂה in the books listed in the Mp. The instances of עֹשֶׂה in these same books are easily located in Even-Shoshan

(p. 921, #1295ff.).

עינ֗

Abbreviation for עִנְיָנָא. Usually occurs with the prefixed preposition ב (בעינ֗). "In this section, context, pericope."

Examples:

a) Amos 1:14 [Mp to וְהִצַּתִּי אֵשׁ] ו֗ ול֗ בעינ֗ "This phrase occurs 6 times (in the Bible), but this is its only occurrence in this context." There is no Mm note giving the six occurrences, but they are given in Ginsburg (I:736, #543; IV:518, #543) as Jer. 21:14; 17:27; 43:12; 50:32; 49:27; Amos 1:14 (in this order). Mm 3051 is attached to the last section of the Mp note (ול֗ בעינ֗) and it pertains only to this context (Amos 1–2). The heading for the note is ל֗ בעיניא ושאר עינינא וְשִׁלַּחְתִּי אֵשׁ "Occurs once in this context, but the rest of the context reads וְשִׁלַּחְתִּי אֵשׁ." This note indicates that וְהִצַּתִּי אֵשׁ occurs only once in the context of Amos 1–2, whereas the alternative phrase וְשִׁלַּחְתִּי אֵשׁ occurs more often. The note is calling attention to two different expressions of a very similar thought. The phrase וְשִׁלַּחְתִּי אֵשׁ occurs six times in Amos 1–2 (1:4, 7, 10, 12; 2:2, 5) as opposed to the one instance of וְהִצַּתִּי אֵשׁ in Amos 1:14. Thus both the Mp note and Mm 3051 serve to protect the minority reading.

b) Gen. 1:6 [Mp to וַיֹּאמֶר אֱלֹהִים] כה֗ ג֗ מנה בטע בעינ֗ "This phrase occurs 25 times (in the Bible), 3 of which have this accent (*zaqef* after *munah*) in this context" [Mm 5]. A list of the 25 occurrences is given. A parallel list can be found in Ginsburg (I:91, #857; IV:105, #857). Elsewhere in the Bible when וַיֹּאמֶר is followed by the divine name, it is יְהוָה [Mm 7]. The three references in the Genesis context which are accented with *zaqef* after *munah* (rather than the other seven instances where *revia'* follows *munah*, Gen. 1:9, 11, 14, 24, 29; 9:12; 17:19) are as follows: Gen. 1:6, 20, 26. This same list is cited by Ginsburg (I:92, #858; IV:105, #858).

עלייה

"Going up, the act of going up."

Example: Exod. 32:4 [Mp to וַיָּצַר] ה֗ וחד מן ג֗ בליש֗ וכל לשון עלייה דכות֗ "One of 5 occurrences of וַיָּצַר, and one of 3 with this meaning, and additionally, all the occurrences with the meaning 'to go up' have the same form" [Mm 1908]. This Mp note is a good illustration for the term עלייה, but it is otherwise a very artificial and convoluted note, created by Weil for *BHS*. The note is really the combination of two notes in L, and the intention of both is to isolate all occurrences of וַיָּצַר. The first note is in Mm 1908: ג֗ וסימנהון: וכל לשון עֲלִיָּה דכותהון (Ex. 32:4; 1 Kgs. 7:15;

2 Kgs. 5:23), "Occurs 3 times with their signs (and excerpts are given for Ex. 32:4; 1 Kgs. 7:15; 2 Kgs. 5:23). And all occurrences with this meaning 'to go up' have the same form." This note (shortened to ג֗ in 1 Kgs. 7:15) relates that the form וַיָּצַר occurs three times. And in addition, whenever the word וַיָּצַר has the meaning "to go up" or something similar, like "move against" or "beseige," the same form is used. Occurrences with the meaning "to go up" are found in 1 Kgs. 20:1; 2 Kgs. 6:24; 17:5; 18:9; Dan. 1:1; 1 Chr. 20:1; and 2 Chr. 28:20. And thus, all 10 occurrences of וַיָּצַר are accounted for. The second note comes from the Mp of 2 Chr. 28:20, which is only ה֗ in L. It is apparently a shortened form of a longer note which perhaps read ה֗ וכל עֲלִיָּה דכות, "The word וַיָּצַר occurs 5 times and all occurrences with a form of the verb עלה or prepositional phrase עָלֶיהָ have the same form." The five occurrences are Exod. 32:4; 1 Kgs. 7:15; 2 Kgs. 5:23; 1 Chr. 20:1; and 2 Chr. 28:20. The remaining occurrences where וַיָּצַר is in close connection with a form of the verb עלה or the prepositional phrase עָלֶיהָ (or both) are 1 Kgs. 20:1; 2 Kgs. 6:24; 17:5 (both); 18:9 (both); and Dan. 1:1. Thus, once again, all ten occurrences of וַיָּצַר are accounted for. The second note is simply another way of annotating the same information described in the first note. It is possible that the second note was originally a misunderstanding of the intention of the first note. In any case, Weil has attempted to combine the two notes for the Mp of *BHS*, and the resulting Mp note is confusing. The form עליה in 1 Chr. 20:1 is a typographical error for עלייה.

עמידה

"Stand, the act of standing." Cf. Hebrew עמד.

Example: Ps. 10:1 [Mp to תַּעֲמֹד בְּרָחוֹק] ל֗ ושאר עמידה מרחוק דכות "This combination is hapax. In the remainder of the occurrences, עמד (to stand) is in combination with מֵרָחוֹק." The other occurrences of some form of עמד in combination with מֵרָחוֹק (or מֵרָחֹק) are Exod. 20:18, 21; 1 Sam. 26:13; 2 Kgs. 2:7; Isa. 59:14; Jer. 51:50; Ps. 38:12. Note that in come cases (e.g., Jer. 51:50), the two words are not adjacent but merely in close proximity.

ענן

"With the meaning of clouds." Written as לשון ענן.

Example: Jer. 10:13 [Mp to נְשִׂאִים] ד֗ חס בנ״ך וכל אורית דכות ב֗ מ֗ ד֗ וחד מן ד֗ מילין לשון ענן "The form נְשִׂאִים occurs 4 times written defectively (with *hireq* under שׂ) in the Prophets and the Writings, and all occurrences in the Pentateuch are like this, with 4 exceptions (נְשִׂיאִם), and this is one of 4 times this word means 'clouds' (instead of 'chief, ruler, head')" [Mm 1367]. The four defective forms

(נְשִׂאִים) in the Prophets and the Writings are given as Josh. 22:14; Jer. 10:13; 51:16; Ps. 135:7. (A similar list occurs in Ginsburg, II:290, #430.) The four exceptions found in the Pentateuch (נְשִׂיאִם instead of נְשִׂאִים) are given as Gen. 17:20; 25:16; Num. 7:10; 27:2. (For a similar list, see Ginsburg, II:290, #429.) Mm 1367 omits any reference to the four instances where this word means "clouds," but BDB, p. 672 (II. נָשִׂיא), gives the following references: Jer. 10:13; 51:16; Ps. 135:7; Prov. 25:14 (these are confirmed by Mp notes accompanying them in *BHS*). There is, of course, some overlapping with the other lists.

עצים

"Trees, wood, timber."

Example: Jer. 3:9 [Mp to הָאֶבֶן] ה֗ דקדמין לעצים "One of 5 cases where stones are mentioned before trees (wood)" [Mm 4157]. The five references are Lev. 14:45; Jer. 3:9; Ezek. 26:12; 1 Chr. 22:15; 2 Chr. 2:13. (See Ginsburg, I:22, #81.) The normal order in which these words occur is for עֵץ to come before אֶבֶן (cf. Deut. 28:36, 64; 29:16; 2 Kgs. 19:18; Isa. 37:19; etc.) The Mp note protects the minority reading.

עשייה

"The verb 'to do, make,' the act of doing or making (cf. עָשָׂה)."

Example: 1 Sam. 22:14 [Mp to כְּדָוִד] ג֗ מיחד וכל עשייה דכות "The form כְּדָוִד is one of 3 unusual occurrences, and wherever it is preceded by a form of the verb 'to do,' it is also written like this" [Mm 1654]. The three unusual occurrences are given as 1 Sam. 22:14; Amos 6:5; Zech. 12:8. The same list occurs in Ginsburg (I:228, #130), with a further commentary on this list in IV:228, #130. Ginsburg states that what makes כְּדָוִד unusual is to find it prefixed with כְּ, since in 16 instances it is prefixed with בְּ. He also gives the six references where כְּדָוִד is preceded by some form of עשה (1 Kgs. 11:6, 33; 15:11; 2 Kgs. 14:3 16:2; 2 Chr. 28:1). This Mp note is designated to safeguard the minority reading.

עשר

See תרי עשר.

"Eighty." פא = "81," פב = "82," פג = "83," etc.

Example: 1 Sam. 7:12 [Mp to וַיָּשֶׂם] פד "This form (with ו consecutive) occurs 84 times (in the Bible)." [Mm lacking] The 84 references are given in E-S, p. 1137, #348–431.

"Open." Abbreviation for פתוחא (cf. סתומא). This refers to the short paragraphs (פרשיות) into which the entire Bible (except Psalms) was divided. Such paragraphs could be either "open" (פתוחא) or "closed" (סתומא). An open paragraph (indicated by פ placed between two verses) had to commence at the beginning of a new line, with the preceding line left partly or wholly blank. The first paragraph in a book is assumed to be open without a written פ, since it begins on the first line of the manuscript. These rules applied to handwritten texts but are no longer valid for printed Bibles, since their line and paragraph divisions are of necessity different from those of ancient manuscripts. However, the original format of L is indicated in *BHS* by the printing of either ס or פ in the space before the beginning of a new paragraph.

פזר

"The accent *pazer.*"

Example: Ps. 104:35 [Mp to הָאָרֶץ] ז בטע פזר "This is one of 7 occurrences of this word with the accent *pazer.*" [Mm lacking]

פינחס

(Preceded by the title רבי, "Rabbi.") "Rabbi Phinehas." Some Masoretes are referred to by name in the Mp notes of L. For example, Ben Asher is mentioned in Dan. 7:10; Ben-Naphtali in Isa. 44:21; and Rabbi Phinehas in Ps. 144:13 and Job 32:3. The latter Masorete is further identified in Mm 3539 as ראש הישיבה, Rosh ha-Yeshivah (cf. Dotan, p. 1423, #3.2.6.2; Ginsburg, I:658, #24).

Example: Job 32:3 [Mp to וּבִשְׁלֹשֶׁת רֵעָיו] כן בטע לרבי פינחס "This phrase is accented thus (*munah* before *zarqa*), according to Rabbi Phinehas" [Mm 3539]. Ps.

114:13 is also cited as another occurrence of *munah* before *zarqa*, also supported by Rabbi Phinehas. However, an ancient manuscript called רובה מחזורה, the "Great Machsor," changes the accentuation in each of these passages to *'azla* before *zarqa*. Mm 3539 mentions yet a third way Job 32:3 is accented, attributed to בעלי טבריה, "the Tiberians," and involving *merekha* before *zarqa*. (Cf. Mm 4010; Ginsburg, *Introduction to the Massoretico-Critical Edition of the Hebrew Bible*, pp. 435f.)

Abbreviation for פלוגתא. "Division of opinion, difference of opinion." This may point to differences of opinion between the various Masoretic traditions.

Examples:

a) Ezra 4:8 [Mp to אִגְּרָה] כת כן ופלג "This form is written correctly, (although) there is a differing opinion." [Mm lacking] The question seems to be whether this word, which is written in Aramaic, should end in ה or א (cf. Ezra 4:11; 5:6).

b) 2 Sam. 7:22 [Mp to בְּכֹל] כת כן ופליג "The form בְּכֹל is written with prefixed בְּ, but there is a difference of opinion" [Mm 4089]. The question here is whether the text should be read בְּכֹל, "in all," or כְּכֹל, "according to all."

c) 2 Sam. 12:25 [Mp to יְדִידְיָה] ל׳ ופלג "This word is found only here, but its authenticity is contested." [Mm lacking] (The word יְדִידְיָה is a name.) The difference of opinion regarding this name is doubtlessly related to David's having named his son Solomon (2 Sam. 12:24), only to have Nathan call him by a totally different and otherwise unknown name.

פלוני

"Someone, so-and-so, a certain person."

Example: Gen. 17:17 [Mp to וַיֹּאמֶר בְּלִבּוֹ] אמירה פלוני בלבו ו׳ "One of 6 occasions in the Bible when a certain person says in his heart." [Mm lacking] Even-Shoshan (p. 586, #495–6, 501, 506–7, 512) indicates the references as Gen. 17:17; 27:41; 1 Kgs. 12:26; Pss. 14:1; 53:2; Est. 6:6. This can be verified by the Mp note which accompanies each of these passages in *BHS*.

"Verse." Abbreviation for the plural form פסוקין. The forms פסוקא and הפסוקים are also found. In *BHS*, this term is usually abbreviated and combined with other abbreviations: מ״פ (within a verse), ס״פ (end of a verse), and ר״פ (beginning of a verse). See examples "b," "c," and "d" as well as the entries for מ״פ, ס״פ, and ר״פ.

Examples:

a) Gen. 22:7 [Mp to וַיֹּאמֶר] ב̇ פסוק דאית בהון ד̇ ויאמר "One of 2 verses in which there are 4 occurrences of ויאמר" [Mm 2019]. The second reference is 1 Kgs. 20:14.

b) Ezek. 5:11 [Mp to וְגַם־אֲנִי] ה̇ מ״פ "This phrase occurs 5 times within verses." (Each of the five times it has the prefixed וְ; the phrase occurs many times within verses as גַּם־אֲנִי.) [Mm 2449] The five references, which are given in the second part of this note are Ezek. 5:11 (2x); 16:43; Hos. 3:3; 2 Chr. 34:27.

c) Ezek. 11:10 [Mp to וִידַעְתֶּם כִּי־אֲנִי יְהוָה] י̇א̇ ס״פ בסיפ̇ "This phrase occurs 11 times at the end of the verse in the book of Ezekiel." [Mm lacking] A concordance enables one to find the 11 occurrences (in exactly this form) in Ezek. 6:7; 7:4; 11:10; 12:20; 13:14; 14:8; 20:38; 25:5; 35:9; 36:11; 37:6.

d) Ezek. 11:9 [Mp to וְהוֹצֵאתִי] ג̇ ר״פ "One of 3 occurrences of this word at the beginning of a verse." [Mm lacking] The three occurrences are found in Isa. 65:9; Ezek. 11:9; 20:34.

Abbreviation for פסיקתא, also written מפסיקין. "*Paseq*," is a vertical stroke (|) placed after a word that has a conjunctive accent. It indicates that there should be a light pause in the reading, but not pronounced enough to require a disjunctive accent. When a word has a *munah* on the stress syllable and is followed by a *paseq*, the combination is known as *legarmeh*, or *munah legarmeh* (cf. also *mehuppak legarmeh* and *'azla legarmeh*). In the majority of cases *munah legarmeh* is followed by the major disjunctive *revia'* (cf. Yeivin, pp. 213–18, #277–85).

Examples:

a) Neh. 8:17 [Mp to מִן־הַשְּׁבִי | סֻכּוֹת] פסיקתא דסיפ̇ "One of the *paseq*s of the book (of Ezra-Nehemiah)" [Mm 3904]. The occurrences are found in Ezra 6:9(2x); 7:17; 10:9; Neh. 2:12, 13 (*Qere*); 8:6, 7(2x), 9, 17, 18; 11:33; 13:15.

b) Lev. 14:6 [Mp to וְאֵת | הַצִּפֹּר] ג̇ ול̇ פסיק̇ "This phrase (with *vav* conjunction on את) occurs 3 times, only one of which is marked with a *paseq*" [Mm 740]. The references are Gen. 15:10; Lev. 14:6, 51. There are five occurrences of הַצִּפֹּר אֶת־, i.e., without *vav* conjunction on את (Lev. 14:5, 6, 7, 50, 53). The Mp note safeguards the minority reading.

Abbreviation for פרשות. See ס̇. The name given to the 54 sections into which the Pentateuch was divided in order to be read in a single year. The beginning of each of these sections (except at the beginning of each book) is indicated in *BHS* by פרש

printed in the center margin of the page (cf. Gen. 6:9; 12:1; 18:1; 23:1; etc.).

1) "The accent *pashta*." 2) Indication that a *patah* is to be pronounced in the tone syllable (but be advised that the term פתח, *patah*, in the Mp can actually indicate *patah qatan*, i.e., *seghol*. Cf. פתח). Plural: פשטין.

Example: Ps. 22:1 [Mp to הַשַּׁחַר] ט פשטין פת ס״פ בסיפ "There are 9 words in the book of Psalms where *patah* (or *seghol*) is to be pronounced in its tone syllable (and followed by) the *sof pasuq*." [Mm lacking] Apparently the original purpose of this Masoretic note was to indicate where the pausal accent *'atnah* is missing and its function has been take over by *revia'*. However, the words so accented still have short vowels in their tone syllables (*patah* or *segol*) instead of the customary long vowel (e.g., *qamets*). There are several different types of *revia'*s used in the three poetical books, and this usage is called "*revia' mugrash* without *geresh*" (cf. Yeivin, p. 270, #367). It is marked by the *revia'* symbol alone without the *geresh* stroke marked above the beginning of the word (i.e., prepositive position). Since *'atnah* is missing in these instances, they are designated in the Mp as ס״פ, that is, to be followed by *sof pasuq* (as opposed to *revia' gadol* or *revia' qatan* both of which also lack the *geresh* stroke but are followed by *'atnah* or *'oleh we-yored*, cf. Yeivin, p. 267, #362). *BHS* marks the nine references with Mp notes in the margin (Pss. 22:1; 31:23; 40:3; 47:10; 55:22; 56:14; 119:14, 59; 137:9). In L, only Pss. 40:3; 47:10; and 55:22 are marked. Of these nine instances, all have *patah* except two with *seghol* (47:10 and 55:22) and one with a *plene holem* (56:14, and see below). This list of occurrences has several complications. Notice that Weil has marked all but three (56:14; 119:59; and 137:9) of the occurrences with a note in the apparatus that has some form of "Textus contra Mp, cf. Mp sub loco." Thus, he apparently had reservations about most of the occurrences and intended to discuss them in his subsequent volume which was never published. However, the three occurrences which are not marked in the apparatus appear to be the problematic occurrences. In 56:14, Weil has the Mp note keyed to the word בְּא֫וֹר which is problematic for several reasons. First, the accent is *revia' mugrash*: it has the *geresh* stroke and occurs after *'atnah* as the last disjunctive accent before *silluq* (Yeivin, p. 269, #366). Second, the word בְּא֫וֹר has no *patah* or *seghol*. Thus, in a similar but slightly different list, Ginsburg (I:653, #233; IV:448, #233) keyed the note to רַגְלַ֔י. But this is equally unacceptable since the *revia'* for רַגְלַ֔י is *revia' qatan*. Another solution would be to interpret the text to which this note was originally attached as having read בְּאֶרֶץ ("in the land of the living" not "in the light of life," cf. Pss. 27:13; 52:7; 116:9; 142:6). However, the *'atnah* on the previous word is still problematic. In Ps. 119:59, a similar situation occurs; the accent for רַגְלַ֔י is *revia' mugrash*. Ginsburg solved this problem by matching the note with אֲמָ֫רְתִּ֥י in 119:57, which seems a more likely candidate. In Ps. 137:9, the only problem is the presence of the *geresh* stroke where we would not expect one on the word עֹלָלַ֗יִךְ. However, this seems to be a scribal error (which Yeivin, p. 270, indicates can happen, even intentionally). Further support for "*revia' mugrash* without *geresh*" is in the previous use of *shalshelet* as a conjunctive in the same sequence (Yeivin, pp. 272–73, #371). Thus, in summary, this note illustrates both the use of the term פשטין and the complexities involved in understanding the intention behind Mp notes. Certainly, it is regrettable that Weil never published his supplementary volume, because his discussion would have been helpful in difficult cases such as this.

"Open." See פ.

1) "*Patah*" 2) "*seghol*" (also called "*patah qatan*"). Abbreviation for פתח.
Examples:

a) Num. 32:32 [Mp to נַחְנוּ] ג̇ ב̇ פת̇ וחד קמ̇ "Occurs 3 times, twice with *patah* and once with qamets" [Mm 1024]. The reference with *qamets* is Gen. 42:11. The references with *patah* are Num. 32:32 and Lam. 3:42.
b) Job 21:18 [Mp to כְּתֶבֶן] ל̇ וכל ליש̇ דכות̇ פת̇ קטן "This is the only occurrence of this form (with prefixed preposition כְּ), but all occurrences of the word are written like this, i.e., with *seghol* (*patah qatan*)."
   Reference source: E-S, p. 1219, #1–7 (תֶּבֶן).

"The letter צ."

Example: 2 Chron. 29:28 [Mp to מַחְצְצְרִים] צ יתיר מן חד (*Qere*) מחצרים "The *Qere* is מַחְצְרִים. One of ? occurrences of superfluous צ." This note is calling attention to words spelled with an extra, unnecessary *tsade*. Apparently, the editors of *BHS* accidentally left out the number of cases of superfluous *tsade*, because the note as it is written does not make sense without the specified number. In L, the note is simply יתיר צ, calling attention to the spelling without numbering the occurrences. The entries in the Masoretic apparatus at the bottom of the page in *BHS* specify other occurrences as 1 Chr. 15:24; 2 Chr. 5:13; 7:6; 13:14.

"90." צׄא = "91," צׄב = "92," צׄג = "93," etc.

Example: Josh. 7:20 [Mp to וַיֹּאמַר] צׄא "Occurs 91 times" (instead of the more common וַיֹּאמֶר). [Mm lacking] The 91 occurrences are listed in Ginsburg, I:90, #842; IV:102f., #842. This list does not include instances in Job where וַיֹּאמַר is preceded either by וַיַּעַן (29x) or by וַיֹּסֶף (3x). When these are added to the 91 mentioned above, the total reaches 123 (cf. E-S, p. 89, #4435–4558). In comparison, וַיֹּאמֶר occurs 1951 times. The Mp note safeguards the minority reading. (Cf. Mynatt, pp. 52–53, #38.)

"The letter צ."

Example: Deut. 32:4 [Mp to הַצּוּר] צדה רבתי בעל "The form הַצּוּר occurs with a large *tsade* (above it?)." [Mm lacking] Two problems arise. First, the text of L has no large *tsade* in this verse. The note, therefore, must have originated in another text tradition. Second, בעל is an enigmatic form. Does it mean "above"? Or is it perhaps related to the information given in Mm 1835, to the effect that the preposition accompanying צוּר or הַצּוּר is עַל, with the exception of three occurrences with אֶל? (Cf. Mynatt, p. 213, #288; E-S, pp. 982f., #8, 18, 19, 23, 24, 38, [1]צוּר.)

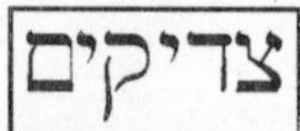

"The righteous."

Example: Ezra 7:6 [Mp הוּא] ה̇ צדיקים בחד ליש "There are 5 occurrences in association with the righteous with the same meaning" [Mm 3908]. This note lists passages where הוּא is used emphatically with reference to (famous) righteous people (Exod. 6:26, 27; Ezra 7:6; 1 Chr. 1:27; 2 Chr. 32:30). Ginsburg discusses this note and also lists five occurrences where הוּא is used emphatically with reference to (infamous) wicked people (Gen. 10:9; 36:43; Num. 26:9; Est. 1:1; 2 Chr. 28:22). Reference source: Ginsburg 1:303, #86; IV:291, #86.

"Form, plan, design." The construct form of צורה (cf. BDB, p. 849, צוּר IV). Used in the combination בצורת הבית. The phrase צורת הבית, "the design of the house (i.e., temple)," refers to the description of the restored temple of God in Ezekiel 40–48 (cf. Ezek. 43:11 for the origin of the term צוּרַת הַבַּיִת).

Examples:

a) Ezek. 40:7 [Mp to אוּלָם] ה מל בצורת הבית "One of 5 occurrences of אוּלָם written *plene* (in contrast to אֻלָם) in 'the design of the house' (i.e., Ezek. 40–48)" [Mm 2957]. The five occurrences of אוּלָם in Ezek. 40–48 are given here as Ezek. 40:7; 41:25, 26; 46:2, 8. A similar list appears in Ginsburg, I:31, #192; IV:35, #192. However, Ginsburg's list omits 41:25 and substitutes in its place 44:3. Obviously, two different textual traditions are reflected here. Examples of אֻלָם in this section of Ezekiel are found in 40:8, 9 (2x), 15, 39, 40, 48 (2x), 49.

b) Ezek. 40:15 [Mp to וְעַל פְּנֵי] ד בצורת הבית "The phrase וְעַל פְּנֵי (written either with or without *vav* conjunction or *maqqef*) occurs 4 times in 'the plan of the house' (Ezek. 40–48)" [Mm 2958]. The Mp note is reversed in this Mm heading: כל צורת הבית דיחזקאל אֶל־פְּנֵי בר מן ד עַל־פְּנֵי "The form אֶל־פְּנֵי appears throughout 'the plan of the house' (Ezek. 40–48), with the exception of the four references, where it appears as עַל־פְּנֵי." The four exceptions are Ezek. 40:15; 42:8; 48:15, 21. Occurrences of אֶל־פְּנֵי can be located by scanning the text of *BHS* (e.g., 41:4, 12, 15, 25; 42:2, 3, 7, 10 [2x], 13; etc.). [Mm 3937] This entry repeats the four references to עַל־פְּנֵי in Ezekiel 40–48. It also lists the nine references to אֶל־פְּנֵי, found outside the book of Ezekiel.

צפק

A mnemonic sequence giving the correct order of the abbreviated words. Cf. סימן for a discussion of this type of note.

Example: Deut. 8:11 [Mp to מִצְוֹתָיו וּמִשְׁפָּטָיו וְחֻקֹּתָיו] ו פסוק מן ג מילין מתחלף צפק סימן "One of 6 verses with some form of these 3 words, varying in order, and צ (מצותיו 'his commandments'), פ (ומשפטיו 'his ordinances'), ק (וחקתיו 'his statutes') is the sign for the correct order of words." [Mm lacking] The six verses (located with the help of Even-Shoshan, p. 699, #153, 163, 165, 166, 176, 177, and verified by the Mp notes in *BHS*) are 1) Deut. 8:11 (צפק); 2) Deut. 11:1 (קפצ); 3) Deut. 26:17 (קצפ); 4) Deut. 30:16 (צקפ); 5) 1 Kgs. 2:3 (קצפ); 6) 1 Kgs. 8:58 (צקפ).

A mnemonic sequence giving the correct order of the abbreviated words. Cf. סימן for a discussion of this type of note.

Example: Deut. 30:16 [Mp to מִצְוֹתָיו וְחֻקֹּתָיו וּמִשְׁפָּטָיו] ו̇ פסוק מן ג̇ מילין מתחלפ̇ צ̇קפ̇ סימן "One of 6 verses with some form of these 3 words, varying in order, and צ̇ (מצותיו 'his commandments'), ק̇ (וחקתיו 'his statutes'), פ̇ (ומשפטיו 'his ordinances') is the sign for the correct order of words." [Mm lacking] The six verses (located with the help of Even-Shoshan, p. 699, #153, 163, 165, 166, 176, 177, and verified by the Mp notes in *BHS)* are 1) Deut. 8:11 (צ̇פ̇ק̇); 2) Deut. 11:1 (ק̇פ̇צ̇), 3) Deut. 26:17 (ק̇צ̇פ̇); 4) Deut. 30:16 (צ̇ק̇פ̇); 5) 1 Kgs. 2:3 (ק̇צ̇פ̇); 6) 1 Kgs. 8:58 (צ̇ק̇פ̇).

"One hundred."

Examples:

a) Gen. 18:3 [Mp to אֲדֹנָי] ק̇ל̇ד̇ "The form אֲדֹנָי occurs 134 times (in the Bible)." [Mm lacking] (This Mp note only counts occurrences of אֲדֹנָי standing alone.) A complete list is found in Ginsburg, I:25f., #115; IV:28f, #115. In addition to the 134 times that אֲדֹנָי stands alone, there are 304 instances where it is followed by יְהוִה. These counts include אֲדֹנָי in all its forms, including those with prefixes. Reference source: For a discussion of the reason for Weil's "Mp sub loco" note, see Mynatt, p. 55, #41.

b) Deut. 31:29 [Mp to בְּעֵינֵי] ק̇ל̇ט̇ ל̇ג̇ מנה בתור "The form בְּעֵינֵי occurs 139 times (in the Bible), 33 of these are in the Pentateuch." [Mm lacking] These can be located in Even-Shoshan, p. 854, #185–323. The 139 occurrences are of this form without additional suffixes or prefixes. The 33 references in the Pentateuch are listed in Mynatt, p. 85, #84. He also discusses the "Mp sub loco" notes on this entry on p. 212, #287. An alternative list of 32 occurrences in the Pentateuch is given by Ginsburg, II:385, #294 (although references from other books of the Bible are included to make up the total).

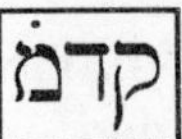

"First, former, preceding." Plural: קדמין.

Examples:

a) Lev. 14:45 [Mp to אֲבָנָיו] ה דקדמין לעצים "This is one of 5 occurrences of a reference to stone(s) preceding a reference to tree(s) (i.e., wood)" [Mm 4157]. The five references are given as Lev. 14:45; Jer. 3:9; Ezek. 26:12; 1 Chr. 22:15; 2 Chr. 2:13. Ginsburg, I:22, #81, provides a list of only four references, from which Jer. 3:9 is missing. The reason for noting the occurrences of אֶבֶן before עֵץ is that in the majority of the cases references to עֵץ come first (cf. Deut. 28:36, 64; 29:16; 2 Sam. 5:11; 2 Kgs. 19:18; Isa. 37:19; etc.).

b) Dan. 2:35 [Mp to כַּסְפָּא וְדַהֲבָא] ד כספא דקדים "In 4 instances כַּסְפָּא ('silver') precedes the reference to דַּהֲבָא ('gold')" [Mm 3800]. The four references are Dan. 2:35, 45; 5:23; Ezra 7:18. This note refers only to Aramaic portions of the Bible (cf. Ginsburg, II:50, #402). For references to דַּהֲבָא listed before כַּסְפָּא in these same Aramaic sections, see Dan. 5:2; Ezra 5:14; 6:5.

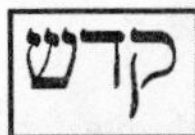

"Sacred, holy, the sacred language (Hebrew)." Often preceded by לשון, as in לשון קדש.

Example: Ps. 61:8 [Mp to מַן] ל לשון קדש "The form מַן occurs only once in Hebrew." [Mm lacking] מַן, the Pi'el imperative 2ms from מָנָה, occurs only here in the Hebrew portions of the Bible. However, the same form, meaning "who?" or "what?" (cf. מִי, מָה), occurs several times in the Aramaic passages in the Bible (cf. Ezra 5:3, 4, 9; Dan. 3:6, 11, 15; etc.).

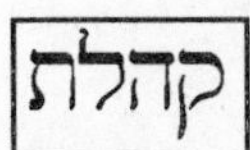

"The book of Ecclesiastes."

Examples:

a) Gen. 6:11 [Mp to לִפְנֵי הָאֱלֹהִים] ו וכל קהלת דכות "This phrase occurs 6 times, in addition to its occurrences in the book of Ecclesiastes" [Mm 4077א]. The six occurrences outside Ecclesiastes are Gen. 6:11; Exod. 18:12; Josh. 24:1; Judg. 21:2; 1 Chr. 13:8; 16:1. Occurrences in Ecclesiastes include 2:26; 5:1; 7:26. There are four occurrences of לִפְנֵי אֱלֹהִים, Pss. 56:13; 61:7; 68:3; 1 Chr. 13:10.

b) Isa. 54:15 [Mp to יִפּוֹל] ו מל וכל משלי וקהלת דכות ב מ ג "Occurs 6 times written *plene* (with *holem-vav*), in addition to occurrences in Proverbs and Ecclesiastes, all of which are written like this, with 3 exceptions (יִפֹּל)." [Mm lacking] Ginsburg, II:283, #292, supplies the references to יִפּוֹל, which are Isa. 10:34; 13:15; 54:15; Ezek. 6:12; Amos 9:9; 1 Chr. 12:20. The three defective forms in Proverbs are 11:5, 14; 13:17. *Plene* forms in Proverbs and Ecclesiastes include Prov. 17:20; 24:16; 28:10, 14, 18; Eccl. 10:8; 11:3.

See שמיעה.

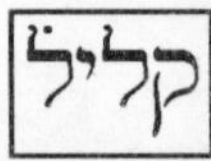

"To be light (of weight), slight, trifling." Cf. Hebrew קלל.

Example: Jer. 3:9 [Mp to מִקֹּל] ל̇ וחס בקליל "This form is unique and defective with (the meaning) to be triflin" [Mm lacking] The word מִקֹּל is a hapax spelled defectively, although there are other *plene* occurrences (e.g., Jer. 4:9). The Mp note specifies the correct meaning for מִקֹּל, since it might otherwise be confused with קוֹל, "voice."

"*qamets*." Plural: קמצין. Also appears in the phrase קמ̇ קטן "*qamets qatan*," i.e., *sere* (cf. פת̇ קטן).

Examples:

a) Ps. 44:4 [Mp to אָ֫רֶץ] יד̇ קמ̇ וכל אתנח וס״פ דכות ב̇ מ̇ ד̇ "There are 14 occurrences of *qamets* in the tone syllable of אָ֫רֶץ, in addition to its occurrences with *'atnah* or *sof pasuq* (*silluq*), which also have *qamets* in the tone syllable, except in four instances (אֶ֫רֶץ)" [Mm 1234]. The 14 occurrences of אָ֫רֶץ (when not accented with *'atnah* or *silluq*) are found in Deut. 32:13; Isa. 14:9, 21; 33:9; 44:23; 49:13; 51:13, 16; 52:10; Jer. 9:18; 16:19; 31:8; Zech. 12:1; Ps. 44:4. The four occurrences with אֶ֫רֶץ, when accented with *'atnah* or *silluq* (instead of the expected אָ֫רֶץ), are found in Pss. 35:20; 48:11; Prov. 30:14, 21. A list roughly parallel to this is given in Ginsburg, I:107, #1097, with additional commentary in IV:129, #1097.

b) Exod. 15:11 [Mp to עֹשֵׂה] ח̇ קמ̇ קטן וכל דברים מלכים תרי עשר תלים קהלת עזרא ד״ה דכות ב̇ מ̇ כב̇ "The form עֹשֵׂה occurs 8 times with *qamets qatan* (*sere*) in the final syllable, in addition to its occurrences in Deut., Kings, the Twelve Prophets, Psalms, Ecclesiastes, Ezra, and Chronicles, where it is also written like this, except in 22 instances (עֹשֶׂה)" [Mm 475]. The first part of this note consists of the eight occurrences of עֹשֵׂה (outside the books listed above). They are found in Exod. 15:11; 35:35; Isa. 19:10; 64:4; Jer. 10:12; 51:15; Prov.

12:22; 22:2. (For an alternate list, reflecting a different Masoretic tradition, see Ginsburg, II:423ff., #860.) The second part of Mm 475 lists the 22 occurrences of עָשָׂה found in the books named above. They are Deut. 5:10; 10:18; 31:21; 2 Kgs. 7:2, 19; Amos 9:12; Nah. 1:9; Zeph. 3:19; Zech. 10:1; Mal. 3:17, 21; Pss. 18:51; 37:7; 104:4; 106:21; 146:6, 7; Eccl. 8:12; Neh. 2:16; 4:11; 6:3; 1 Chr. 18:14. (For a slightly different list, see Ginsburg, II:423, #854.) The many references to עָשָׂה in the group of books listed above could be found in a concordance (cf. E-S, p. 921, #1372–1412).

קׄפׄצׄ

A mnemonic sequence giving the correct order of the abbreviated words. Cf. סִימָן for a discussion of this type of note.

Example: Deut. 11:1 [Mp to וְחֻקֹּתָיו וּמִשְׁפָּטָיו וּמִצְוֹתָיו] ו פסוק מן ג מילין מתחלפ קׄפׄצׄ סימן "One of 6 verses with some form of these 3 words, varying in order, and ק (וחקתיו 'his statutes'), פ (ומשפטיו 'his ordinances'), צ (מצותיו 'his commandments') is the sign for the correct order of words." [Mm lacking] The six verses (located with the help of Even-Shoshan, p. 699, #153, 163, 165, 166, 176, 177, and verified by the Mp notes in *BHS)* are 1) Deut. 8:11 (צׄפׄקׄ); 2) Deut. 11:1 (קׄפׄצׄ); 3) Deut. 26:17 (קׄצׄפׄ); 4) Deut. 30:16 (צׄקׄפׄ); 5) 1 Kgs. 2:3 (קׄצׄפׄ); 6) 1 Kgs. 8:58 (צׄקׄפׄ).

קׄצׄפׄ

A mnemonic sequence giving the correct order of the abbreviated words. Cf. סִימָן for a discussion of this type of note.

Example: Deut. 26:17 [Mp to וְחֻקָּיו וּמִצְוֹתָיו וּמִשְׁפָּטָיו] ו פסוק מן ג מילין מתחלפ קׄצׄפׄ סימן "One of 6 verses with some form of these 3 words, varying in order, and ק (וחקתיו 'his statutes'), צ (מצותיו 'his commandments'), פ (ומשפטיו 'his ordinances') is the sign for the correct order of words." [Mm lacking] The six verses (located with the help of Even-Shoshan, p. 699, #153, 163, 165, 166, 176, 177, and verified by the Mp notes in *BHS)* are 1) Deut. 8:11 (צׄפׄקׄ); 2) Deut. 11:1 (קׄפׄצׄ); 3) Deut. 26:17 (קׄצׄפׄ); 4) Deut. 30:16 (צׄקׄפׄ); 5) 1 Kgs. 2:3 (קׄצׄפׄ); 6) 1 Kgs. 8:58 (צׄקׄפׄ).

"Read, or to be read." Alternate form: ק̇, used in *Ketiv/Qere* combinations.

Examples:

a) Isa. 44:24 [Mp to מֵי אִתִּי] חד מן ח̇ כת̇ ב̇ מילין וקר̇ חדה (*Qere*) מאתי "The phrase מִי אִתִּי should be read as מֵאִתִּי. This is one of 8 instances where that which is written as two words should be read as one" [Mm 214]. The second part of this note lists the eight passages with their divided words as Judg. 16:25; 1 Sam. 9:1; 24:9; Isa. 9:6; 44:24; Lam. 1:6; 4:3; 2 Chr. 34:6.

b) Judg. 20:13 [Mp to ...] בני חד מן י̇ קר̇ ולא כת̇ "The word בני should be placed with the vowels in the text (resulting in בְּנֵי). This is one of 10 instances where a word is to be read although it is not written." [Mm 2745] The ten references with the missing words are Judg. 20:13; 2 Sam. 8:3; 16:23; 18:20; 2 Kgs. 19:31, 37; Jer. 31:38; 50:29; Ruth 3:5, 17. See Chapter 3 for a discussion of this phenomenon.

c) 2 Sam. 13:33 [Mp to אִם] אם חד מן ח̇ כת̇ ולא קר̇ "The word אִם is one of 8 words which are written (in the text) but should not be read" [Mm 2752]. The eight references with the superfluous words are 2 Sam. 13:33; 15:21; 2 Kgs. 5:18; Jer. 38:16; 39:12; 51:3; Ezek. 48:16; Ruth 3:12. See Chapter 3 for a discussion of this phenomenon. *BHS* points this word in error; cf. *BHK* where they are absent.

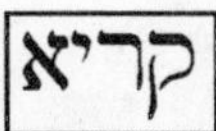

"The entire Bible."

Examples:

a) Num. 3:39 [Mp to פְּקוּדֵי] כל קריא מל ב̇ מ̇ א̇ "Always written *plene* (with *shureq*) throughout the Bible, with one exception" (פְּקֻדֵי 2 Kgs. 11:15).

b) Ps. 89:51 [Mp to רַבִּים עַמִּים] ל̇ וכל קריא חלוף עמים רבים "These words occur only here (in this order), and elsewhere throughout the Bible their order is reversed to read עמים רבים." [Mm lacking] Examples of these words in their customary order can be seen in E-S, p. 888, #1661, 1668, 1677, 1679–88, 1695.

See מיתא.

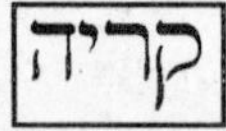

"Name of a city or a place." Usually preceded by שם.

Examples:

a) 1 Sam. 2:29 [Mp to מָעוֹן] ד̇ וכל שם קריה ואנש דכות "The form מָעוֹן occurs 4 times (in the Bible), in addition to its occurrences as the name of a place or of a person (or people)." [Mm lacking] Ginsburg, II:238, #607, lists the first four references as 1 Sam. 2:29, 32; Ps. 71:3; 90:1. That these are the intended references can be verified by the Mp note placed beside each in *BHS*. מָעוֹן is

used as a place name in Josh. 15:55; 1 Sam. 23:24, 25 (2x); 25:2. As a personal (or gentilic) name, it occurs in 1 Chr. 2:45 (2x); Judg. 10:12.
Reference source: E-S, pp. 686f.

b) Josh. 15:42 [Mp to וְעָשָׁן] ה̇ שם קריה "The word עָשָׁן occurs 5 times as the name of a city" [Mm 1346]. The five references are given as Josh. 15:42; 19:7; 1 Chr. 4:32; 6:44; 1 Sam. 30:30 (the latter as בּוֹר־עָשָׁן). The purpose of the Mp note placed beside these references is to distinguish the occurrences of עָשָׁן as the name of a city and its more frequent use as a simple noun meaning "smoke" (cf. Judg. 20:40; Isa. 6:4; Ps. 18:9; etc.).

"Bald," or "bare," i.e., without a prefixed *vav*.

Example: 1 Chr. 23:29 [Mp to לְמִנְחָה] קרחא בפסוק "This form is written without prefixed *vav* in this verse" [Mp sub loco]. לְמִנְחָה stands in a series of words prefixed with the preposition לְ, but all the others also have a prefixed *vav*. לְמִנְחָה alone stands without *vav*.

ר

"The letter ר."

Example: Gen. 10:3 [Mp to וְרִיפַת] ל̇ כת ר "This name (Riphath) occurs only once written with *resh*." [Mm lacking] However, the same person is referred to as דִּיפַת (Diphath) in 1 Chr. 1:6. The note in Gen. 10:3 has been marked "Mp sub loco" because L originally had only ל̇ as its Mp note. Weil has expanded this note to read ל̇ כת ר to make it match the Mp note to 1 Chr. 1:6 (cf. Mynatt, p. 44 , #25).

"Beginning, start, head." Cf. ר״פ.

Example: Deut. 18:16 [Mp to מֵעִם יְהוָה] ט̇ ומן ראש דמלכים עד וירא כל ישראל דכות̇ "This combination occurs nine times in addition to the occurrences from the beginning of the book of Kings until וַיַּרְא כָּל־יִשְׂרָאֵל, which are like them" [Mm 3417]. The Hebrew phrase cited by this note is the first three words from 1 Kgs. 12:16. Citing an excerpt is the usual method in the Masorah of noting a verse reference. This Mp note is accounting for all of the occurrences of the combination מֵעִם יְהוָה. The note says that מֵעִם יְהוָה occurs nine times (Deut. 18:16; 29:17; 1 Sam. 3:28; Isa. 7:11; 8:18; 28:29; 29:6; Ps. 121:2; Ruth 2:12) plus the instances which occur between the beginning of the book of Kings and 1 Kgs. 12:16 (where there are three occurrences, 2:33; 11:9; and 12:15). Thus, all of the occurences of the combination מֵעִם יְהוָה are accounted for.

רביׄע

"Fourth." Abbreviation for רְבִיעָאָה.

Example: Job 36:23 [Mp to מִי] ג ר״פ מי וג מילין רביׄע ומי וכל פסוקׄ דאית בהון ח מילין "There are 3 instances where the word מִי occurs at the beginning of a verse with 3 words (following) and the fourth word is וּמִי. And all of these verses contain 8 words" [Mm 3552]. This note is calling attention to three unusual verses. They all have מִי at the beginning of the verse and three more words follow before the fourth word which is וּמִי. In each of the verses, there is a total of eight words (Job 34:13; 36:23; Ps. 24:3). The word מִי never appears elsewhere at the beginning of a verse, but there are several other instances where the sequence מִי plus three words plus וּמִי occurs in the middle of a verse (2 Sam. 7:18; 20:11; 1 Chr. 17:16; etc.).

רבי פינחס

See פינחס.

רבים

"Plural." Sometimes in the combination לשון רבים.

Example: Num. 13:22 [Mp to וַיָּבֹא] ח סביׄר לשון רבים "One of 8 cases where it is wrongly supposed that a plural form should be used (instead of the singular וַיָּבֹא)." [Mm lacking] However, Ginsburg (I:170, #119a; IV:185, #119a) lists 12 cases where וַיָּבֹאוּ might wrongly be suggested as a correction for וַיָּבֹא (since its subject is plural). The last four references in Ginsburg are problematic, and only the first eight match the Mp notes in *BHS*. They are Num. 13:22; 2 Sam. 3:22; Isa. 45:24; Ezek. 14:1; 20:38; 23:44; 36:20; Jer. 51:48.

רבתי

"Large, larger than normal."

Example: Num. 27:5 [Mp to [מִשְׁפָּטָן] ל נון רבתי "This is the only occurrence of a large *nun*." Cf. the text of *BHS*, where the final nun is larger than normal; also see chapter 3 on the Proto-Masoretic Text.

רגלי

(See the example under מנין.)

רוח

"Spirit."

Example: Gen. 1:2 [Mp to [וְרוּחַ אֱלֹהִים] ח ב מנה בליש וכל שמואל דכות ב מ ה רוח יי "One of 8 occurrences of רוּחַ אֱלֹהִים (in the Bible), 2 of which have this same form (with prefixed *vav*, see 2 Chr. 24:20), in addition to references (to the divine Spirit) in the book of Samuel, which are also written like this, with the exception of 5 references to רוּחַ יְהוָה." [Mm lacking] Ginsburg (II:572, #240) supplies the missing information. The eight references to רוח אלהים are Gen. 1:2; 41:38; Exod. 31:3; 35:31; Num. 24:2; Ezek. 11:24; 2 Chr. 15:1; 24:20. The five references to רוח יהוה in the books of Samuel are 1 Sam. 10:6; 16:13, 14; 19:9; 2 Sam. 23:2. All of the above can be verified by checking the Mp notes in *BHS*. See also Mynatt, p. 91, #90.

רות

"The book of Ruth."

Example: Isa. 32:12 [Mp to [שְׂדֵי] ו כת י וכל רות דכות ב מ ב "This form occurs 6 times spelled with י, and it is always spelled this way in the book of Ruth, with 2 exceptions" [Mm 2329]. This Mp note is distinguishing between occurrences of שְׂדֵי and שְׂדֵה. Prefixes are ignored with the result that various different forms are included. The note is saying that שְׂדֵי occurs six times (2 Sam. 1:21; Isa. 32:12; Ps. 132:6; Prov. 23:10; Neh. 12:44; 2 Chron. 31:19), and שְׂדֵי is the usual spelling in Ruth (1:1, 2, 6, 22; 2:6). But there are two exceptions where שְׂדֵה occurs in Ruth (1:6; 4:3).

ריח

"Odor, scent." See example under ניחח.

ר״פ

"Beginning of the verse." Abbreviation for ראש פסוק (cf. סוף פסוק).

Examples:

a) Lev. 13:9 [Mp to [נֶגַע] יא ר״פ וס״פ נ "One of 11 instances where nun is found at the beginning and at the end of the verse" [Mm 729]. The 11 references are Lev. 13:9; Num. 32:32; Deut. 18:15; Jer. 50:8; Pss. 46:5; 77:21; 78:12; Prov. 7:17; 20:27; Song 4:11; 1 Chr. 12:2.

b) Lev. 22:24 [Mp to וּמָעוּךְ] ל̇ וחד מן י̇ פסוק̇ מן ד̇ מילין נסבין ו ר״פ "This form is found only here, and this is one of 10 verses with 4 words at the beginning of the verse prefixed with *vavs*" [Mm 4162]. The ten verses are Lev. 22:24; Deut. 7:13; Josh. 15:32, 36; 19:26, 28; 2 Sam. 17:29; 1 Chr. 3:20; 12:5; 2 Chr. 5:1.

"Lacking *dagesh* forte." The opposite of this is דגשׁ, "with *dagesh* forte."
Examples:

a) Gen. 2:25 [Mp to עֲרוּמִּים] ד̇ מל̇ ב̇ דגש וב̇ רפי̇ "This form is written *plene* (with *shureq*) 4 times, 2 times with *dagesh* (in מ) and 2 times without *dagesh* (in מ)" [Mm 18]. עֲרוּמִּים occurs in Gen. 2:25 and Job 22:6 (there is a typographical error in the Mp; ופי̇ should be רפי̇). עֲרוּמִים occurs in Job 5:12 and 15:5.

b) Gen. 4:9 [Mp to הֲשֹׁמֵר] ל̇ רפי̇ "This form occurs only once without *dagesh* (in the שׁ)." [Mm lacking] This indicates that the ה prefixed to the Qal participle is the interrogative ה rather than the ה of the definite article (cf. Ps. 146:6).

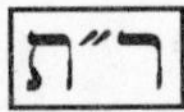

"Beginning of the word." Abbreviation for ראשׁ תיבותא. Cf. ס״ת.

Example: 1 Sam. 14:32 [Mp to שָׁלָל] חד מן יג̇ חס̇ ה ר״ת בליש̇ (*Qere*) השלל "One of 13 words lacking the ה of the definite article at the beginning of the word in this and similar forms" [Mm 1856]. The 13 words are found in the following references: 1 Sam. 14:32; 2 Sam. 23:9; 1 Kgs. 4:7; 7:20; 15:18; 2 Kgs. 11:20; 15:25; Jer. 10:13; 17:19; 40:3; 52:32; Ezek. 18:20; Lam. 1:18.

"The letter ש representing either שׁ or שׂ."

Example: Judg. 4:18 [Mp note to בַּשְׂמִיכָה] יׄ כת שׂ ולׄ בליש "One of 10 words written with שׂ, and בַּשְׂמִיכָה occurs nowhere else" [Mm 1411]. The heading to this note further clarifies the Mp note: יׄ כתׄ ש וקרין ס וסימנהון "These are the 10 words written שׂ but pronounced ס, and their references." The ten words are as follows: (Judg. 4:18) בַּשְׂמִיכָה; (Isa. 3:17) וְשִׂפַּח (for וְסִפַּח); (Isa. 5:5) מְשׂוּכָּתוֹ; (Ezek. 41:16) שְׂחִיף; (Hos. 8:4) הֵשִׂירוּ (from שָׂרַר); (Hos. 9:12) בְשׂוּרִי (for בְּסוּרִי); (Job 40:31) בְשֻׂכּוֹת; (Eccl. 12:11) וּכְמַשְׂמְרוֹת (for מַסְמְרוֹת); (Lam. 2:6) שֻׂכּוֹ (for סֻכּוֹ, Jer. 25:30); (Lam 3:8) שָׂתַם (for סָתַם, 2 Chr. 32:30). The significance of this note is that it reflects an early stage in the formation of the Hebrew text, a stage during which the use of ס seems to have been more widespread than at a later stage, when ס was slowly replaced by שׂ. Some words have survived with both spellings, but most have not. For an early dialectical difference between שׁ and ס, see Judg. 12:6.

שאר

"The remainder, the others, the rest." This term is used to refer to other texts which are similar to the one marked by the Mp note. Yet they are different in some significant way such as vocabulary or meaning.

Examples:

a) Deut. 4:5 [Mp to בָאִים שָׁמָּה לרשתה] בׄ ושאר עברים שמה לרשתה "The phrase 'going there to possess' occurs twice (cf. Deut. 30:18), and all the rest refer to 'passing over there to possess.'" In this case, the "rest" refers to other similar expressions, the difference being עֹבְרִים versus בָאִים. [Mm lacking] References to "passing over to possess" are found in Deut. 4:14; 6:1; 11:8, 11; etc.

b) Ruth 4:10 [Mp to אֵשֶׁת מַחְלוֹן קָנִיתִי] לׄ ושאר אשת המת "This is the only time Ruth is described as the 'wife of Mahlon'; the remaining reference (Ruth 4:5) speaks of her as 'the wife (widow) of the dead man.'"

שבט

"Tribe, clan."

Example: Num. 2:14 [Mp to רְעוּאֵל] ל׳ בשבט "The name Reuel occurs only once in the section on the tribes." [Mm lacking] Here שבט is a designation for a particular context of scripture, the section on the tribes in Num. 1:20–2:34. The note is saying that this name occurs only once in this section. However, note that this same person is referred to by the name דְּעוּאֵל in other texts (Num. 1:14; 7:42, 47; 10:20). See Mynatt, pp. 156–58, #192.

שובה

"To return, the act of returning."

Example: 2 Chr. 19:1 [Mp to וַיָּשָׁב] ה׳ שובה לירושלם "One of 5 references to (someone) returning to Jerusalem" [Mm 3963]. The five references are given as Zech. 1:16; Ezra 2:1; Neh. 7:6; 2 Chr. 19:1; 34:7.

שינה

"To sleep, the act of sleeping."

Example: Jer. 51:39 [Mp to שְׁנַת] ה׳ בשינה "This word occurs 5 times with reference to sleep" [Mm 2756]. The purpose of this note is to distinguish between the two uses of שְׁנַת in the Bible. It occurs numerous times as the construct form of שָׁנָה, "year," in which case it means "year of" (cf. Gen. 41:50; Lev. 25:5; Isa. 61:2; etc.). In five instances, however, it is the construct form of שֵׁנָה, "sleep" (from יָשֵׁן), meaning "the sleep of" (cf. Jer. 51:39, 57; Ps. 132:4; Eccl. 5:11; Est. 6:1).

שיר השירים

"Song of Songs."

Example: Num. 31:18 [Mp to בַּנָּשִׁים] ל׳ וכל שיר השירים דכות "This form occurs only here and in the book of Song of Songs, where it is always written like this." [Mm lacking] Even-Shoshan (p. 124, #684–86) lists three occurrences in Song of Songs (1:8; 5:9; 6:1).

שלשׁ ספרים

"Three Books (Psalms, Job, Proverbs)." Cf. אמ״ת.

Example: Ps. 87:5 [Mp to וּלְצִיּוֹן] ב׳ וחד מן ה׳ בטע ר״פ בשלשׁ ספרים "One of 2 occurrences of this form, and one of 5 words with this accent (*'azla legarmeh*) at the beginning of the verse in the Three Books" [Mm 3346]. וּלְצִיּוֹן (or וּלְצִיּוֹן) occurs in Zech. 1:14 and Ps. 87:5. [Mm 3654] The five words with *'azla legarmeh* at the beginning of the verse are found in Pss. 2:2; 5:11; 87:5; Prov. 6:14; 30:15.

שם

"Personal or place name(s)." Alternative spelling שום. Alternate form שמואתא.

Examples:

a) Josh. 15:24 [Mp to וְטֶלֶם] בׄ חד שם קריה וחד שם ברנש "Occurs twice, once as the name of a city, and once as a man's name" [Mm 1328]. טֶלֶם as the name of a town occurs in Josh. 15:24, and as a man's name in Ezra 10:24.

b) Exod. 29:40 [Mp to וְרֶבַע] בׄ וכל שם אנש דכות "The form רֶבַע occurs twice, in addition to its occurrences as a man's name." [Mm lacking] Twice רֶבַע signifies "a fourth (of something)." The references are Exod. 29:40 and 1 Sam. 9:8. רֶבַע as a man's name (Reba) is found in Num. 31:8 and Josh. 13:21. (Cf. E-S, p. 1058, #1–2 [[1]רֶבַע] and #1–2 [[2]רֶבַע].)

c) Isa. 6:6 [Mp to רִצְפָּה] לׄ וכל שם אית דכות "The form רִצְפָּה occurs only once (meaning 'a live coal'), and elsewhere it is used as a woman's name." [Mm lacking] The references to a woman's name (Rizpah) are found in 2 Sam. 3:7; 21:8, 10, 11.

שמואל

"The book of Samuel."

Example: 2 Sam. 14:32 [Mp to בָא] הׄ חס בשמואל ובכתיב ולׄ מנהׄ בסיפׄ "This form is written defectively (instead of בוֹא) 5 times in Samuel and the Writings, and this is its only occurrence in this book (Samuel)" [Mm 169]. This list is in two parts. The first gives 14 references where the *plene* form (בוֹא) occurs in the Pentateuch and the Prophets (omitting its occurrences in the Writings). The second part of the Mm note gives the defective form's occurrences in Samuel and the Writings, which include 2 Sam. 14:32; Ps. 105:19; 126:6; Est. 5:14; 2 Chr. 25:8. For additional data and accompanying commentary on the incidence of בוֹא (בָא), see Ginsburg, I:168, #80–81; IV:180, #80–81.

שמואתא

See שם and מׄתא.

שמיעה

"To hear, the act of hearing."

Example: Gen. 3:17 [Mp to שָׁמַעְתָּ לְקוֹל] יזׄ שמיעה לקול "There are 17 references to (someone) hearing a voice" [Mm 23]. The heading to Mm 23 is "יזׄ שָׁמַעְתָּ לְקוֹל", the same as the Mp note in Gen. 3:17, and the references are given as Gen. 3:17; 16:2;

Exod. 3:18; 4:8, 9; 15:26; 18:24; Judg. 2:20; 1 Sam. 2:25; 28:22, 23; 1 Kgs. 20:25; 2 Kgs. 10:6; Jer. 18:19; Hab. 3:16; Pss. 58:6; 81:12; Song 8:13. However, there are two problems with this list: 1) There are 18 references given, not 17 as specified by both the Mp note and Mm 23. The error in the list is 1 Sam. 28:22, which has בְּקוֹל, not לְקוֹל. 2) Mm 23 has omitted the occurrence in 1 Sam. 15:1. Notice also that the Mp note in 1 Sam. 15:1 is יח (both in *BHS* and L). It appears that this Mp note includes the 17 correct occurrences listed above, *plus* 1 Sam. 15:1. Thus, the Mp note יח in 1 Sam. 15:1 gives an accurate accounting of the occurrences, whereas Mm 23 is in error. In L, the occurrence in Gen. 3:17 also has the Mp note יח, although Weil has changed it to יז שמיעה לקול, as noted above.

שמשון

See כפתוי שמשון.

שנאה

"Hatred, enmity (enemy)." Combined with לשון.

Example: 1 Sam. 28:16 [Mp to עָרֶךָ] ח לשון שנאה "There are 8 occurrences of ערך (or variations thereof) meaning enmity (or enemy)." [Mm lacking] Ginsburg (II:418, #758a, 758b) lists eight occurrences with this meaning, but some of his references are problematic. The list he gives includes 1 Sam. 28:16 (עָרֶךָ); Isa. 14:21 (עָרִים); Mic. 5:11 (for 5:10?) (עָרֵי); 5:13 (עָרֶיךָ); Pss. 9:7 (וְעָרִים); 139:20 (עָרֶיךָ); Dan. 4:16 (לְעָרָיךְ); Ezra 4:14 (which seems to have been listed in error). A careful examination of these passages in *BHS* indicates that the following were included in the eight, as verified by the accompanying Mp notes: 1 Sam. 28:16; Isa. 14:21; Mic. 5:10 (rather than 5:11); 5:13; Pss. 9:7; 139:20; Dan. 4:16. Since this list omits Ezra 4:14, a replacement must be found to arrive at a total of eight occurrences. A search of Even-Shoshan reveals a second meaning for עִיר (p. 862) as "adversary," and refers to Jer. 15:8 and Hos. 11:9 as instances of its usage. Only Jer. 15:8 is accompanied by an Mp note indicating that it is the reference missing from Ginsburg's list. Incidentally, this suggests the possibility of translating בְּעִיר in Hos. 11:9 in a way that better suits the context.

שפטים

"The book of Judges."

Example: Gen. 26:32 [Mp to וַיַּגִּדוּ] ד חס וכל שפטים ושמואל דכות ב מ ב מל "This form occurs 4 times written defectively (*hireq* instead of *hireq-yod*), in addition to its occurrences in Judges and Samuel, which are also defective, with two exceptions, which are *plene* (with *hireq-yod*)" [Mm 195]. The four defective forms (outside Judges and Samuel) are found in Gen. 26:32; 45:26; 2 Kgs. 7:15; 18:37. The two *plene* forms referred to above are found in 1 Sam. 11:9; 14:33. This same list can be found in Ginsburg, II:273, #81.

ת

"The letter ת."

Example: Exod. 40:4 [Mp to וְהַעֲלֵיתָ] לׄ וטעם באות ת "This is the only occurrence of this form, and it is accented on the letter ת, i.e., on the final syllable (מִלְרַע)." [Mm lacking]

תׄגׄמׄכׄפׄוׄסׄ

A mnemonic device giving the correct order of the abbreviated words. Cf. סימן for a discussion of this type of note.

Example: Deut. 7:1 [Mp to הַחִתִּי...הַיְבוּסִי] סימן תׄגׄמׄכׄפׄוׄסׄ "The sign for the correct order of words is תׄ (הַחִתִּי 'the Hittites'), גׄ (הַגִּרְגָּשִׁי 'the Girgashites'), מׄ (הָאֱמֹרִי 'the Amorites'), כׄ (הַכְּנַעֲנִי 'the Canaanites'), פׄ (הַפְּרִזִּי 'the Perizzites'), וׄ (הַחִוִּי 'the Hivites'), סׄ (הַיְבוּסִי 'the Jebusites')" [Okhl 274].

תגרייא

"Merchant, trader."

Example: Job 40:30 [Mp to כְּנַעֲנִים] גׄ ולׄ לשון תגרייא "This word (in its plural form) occurs 3 times, but only here does it mean 'merchants'." [Mm lacking] Ginsburg (II:49, #391) lists the three references as Obad. 20; Job 40:30; Neh. 9:24. The Mp notes in *BHS* match these three references.

תׄדׄמׄקׄ

"An abbreviated reference to the Twelve Prophets (תׄ for תרי עשר), Chronicles (דׄ for דברי הימים), Proverbs (מׄ for משלי), and Ecclesiastes (קׄ for קהלת)."

Example: Ps. 90:11 [Mp to יוֹדֵעַ] יׄ מלׄ וכל תׄדׄמׄקׄ דכות בׄ מׄ גׄ חסׄ "Occurs 10 times written *plene* (with *holem-vav*), in addition to its occurrences in the Twelve Prophets, Chronicles, Proverbs, and Ecclesiastes, where it is also written *plene*, except in 3 instances where it is defective (with *holem* only)." [Mm lacking] Ginsburg (I:708ff., #141) lists the ten *plene* forms (outside the books mentioned above) as occurring in 1 Sam. 26:12; 2 Sam. 12:22; Isa. 29:11; Jer. 29:23 (*Qere*); Pss. 1:6; 37:18; 90:11; Ruth 3:11; Est. 4:14; Neh. 10:29. The three defective forms found among the four books listed above are in Prov. 28:2; 29:7; Eccl. 8:7.

"The Torah, Pentateuch." Abbreviation for תורה. Cf. אורית (אוֹר). Usually found with prefixed preposition ב (בתוֹר).

Example: Gen. 48:11 [Mp to רְאֹה] יו כת ה בתוֹר ול בליש "There are 16 words in the Pentateuch that are written with (final) ה (where one would expect *vav* instead), and this is the only occurrence of רְאֹה in the Bible (Qal infinitive construct)" [Mm 598]. The 16 words are found in Gen. 48:11; 49:11 (2x); Exod. 2:19; 15:1, 21; 17:14; 19:13; 22:4, 26; 32:17, 25; Lev. 23:13; Num. 10:36; 23:8; Deut. 34:7. See Mynatt, p. 128, #144.

"Word." Abbreviation for תיבותא. See ס״ת and ר״ת. When תיבותא is cited in an Mp note, it is usually abbreviated as ת, especially in the combinations ר״ת (beginning of the word") or ס״ת ("end of the word"). Examples of this usage can be found under ר״ת and ס״ת.

תֹּכֹה

Abbreviation for תורה כל המחלה, "the Torah is כל המחלה." תֹּכֹה is a mnemonic sign giving the correct form for the phrase כָּל־מַחֲלָה in the Torah. This phrase occurs only three times in the Bible (Exod. 15:26; 1 Kgs. 8:37; 2 Chr. 6:28), and each occurrence varies slightly from the other two.

Exod. 15:26	כָּל־הַמַּחֲלָה	תֹּכֹה = תורה כל המחלה
1 Kgs. 8:37	כָּל־מַחֲלָה	מֹכֹם = מלכים כל מחלה
2 Chr. 6:28	וְכָל־מַחֲלָה	דוֹם = דברי הימים וכל מחלה

Thus, mnemonic signs were developed as reminders of the correct form in each case. Cf. סימן for a discussion of mnemonic signs.

Example: Exod. 15:26 [Mp to כָּל־הַמַּחֲלָה] ל תֹּכֹה סימן "This combination occurs only once, and תֹּכֹה is its sign." The mnemonic sign in unabbreviated form is תורה כל המחלה, and it indicates that, in the Torah, the correct form of this phrase is

כָּל־מַחֲלָה, with no prefixes attached to מַחֲלָה. This form is in contrast to two other occurrences (1 Kgs. 8:37; 2 Chr. 6:28), which are slightly different [Mm 4166].

תלדות

"Generations."

Example: Gen. 25:7 [Mp to וְאֵלֶּה] יז ר״פ בתור וכל תלדות דכות ב מ ד "The word וְאֵלֶּה occurs 17 times at the beginning of the verse in the Pentateuch in addition to its occurrences before the word תלדות ("generations"), where it also is written like this, except in four instances (where it is written as אֵלֶּה תּוֹלְדֹת)" [Mm 267]. The 17 occurrences of וְאֵלֶּה are listed as Gen. 25:7, 17; 36:13, 14, 17, 18, 23, 24, 25, 26, 31; Exod. 21:1; 28:4; Num. 13:4; 26:36, 57; Deut. 27:13 [Mm 48]. The four occurrences of אֵלֶּה תּוֹלְדֹת (at the beginning of the sentence) are found in Gen. 2:4; 6:9; 11:10; 37:2. For examples of וְאֵלֶּה תּוֹלְדֹת, see Gen. 10:1; 11:27; 25:12, 19; 36:1, 9; Num. 3:1.

תלויות

"Raised, suspended." Usually preceded by אותיות. See אוֹת.

Example: Judg. 18:30 [Mp to מְנַשֶּׁה] ד אותיות תלויות "One of 4 suspended letters" [Mm 3557]. The references where the raised letters occur are Judg. 18:30; Ps. 80:14; Job 38:13, 15. (See chapter 3 on the Proto-Masoretic Text.)

תלים

"The book of Psalms."

Example: Isa. 64:4 [Mp to וְעֹשֵׂה] ח קמ קטן וכל דברים מלכים תרי עשר תלים קהלת עזרא ד״ה דכות ב מ כב "The form עֹשֵׂה (or עֹשֵׂי) occurs 8 times with *qamets qatan* (*sere*) in the final syllable, in addition to its occurrences in Deuteronomy, Kings, the Twelve Prophets, Psalms, Ecclesiastes, Ezra, and Chronicles, in which books it also appears as עֹשֵׂה, with 22 exceptions (עֹשֶׂה)" [Mm 475]. This note furnishes two separate lists. The first contains the eight references to עֹשֵׂה (outside the additional books listed above). The second contains the 22 references to עֹשֶׂה occurring in these same books. (The lists may be found in the second example under קמ.)

תלת

"Three, third, or *seghol*" (because it has three dots or points).

Examples:

a) Gen. 42:22 [Mp to וְגַם] כג פסוק וגם ובתר תלת מילין "In 23 verses (in the Bible) וגם is followed by (only) 3 words" [Mm 1629]. This means וגם is the fourth word from the end of the verse in all these references. The 23 references are given as Gen. 42:22; Exod. 21:35; 33:12; Num. 24:24, 25; 1 Sam. 18:5; 2 Sam. 15:19; 19:41; 21:20; 2 Kgs. 13:6; Isa. 7:20; Jer. 10:15; Ezek. 5:11; 16:29; 24:3; Hos. 4:3; Zech. 11:8; Ps. 78:21; Prov. 16:4; Eccl. 6:7; 1 Chr. 10:13; 20:6; 2 Chr. 28:2.

b) Deut. 1:31 [Mp to אֲשֶׁר] ח̇ פסוק מן ד̇ מילין דמיין ותלת משני "One of 8 verses (in the Bible), in each of which the same word occurs 4 times, except that the third occurrence differs from the others." [Mm lacking] This note is difficult to decipher, since there seem to be multiple traditions about the number and identification of the relevant verses. Ginsburg (I:416, #107; IV:342f., #107) puts the number of the verses at seven, and then fails to identify one of the seven. The six he identifies are Gen. 41:26; Deut. 1:31; Isa. 30:16; 1 Sam. 9:4; Ezek. 48:16; Ezra 8:16. These verses match the Mp notes in *BHS*, and so are to be regarded as part of the eight. But this still leaves two to be sought elsewhere. One can be found in Isa. 31:1, as verified by the Mp note accompanying this verse. The location of the other, however, remains a mystery.

c) Gen. 26:25 [Mp to וַיֶּט־] ב̇ מנוקדין בתלת "This form occurs twice pointed with *seghol*" (rather than וַיֵּט, Gen. 12:8; 35:21; etc.). [Mm lacking] The other occurrence of וַיֶּט־ is in 1 Chr. 15:1. In both instances *sere* is shortened to *seghol* because this word is joined to the following word by *maqqef.*

תׄמׄכׄפׄוׄסׄ

A mnemonic sequence giving the correct order of the abbreviated words. Cf. סימן for a discussion of this type of note.

Example: Deut. 20:17 [Mp to הַחִתִּי...הַיְבוּסִי] סימן תׄמׄכׄפׄוׄסׄ "The sign for the correct order of words is ת̇ (הַחִתִּי 'the Hittites'), מ̇ (הָאֱמֹרִי 'the Amorites'), כ̇ (הַכְּנַעֲנִי 'the Canaanites'), פ̇ (הַפְּרִזִּי 'the Perizzites'), ו̇ (הַחִוִּי 'the Hivites'), ס̇ (הַיְבוּסִי 'the Jebusites')" [Okhl 274].

תׄמׄפׄוׄסׄ

A mnemonic sequence giving the correct order of the abbreviated words. Cf. סימן for a discussion of this type of note.

Example: 2 Chr. 8:7 [Mp to הַחִתִּי...הַיְבוּסִי] סימן תׄמׄפׄוׄסׄ "The sign for the correct order of words is ת̇ (הַחִתִּי 'the Hittites'), מ̇ (הָאֱמֹרִי 'the Amorites'), פ̇ (הַפְּרִזִּי 'the Perizzites'), ו̇ (הַחִוִּי 'the Hivites'), ס̇ (הַיְבוּסִי 'the Jebusites')" [Okhl 274].

תנוּפׄ

"Wave-offering, elevation offering." Abbreviation for תנופה (cf. BDB, p. 632).

Example: Isa. 33:20 [Mp to חֲזֵה] ג̇ וכל תנופ̇ דכות "The form חֲזֵה (Qal imperative 2ms

from חזה) occurs 3 times, and חֲזֵה (noun ms construct), meaning 'breast' (of the wave-offering) is written like it" [Mm 3812]. חֲזֵה (as a verb) occurs in Isa. 33:20; 48:6; Dan. 3:19. As a (construct) noun, it occurs (in conjunction with a wave-offering) in Exod. 29:27; Lev. 7:34; 10:14, 15; Num. 6:20; 18:18.
Reference sources: BDB, p. 302 (I. חזה for verb), p. 303 (II. חזה for חָזֶה, "breast"); E-S, p. 354 (חָזֶה, #6–11).

תנ֯

"Second, the second in a series." Abbreviation for תנינא.

Example: Gen. 39:22 [Mp to הָאֲסִרִם] ל חס י תנ֯ "This form is unique in that the second *hireq* is lacking an accompanying *yod*" [Mm 3310]. This note lists two occurrences of this form written *plene* (אֲסִירִים), as well as the one form written defectively. The *plene* forms are found in Ps. 68:7 and Job 3:18.

תסמכ֯

A mnemonic sequence giving the correct order of the abbreviated words. Cf. סימן for a discussion of this type of note.

Example: Num. 13:29 [Mp to הַחִתִּי...וְהַכְּנַעֲנִי] סימן תסמכ֯ "The sign for the correct order of words is ת (הַחִתִּי 'the Hittites'), ס (הַיְבוּסִי 'the Jebusites'), מ (הָאֱמֹרִי 'the Amorites'), כ (הַכְּנַעֲנִי 'the Canaanites')" [Okhl 274].

תקוני ספרים

"The emendations (or euphemisms) of the scribes, also called *Tiqqune Sopherim.*" An ancient tradition lists 18 passages which have been emended for theological traditions. Most were designed to remove irreverent statements or inferences about God. These emendations usually involved minor changes such as the omission of one or more consonants or words, or the transposition of consonants or words within a verse. For instance, the statement in Gen. 18:22, to the effect that the LORD stood before Abraham, was regarded as unworthy of the divine glory, and was emended to its present state, which has Abraham standing before the LORD. Some of the emendations were even more subtle than this. The *Tiqqune Sopherim* are never mentioned in the Mp notes in *BHS*, although some (but not all) are noted in the text critical apparatus at the bottom of the page. The 18 include Gen. 18:22; Num. 11:15; 12:12; 1 Sam. 3:13; 2 Sam. 16:12; 20:1; 1 Kgs. 12:16; Jer. 2:11; Ezek. 8:17; Hos. 4:7; Hab. 1:12; Zech. 2:12; Mal. 1:13; Job 7:20; 32:3; Lam. 3:20; 2 Chr. 10:16.
Reference sources: C. McCarthy, *The Tiqqune Sopherim*; E.J. Revell, "Scribal Emendations," *Anchor Bible Dictionary*, V:1011f.; Ginsburg, *Introduction to the*

Massoretico-Critical Edition of the Hebrew Bible, pp. 347–63. Also see chapter 3 on Proto-Masoretic Text.

תרגום

"The language of the Targum, i.e., Aramaic." Usually accompanied by לשון. Cf. ארמי.

Example: Dan. 2:10 [Mp to יוּכַל] ל̇ בלשון תרגום "This is the only occurrence of this form in the Aramaic language." [Mm lacking] The form involved here is Pe'il imperfect 3ms from יְכִל (cf. BDB, p. 1095). It occurs frequently as a Qal imperfect form of יָכֹל, and its occurrence in Aramaic is thought to be a Hebraism. Reference source: E-S, pp. 466f., #119–59.

תרי

"Two, second." Alternate form: תרתין.

Examples:

a) Gen. 46:20 [Mp to פּוֹטִי פֶרַע] ג̇ כת̇ תרתין מילין "'Potiphera' occurs 3 times written as two words (Poti Phera)." [Mm lacking] A concordance will show that this name of Joseph's father-in-law, the priest of On, occurs only three times (Gen. 41:45, 50; 46:20), and always as two words.

b) Judg. 11:6 [Mp to וְהָיִיתָה] ג̇ חד כת̇ י וב̇ כת̇ תרי י "Occurs 3 times, once written (defectively) with a single *yod*, and twice written (*plene*) with a second *yod*" [Mm 1755]. The *plene* occurrences are in Judg. 11:6; 2 Sam. 5:2. The only defective occurrence is in 2 Sam. 10:11.

c) Job 38:1 [Mp to מֵאֲשֶׁתַּם] חד מן הי̇ כת̇ מילה חדה וקר̇ תרי (*Qere*) מאש תם "The *Qere* is מאש תם. One of 15 occurrences written as one word but read as two" [Mm 214]. The note is marking 15 times that two words are written as one. According to Mm 214, the fifteen are Gen. 30:11; Exod. 4:2; Deut. 33:2; Isa. 3:15; Jer. 6:29; 18:3; Ezra 8:6; Pss. 10:10; 55:16; 123:4; Job 38:1; 40:6; Neh. 2:13; 1 Chr. 9:4; 27:12. Mm 214 also includes a further note, that there are eight instances where the opposite is the case, where words written as one should be read as two (Judg. 16:25; 1 Sam. 9:1; 24:9; Isa. 9:6; 44:24; Lam. 1:6; 4:3; 2 Chr. 34:6).

תרי עשר

"The Book of the Twelve Prophets."

Example: Deut. 10:10 [Mp to וְאָנֹכִי] ט̇ ר״פ וכל תרי עשר דכות "This form occurs at the beginning of the verse 9 times (in the Bible), in addition to its occurrences at the beginning of the verse in the Twelve Prophets, where it is also written like this (with the prefixed *vav*)" [Mm 1472]. A similar list occurs in Ginsburg (I:100, #978; IV:118, #978). The nine occurrences (outside the Book of the Twelve) are in Deut. 10:10;

31:18; Judg. 11:27; 2 Sam. 3:39; Isa. 51:15; 66:18; Jer. 2:21; 3:19; Ps. 22:7. This form (with prefixed *vav*) begins a verse five times in the book of the Twelve: Hos. 11:3; 12:10; 13:4; Amos 2:9, 10.

BIBLIOGRAPHY

This bibliography concludes with a collection of reviews of *BHS*.

Abrahams, I. "Note to *JQR*, XVI, P. 392, L. 25." *Jewish Quarterly Review* 16 (1903–4) 602.

Abulafia, Meir ben Todras ha–Levi. *Masoret Siyag la–Torah.* Tel Aviv: Tsiyon, 1968.

Adler, C. "On a Hebrew Manuscript of the Year 1300." *American Journal of Semitic Languages and Literature* 1 (1884–85) 80–85.

Albrecht, K. "Die sogennanten Sonderbarkeiten des masoretischen Textes." *Zeitschrift für die alttestamentliche Wissenschaft* 39 (1921) 160–69.

Albrektson, B. "Reflections on the Emergence of a Standard Text of the Hebrew Bible." *Supplements to Vetus Testamentum* 29 (1978) 49–65.

Albright, W.F. "On Dr. Gordis's Communication." *Journal of Biblical Literature* 57 (1938) 332–333.

Allony, N. "El prefacio del libro 'Horaiat Hakore' de Ibn Balam." *Estudios Masoreticos: Proceedings of the 5th Congress of IOMS.* Textos y Estudios "Cardenal Cisneros", 33. Madrid: Instituto "Arias Montano" CSIC, 1983.

Azcárraga Servert, M.J. "El *ketîb/qerê* en el libro de Josué del Códice de Profetas de el Cairo." *Proceedings of the Eleventh Congress of IOMS*. Jerusalem: Magnes Press, 1994.

________. "El libro de Isaías en el *Minhat Say*. *Estudios Masoreticos: Proceedings of the 10th Congress of IOMS*. Madrid: Instituto de Filología, CSIC, Departamento de Filología Bíblica y de Oriente Antiquo, 1993.

________. *Minhat Say de Y. S. de Norzi: Profetas Menores.* Textos y Estudios "Cardenal Cisneros," 40. Madrid: Instituto de Filología, CSIC, Departamento de Filología Bíblica y de Oriente Antiquo, 1987.

________. "Les Notes *ma'arvaé–madinhaé* dans le manuscript du Caire." *Proceedings of the Ninth International IOMS Congress (1989).* Masoretic Studies, No. 8. Missoula, MT: Scholars Press, 1992.

Bacher, W. "A Contribution to the History of the Term 'Massorah'." *Jewish Quarterly Review* 3 (1890–91) 785–790.

________. "Notes on JQR." *Jewish Quarterly Review* 18 (1905–6) 146–48.

Baer, S.I. "The Daghesh in Initial Letters." *Hebraica* 1 (1884–5) 142–152.

Barnes, W.E. "Ancient Corrections in the Text of the Old Testament (Tikkun Sopherim)." *Journal of Theological Studies* 1 (1900) 387–414.

________. "The Septuagint and the Massoretic Text, Two Interesting Passages." *Ex-*

pository Times 6 (1894–95) 223–25.

Barr, J. "A New Look at Kethib–Qere." *Oudtestamentische Studien* 21 (1981) 19–37.

Barrow, J.W. "On a Hebrew MS. of the Pentateuch, from the Jewish Congregation at Kai–fung–fu in China." *Journal of the American Oriental Society* 9 (1869–71) liii.

Barthélemy, D. "Les ruines de la tradition des soferim dans le manuscrit d'Alep: la gageure de Shelomoh ben Buya`a." *Revue Biblique* 99 (1992) 7–39.

________. "Texte, massores, et facsimilé du manuscrit d'Alep." *Salvacion en la Palabra...en memoria Alejandro Díez Macho*. Madrid: Ediciones Cristiandad, 1986.

Beck, A.B., ed., *The Leningrad Codex: A Facsimile Edition*. Grand Rapids, MI: Eerdmans, 1997.

Bee, R.E. "Use of Statistical Methods in Old Testament Studies." *Vetus Testamentum* 23 (1973) 257–72.

Beecher, W.J. "Had the Massorites the Critical Instinct?" *Old and New Testament Student* 2 (1882–3) 1–7.

Ben–David, A. "The Differences between Ben Asher and Ben Naftali." *Tarbiz* 26 (1956–7) #4, IV–V (Hebrew).

Ben–David, I. "Disjunctive Accents–*Imperatores* and *Quasi Imperatores*." *Proceedings of the Ninth International IOMS Congress (1989)* (Hebrew Section). Masoretic Studies, No. 8. Missoula, MT: Scholars Press, 1992.

Ben–Zvi, I. "The Codex of Ben Asher." *Textus* 1 (1960) 1–16.

Beyer, K. "Für einen Ergänzungsband zur Biblia Hebraica Stuttgartensia." *Zeitschrift für die Alttestamentliche Wissenschaft* 85 (1973) 231.

Birnbaum, E. "The Michigan Codex. An Important Hebrew Bible Manuscript Discovered in the University of Michigan Library." *Vetus Testamentum* 17 (1967) 373–415.

Birnbaum, S.A. *The Hebrew Scripts*. London: Paleographica, 1971.

Blank, S. "A Hebrew Bible MS in the Hebrew Union College Library." *Hebrew Union College Annual* 8 & 9 (1931–32) 229–55.

Blau, L. "Massoretic Studies." *Jewish Quarterly Review* 8 (1895–6) 343–359; 9 (1896–7) 122–144, 471–490.

Breuer, M. *Aleppo Codex and the Accepted Text of the Bible*. Jerusalem: Mosad Harav Kook, 1976.

________. "Dividing the Decalogue into Verses and Commandments." *Ten Commandments in History and Tradition*. Ed. B. Segal and G. Levi. Jerusalem: Magnes Press, 1990.

Brown, F., S.R. Driver, and C.A. Briggs, eds. *A Hebrew and English Lexicon of the Old Testament*. Oxford: Clarendon Press, 1951.

Busi, G. *Horayat ha–qorè: una grammatica ebraica del secolo XI*. Frankfurt: Peter D. Lang, 1984.

Butin, R.F. "The Extraordinary Points in the Massoretic Text." *New York Review* 1

(1905–6) 771–81.

________. *The Ten Nequdoth of the Torah.* 1906; rpt. New York, NY: Ktav, Inc., 1969.

Casper, L. "Masorah." *The Jewish Encyclopedia,* Vol. VIII. New York, NY: Funk and Wagnalls Co., 1904.

Cassuto, P. "Masoretic Lists and Matres Lectionis." *VIII International Congress of the International Organization for Masoretic Studies (1988).* Masoretic Studies, No. 6. Missoula, MT: Scholars Press, 1990.

________. "*Qeré/ketiv* dans le manuscrit Londres Or. 4445." *Proceedings of the Eleventh Congress of IOMS.* Jerusalem: Magnes Press, 1994.

________. "*Qere–Ketiv* et linéarité du text biblique aux vues méthodes informatiques." *Proceedings of the Ninth International IOMS Congress (1989).* Masoretic Studies, No. 8. Missoula, MT: Scholars Press, 1992.

________. "Qeré–Ketiv et Massora Magna dans le Manuscrit B19a." *Textus* 15 (1990) 85–118.

Chiesa, B. *L'Antico Testamento Ebraico secondo la tradizione palestinese.* Turin: Bottega d'Erasmo, 1978.

________. *The Emergence of Hebrew Biblical Pointing.* Frankfurt: Peter D. Lang, 1979.

Chomsky, W. "The History of Our Vowel System in Hebrew." *Jewish Quarterly Review* 32 (1941–42) 26–49.

Christensen, D.L. "The Masoretic Accentual System and Repeated Metrical Refrains in Nahum, Song of Songs, and Deuteronomy." *VIII International Congress of the International Organization for Masoretic Studies (1988).* Masoretic Studies, No. 6. Missoula, MT: Scholars Press, 1990.

Cohen, M.B. "Masoretic Accents as a Biblical Commentary." *Journal of the Ancient Near Eastern Society* 4 (1972) 2–11.

________. *The System of Accentuation in the Hebrew Bible.* Minneapolis, MN: Milco Press, 1969.

Cohen, M. and D. Freedman. "The Dual Accentuation of the Ten Commandments." *1972 and 1973 Proceedings of IOMS.* Masoretic Studies, No. 1. Missoula, MT: Scholars Press, 1974.

________, and D.B. Freedman. "Snaith Bible: A Critical Examination of the Hebrew Bible Published in 1958 by the British and Foreign Bible Society." *Hebrew Union College Annual* 45 (1974) 97–132.

Corré, A.D. "Phonemic Problems in the Masora." *Essays Presented to Chief Rabbi I. Brodie.* Jews' College Publications, New Series, No. 3. Ed. H. J. Zimmels, et al. London: Soncino Press, 1966.

Costacurta, B. "Implicazioni Semaniche in alcuni casi de *qere–ketib.*" *Biblica* 71 (1990) 239–77.

Courtenay, J.B. "The Masora." *British Quarterly Review* 73 (1881) 310–41.

Crosby, H. "A Question." *Old and New Testament Student* 4 (1884–85) 279.

Crown, A.D. "Studies in Samaritan Scribal Practices and Manuscript History, pt. 3: Columnar Writing and the Samaritan Masorah." *Bulletin of John Rylands Library* 1 (1984) 349–81.

Dahood, M. "Isaiah 53:8–12 and Massoretic Mis–constructions." *Biblica* 63 (1982) 560–570.

Danker, F.W. "Aids to Bible Study: the Hebrew Old Testament." *Concordia Theological Monthly* 29 (1958) 902–18.

Davidson, A.B. *Outlines of Hebrew Accentuation: Prose and Poetical.* London: Williams and Norgate, 1861.

Dérenbourg, J. "Manuel du lecteur d'un auteur inconnu." *Journal Asiatique*, 6ème série, Tome xvi (1870) 309–550.

Díaz-Esteban, F. "References to Ben Asher and Ben Naftali in the Masora Magna Written in the Margins of MS Leningrad B19a." *Textus* 6 (1968) 62–74.

________. "The Sefer Okla W'Okla as a Source of Not Registered Biblical Textual Variants." *Zeitschrift für die alttestamentliche Wissenschaft* 70 (1958) 250–53.

________. *Sefer Oklah we–Oklah.* Madrid: Consejo Superior de Investigaciones Cientificos, 1975.

________. "Texto hebreo y targum arameo de un fragmento de la geniza dal Cairo con punctuation babilonica." *Boletin de la Assocation Espanole de Orientalistes* 10 (1974) 201–213.

Dietrich, M. *Neue palästinisch punktierte Bibelfragmente.* Leiden: Brill, 1968.

Díez-Macho, A. "Fragmento del texto hebreo y arameo del libro de Numerus escritto en una muy antigua megilla en el sistema babilonico." *Sefarad* 17 (1957) 386–88.

________. "A Fundamental Manuscript for an Edition of the Babylonian Onkelos to Genesis." *Zeitschrift für die alttestamentliche Wissenschaft* 70 (1958) 250–53.

________. "Importants manuscrits hébreux et araméens aux Etats–Unis." *Supplements to Vetus Testamentum* 4 (1957) 49–65.

________. "A New Fragment of Isaiah with Babylonian Pointing." *Textus* 1 (1960) 132–43.

________. "A New List of So–called 'Ben Naftali' Manuscripts, Preceded by an Inquiry into the True Character of These Manuscripts." *Hebrew and Semitic Studies.* Festschrift G. R. Driver. Ed. D. W. Thomas and W. D. McHardy. Oxford: Clarendon Press, 1963.

________. "Onquelos manuscript with Babylonian Transliterated Vocalization in the Vatican Library." *Vetus Testamentum* 8 (1958) 113–33.

________. *The Pentateuch: with the Masorah Parva and Masorah Magna and with Targum Onkelos: Ms. Vat. heb. 448, Facsimile ed.* Jerusalem: Makor Publishing,

1977.

________. *Targum to the Former Prophets: Codex New York 229* (Facsimile). Jerusalem: Makor, 1974.

Diez–Merino, L. *La biblia babilonica.* Madrid: Consejo Superior de Investigaciones Cientificos, 1975.

________. "La Masora Targumica." *Estudios Biblicos* 44 (1986) 305–318.

________. "The Targumic Masora of the Vat Ebr 448." *Estudios Masoreticos: Proceedings of the 5th Congress of IOMS.* Textos y Estudios "Cardenal Cisneros", 33. Madrid: Instituto "Arias Montano" CSIC, 1983.

Dotan, A. "The Beginnings of Masoretic Vowel Notation." *1972 and 1973 Proceedings of IOMS.* Masoretic Studies, No. 1. Missoula, MT: Scholars Press, 1974.

________. *Ben Asher's Creed.* Masoretic Studies, No. 3. Missoula, MT: Scholars Press, 1977.

________. "Deviation in Gemination in the Tiberian Vocalization." *Estudios Masoreticos: Proceedings of the 5th Congress of IOMS.* Textos y Estudios "Cardenal Cisneros", 33. Madrid: Instituto "Arias Montano" CSIC, 1983.

________. "Elijah Levita." *Encyclopedia Judaica*, vol. XI. New York, NY: The Macmillan Co., 1971.

________. *The Hebrew Bible according to the Aaron ben–Asher text of the Leningrad Manuscript* (Hebrew). Tel Aviv: The School of Jewish Studies, Tel Aviv University, 1971.

________. "Masorah." *Encyclopedia Judaica*, Vol. XVI. Jerusalem, NY: MacMillan Co., 1971.

________. "Masoretic Rubrics of Indicated Origin in Codex Leningrad (B19a)." *VIII International Congress of the International Organization for Masoretic Studies (1988).* Masoretic Studies, No. 6. Missoula, MT: Scholars Press, 1990.

________. "De la Massora à la grammaire les débuts de la pensée grammaticale dans l'hébreu." *Journal Asiatique* 278 (1990) 13–30.

________. "The Minor *Ga`ya.*" *Textus* 4 (1964) 55–75.

________. "The Problem of *dehiq* and *até mérahiq.*" *Fourth World Congress of Jewish Studies* 2 (1968) 186.

________, ed. *Proceedings of the Ninth International IOMS Congress (1989).* Masoretic Studies, No. 8. Missoula, MT: Scholars Press, 1992.

________, ed. *Proceedings of the 11th Congress of the IOMS.* Jerusalem: Magnes Press, 1994.

________. "Reflections Towards a Critical Edition of Pentateuch Codex Or. 4445." *Estudios Masoreticos: Proceedings of the 10th Congress of IOMS.* Madrid: Instituto de Filología, CSIC, Departamento de Filología Bíblica y de Oriente Antiquo, 1993.

________. "The Relative Chronology of Hebrew Vocalization and Accentuation." *Pro-*

ceedings of the American Academy for Jewish Research 48 (1981) 87–99.

________, ed. *Sefer Dikduke ha–Te`amim*. Jerusalem: Academy of the Hebrew Language, 1967.

________. *Thesaurus of the Tiberian Masorah.* Tel Aviv: Tel Aviv University, 1977.

________, ed. *Torah, Nevi'im, u–Khetuvim.* Tel Aviv: Adi, 1973.

________. "Vestiges of the Masora in Saadia Gaon's Grammar." *Proceedings of the Eleventh Congress of IOMS* (Hebrew Section). Jerusalem: Magnes Press, 1994.

________. "Was the Aleppo Codex Actually Vocalized by Aharon Ben Asher? " *Tarbiz* 34 (1964–5) 136–55 (Hebrew).

Driver, G.R. "Abbreviations in the MT." *Textus* 1 (1960) 112–31.

________. "Once Again Abbreviation." *Textus* 4 (1963) 76–94.

Edelmann, R. "Masoret and its Historical Background." *Salo Wittmayer Baron*. Ed. S. Lieberman and Hyman Arthur. Jerusalem: American Academy for Jewish Research, 1975.

________. "Soferim–Massoretes, 'Massoretes'–Nakdanim." *In Memoriam Paul Kahle*. Ed. Matthew Black. Berlin: Alfred Topelmann, 1968.

Eldar, I. "The Art of Correct Reading of the Bible." *Proceedings of the Ninth International IOMS Congress (1989).* Masoretic Studies, No. 8. Missoula, MT: Scholars Press, 1992.

________. "Hebrew Reading Traditions of the Jewish Communities." *VIII International Congress of the International Organization for Masoretic Studies (1988)*. Masoretic Studies, No. 6. Missoula, MT: Scholars Press, 1990.

________. "Mukhtasar (An Abridgement of) Hidayat al–Qari: a Grammatical Treatise Discovered in the Genizah." *Genizah Research after Ninety Years*. University of Cambridge Oriental Publications 47. Ed. J Blau and S Reif. Cambridge: Cambridge University Press, 1992.

Elder, I. "The Law of '*WY*' *H* and *BGDKP*' *T*." *Hebrew Union College Annual* 55 (1984) 1–14.

Engberg, G. "Greek Ekphonetic Neumes and Masoretic Accents." *Studies in Eastern Chant* 1 (1966) 37–44.

Eissfeldt, O. *The Old Testament, An Introduction.* New York, NY: Harper and Row, 1965.

Elliger, K. and W. Rudolph, ed. *Biblia Hebraica Stuttgartensia.* Stuttgart: Deutsche Bibelstiftung, 1967–77.

Even–Shoshan, A., ed. *A New Concordance of the Old Testament.* 2nd ed. Grand Rapids, MI: Baker Book House, 1990.

Fassberg, S.E. "The Origin of the Ketib/Qere in the Aramaic Portions of Ezra and Daniel." *Vetus Testamentum* 39 (1989) 1–12.

Fishbane, M. "Biblical Colophons, Textual Criticism, and Legal Analogies." *Catholic*

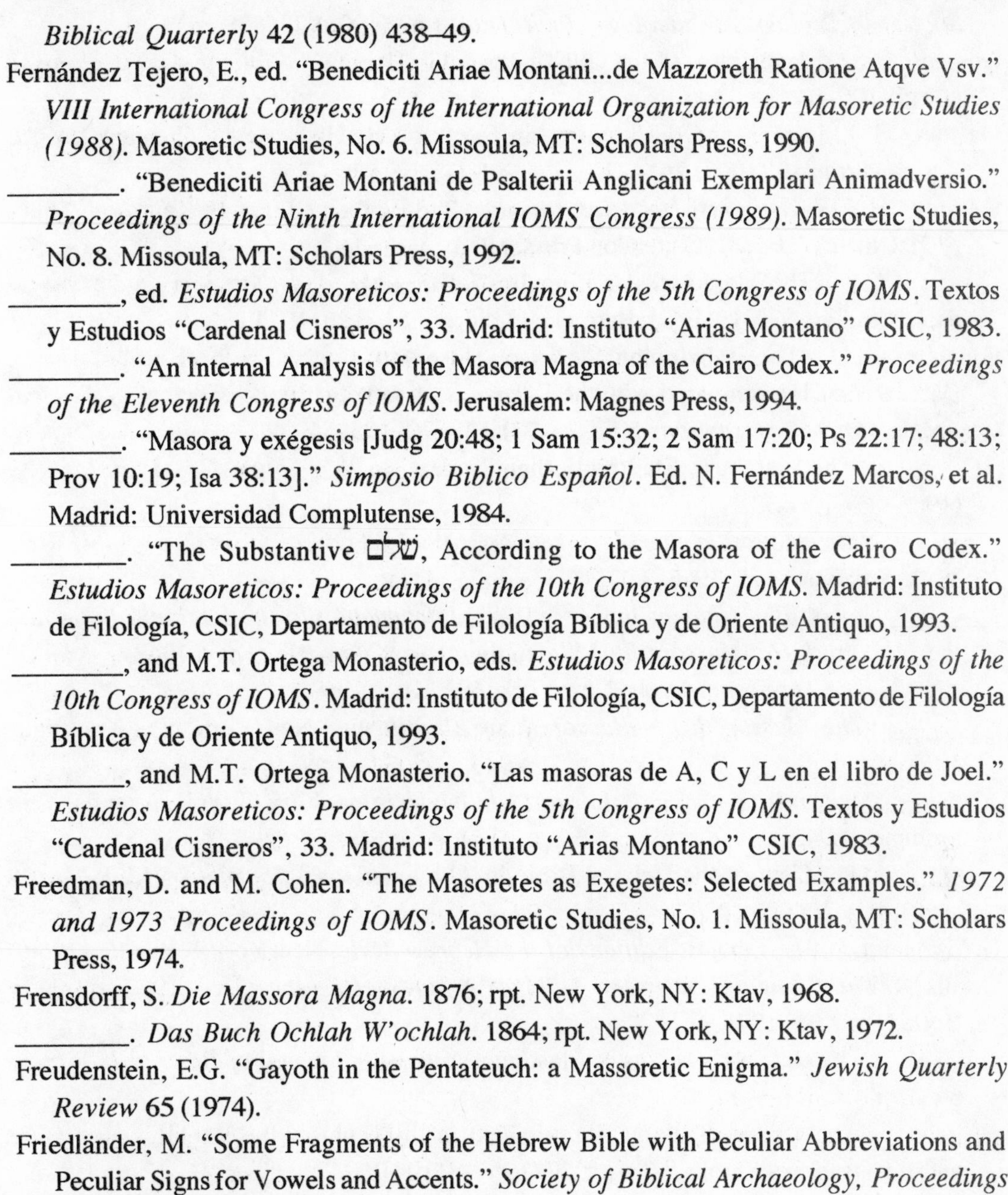

Biblical Quarterly 42 (1980) 438–49.

Fernández Tejero, E., ed. "Benediciti Ariae Montani...de Mazzoreth Ratione Atqve Vsv." *VIII International Congress of the International Organization for Masoretic Studies (1988)*. Masoretic Studies, No. 6. Missoula, MT: Scholars Press, 1990.

________. "Benediciti Ariae Montani de Psalterii Anglicani Exemplari Animadversio." *Proceedings of the Ninth International IOMS Congress (1989)*. Masoretic Studies, No. 8. Missoula, MT: Scholars Press, 1992.

________, ed. *Estudios Masoreticos: Proceedings of the 5th Congress of IOMS*. Textos y Estudios "Cardenal Cisneros", 33. Madrid: Instituto "Arias Montano" CSIC, 1983.

________. "An Internal Analysis of the Masora Magna of the Cairo Codex." *Proceedings of the Eleventh Congress of IOMS*. Jerusalem: Magnes Press, 1994.

________. "Masora y exégesis [Judg 20:48; 1 Sam 15:32; 2 Sam 17:20; Ps 22:17; 48:13; Prov 10:19; Isa 38:13]." *Simposio Biblico Español*. Ed. N. Fernández Marcos, et al. Madrid: Universidad Complutense, 1984.

________. "The Substantive שׁלם, According to the Masora of the Cairo Codex." *Estudios Masoreticos: Proceedings of the 10th Congress of IOMS*. Madrid: Instituto de Filología, CSIC, Departamento de Filología Bíblica y de Oriente Antiquo, 1993.

________, and M.T. Ortega Monasterio, eds. *Estudios Masoreticos: Proceedings of the 10th Congress of IOMS*. Madrid: Instituto de Filología, CSIC, Departamento de Filología Bíblica y de Oriente Antiquo, 1993.

________, and M.T. Ortega Monasterio. "Las masoras de A, C y L en el libro de Joel." *Estudios Masoreticos: Proceedings of the 5th Congress of IOMS*. Textos y Estudios "Cardenal Cisneros", 33. Madrid: Instituto "Arias Montano" CSIC, 1983.

Freedman, D. and M. Cohen. "The Masoretes as Exegetes: Selected Examples." *1972 and 1973 Proceedings of IOMS*. Masoretic Studies, No. 1. Missoula, MT: Scholars Press, 1974.

Frensdorff, S. *Die Massora Magna*. 1876; rpt. New York, NY: Ktav, 1968.

________. *Das Buch Ochlah W'ochlah*. 1864; rpt. New York, NY: Ktav, 1972.

Freudenstein, E.G. "Gayoth in the Pentateuch: a Massoretic Enigma." *Jewish Quarterly Review* 65 (1974).

Friedländer, M. "Some Fragments of the Hebrew Bible with Peculiar Abbreviations and Peculiar Signs for Vowels and Accents." *Society of Biblical Archaeology, Proceedings* 18 (1896) 86–98.

Fruchtman, M. "Grammar, Masora, and Linguistic Approach in Abraham ben 'Azri'el's *'Arugat Ha–Bosem*." *Proceedings of the Eleventh Congress of IOMS* (Hebrew Section). Jerusalem: Magnes Press, 1994.

Gaster, M. "A Codex of the Bible according to the Massora of Ben Naphtali and the Oriental Tradition. *Bible Magazine* 3 (1915) 923–38.

________. "Hebrew Illuminated MSS. of the Bible of the IXth and Xth Centuries."

Society of Biblical Archaeology, Proceedings 22 (1900) 226–39.

Gehman, H.S. "Manuscripts of the Old Testament in Hebrew." *Biblical Archaeologist* 8 (1945) 100–03.

Gertner, M. "Masorah and the Levites, an Essay in the History of a Concept." *Vetus Testamentum* 10 (1960) 241–72.

Gesenius, H.F.W. *Gesenius' Hebrew Grammar*. 2nd English ed. Ed. E. Kautzsch. Trans. A. E. Cowley. Oxford: Clarendon Press, 1983.

Gibson, J.C.L. "The Massoretes as Linguists." *Language and Meaning*. Oudtestamentische Studien, Vol. 19. Ed. J. Barr, et al. Leiden: E. J. Brill, 1974.

Ginsburg, C.D. "The Babylonian Codex of Hosea and Joel, also the Book of Jonah, Dated 916 A.D., compared with the Received Massoretic Texts." *Society of Biblical Archaeology, Transactions* 5 (1876–77) 129–76, 475–549.

________. "The Hamburg Stadtbibliothek Codex No. 1," *Journal of Philology* 29 (1903–04) 126–38.

________. *Introduction to the Massoretico-Critical Edition of the Hebrew Bible*. New York, NY: Ktav, Inc., 1966.

________. *Jacob Ben Chayim Ibn Adonijah's Introduction to the Rabbinic Bible and the Massoreth Ha–Massoreth of Elias Levita*. New York, NY: Ktav, 1968.

________. *The Massorah*. 4 vols. New York, NY: Ktav, 1968.

________. *The Massoreth ha–Massoreth of Elias Levita*. New York, NY: Ktav, Inc., 1968.

________. *Masoretico–Critical Edition of the Hebrew Bible*. 2 vols. Vienna: Carl Fromme, 1894.

________. "The Text of the Hebrew Bible in Abbreviations," *Journal of Philology* 28 (1901–03) 254–70.

Goldschmidt, L. *The Earliest Editions of the Hebrew Bible*. New York, NY: Ktav, 1950.

Gordis, R. *The Biblical Text in the Making, A Study of Ketibh–Qere*. 1937; rpt. New York, NY: Ktav, 1971.

________. "The Date and Origins of Masoretic Activity." *Journal of Biblical Literature* 69 (1950) x.

________. "The Origin of the Masoretic Text in the Light of the Rabbinic Literature and the Dead Sea Scrolls." *Tarbiz* 27 (1957–8) III–IV.

________. "A Reply to One of Professor Albright's Reviews." *Journal of Biblical Literature* 57 (1938) 329–331.

Goshen–Gottstein, M.H. *The Aleppo Codex* (Facsimile). Jerusalem: Magnes Press, 1976.

________. "The Aleppo Codex and Ben Buya'a the Scribe."*Tarbiz* 33 (1963–4) #2, V.

________. "The Aleppo Codex and the Rise of the Masoretic Text." *Biblical Archaeologist* 42 (1979) 145–63.

________. "The Authenticity of the Aleppo Codex." *Textus* 1 (1960) 17–58.

________, ed. *Biblia Rabbinica.* Jerusalem: Makor Publishing, 1972.

________. "Biblical Manuscripts in the United States." *Textus* 2 (1962) 28–59.

________. "Hebrew Biblical Manuscripts: Their History and Their Place in the HUBP Edition." *Biblica* 48 (1967) 243–90.

________. "A Recovered Part of the Aleppo Codex." *Textus* 5 (1966) 53–59.

________. "The Rise of the Tiberian Bible Text. *Biblical and Other Studies.* Ed. A. Altmann. Cambridge, MA: Harvard University Press, 1963.

Gottheil, R. "Bible Editions." *The Jewish Encyclopedia*, Vol. III. New York, NY: Funk and Wagnalls Co., 1905.

________. "Notes to JQR." *Jewish Quarterly Review* 18 (1905–6) 566.

________. "Some Hebrew Manuscripts in Cairo." *Jewish Quarterly Review* 17 (1904–5) 609–55.

Gutmann, J. "Masorah Figurata in the Mikdashyah: The Messianic Solomonic Temple in a 14th–Century Spanish Hebrew Bible Manuscript." *VIII International Congress of the International Organization for Masoretic Studies (1988).* Masoretic Studies, No. 6. Missoula, MT: Scholars Press, 1990.

________. "Masorah Figurata: The Origins and Development of a Jewish Art Form." *Estudios Masoreticos: Proceedings of the 5th Congress of IOMS.* Textos y Estudios "Cardenal Cisneros", 33. Madrid: Instituto "Arias Montano" CSIC, 1983.

Hall, I.H. "A Note in Reference to the 'Massora Among the Syrians.'" *American Journal of Semitic Languages and Literature* 2 (1885–6) 95–97.

Halpern, B. "Descriptive Catalogue of Genizah Fragments in Philadelphia." *Jewish Quarterly Review*, N.S. 12 (1921–22) 397–433.

Haran, M. "Bible Scrolls in Eastern and Western Jewish Communities from Qumran to the High Middle Ages." *Hebrew Union College Annual* 56 (1985) 21–62.

Harman, H.M. "Some Observations upon Tikkun Sopherim." *American Journal of Semitic Languages and Literature* 4 (1887–88) 34–42.

Harper, W.R. "The True Massoretic Text." *Old and New Testament Student* 2 (1882–83) 27–28.

Harris, I. "The Rise and Development of the Massorah." *Jewish Quarterly Review* 1 (1888–9) 128–42, 223–57.

Harviainen, T. "Karaite Arabic Transcriptions of Hebrew in the Saltykov–Shehedrin Public Library in St. Petersburg." *Estudios Masoreticos: Proceedings of the 10th Congress of IOMS*. Madrid: Instituto de Filología, CSIC, Departamento de Filología Bíblica y de Oriente Antiquo, 1993.

________. "A Karaite Bible Transcription with Indiscriminate Counterparts of Tiberian *qames* and *holam* (MS. Firkovitsh II, Arab.–evr.1)." *Proceedings of the Eleventh Congress of IOMS*. Jerusalem: Magnes Press, 1994.

________. "The Karaites of Lithuania at the Present Time and the Pronunciation Tradition of Hebrew among them: A Preliminary Survey." *Proceedings of the Ninth International IOMS Congress (1989)*. Masoretic Studies, No. 8. Missoula, MT: Scholars Press, 1992.

________. "On the Vocalism of the Closed Unstressed Syllables in Hebrew." *Studia Orientalia 48/1*. Helsinki, 1977.

Herzog, A. "Masoretic Accents (Musical Rendition)." *Encyclopedia Judaica*, Vol. XI. Jerusalem: Macmillan Co., 1971.

Hyvernat, H. "Petite introduction à l'étude de la Massore." *Revue Biblique*, 11 (1902) 551–63; 12 (1903) 529–42; 13 (1904) 521–46; 14 (1905) 203–34, 515–42.

Japhet, I.M. *Die Accente der heiligen Schrift*. Frankfurt: J. Kaufmann, 1896.

Jellinek, A. *Jedidjah Salomo Norzi's Einleitung, Titelblatt and Schlusswort zu seinem masoretischen Bibelcommentar*. Wien: Brüder Winter, 1876.

Kahle, P.E. "The Ben Asher Text of the Hebrew Bible." *Orientalia Suecana* 4 (1955) 43–52.

________. *The Cairo Geniza*. Oxford: Blackwell, 1959.

________. "Die hebräischen Bibelhandschriften aus Babylonien." *Zeitschrift für die Alttestamentliche Wissenschaft*, 46 (1928) 113–37.

________. "The Hebrew Ben Asher Bible Manuscripts." *Vetus Testamentum* 1 (1951) 161–167.

________. *Masoreten des Ostens*. Hildesheim: G. Olms, 1966.

________. *Masoreten des Westens*. Hildesheim: G. Olms, 1967.

________. *Der Masoretische Text des Alten Testaments*. Hildesheim: G. Olms, 1966.

________. "The Massoretic Text of the Bible and the Pronunciation of Hebrew." *Journal of Jewish Studies* 7 (1956) 133–54.

________. "Pre-Masoretic Hebrew." *Textus* 2 (1962) 1–7.

________. "Die Punktation der Masoreten." *Beihefte zur Zeitschrift für die Alttestamentliche Wissenschaft* 41 (1925) 167–72.

________. "The Reputed Ancient Hebrew Bible at Cambridge." *Journal of Theological Studies* 32 (1930–31) 69–71.

Kellermann, D. "Korrektur, Variante, Wahllesart: ein Beitrag zum Verständnis der K1'/Q1w–Fälle." *Biblische Zeitschrift*, N.S. 24 (1980) 57–75.

Kennedy, J. "Plea for a Fuller Criticism of the Massoretic Text, with Illustrations from the First Psalm." *Expositor, 8th Ser*. 5 (1913) 378–84.

Khan, G. "The Importance of the Karaite Transcriptions of the Hebrew Bible for the Understanding of the Tiberian Masora." *Proceedings of the Ninth International IOMS Congress (1989)* (Hebrew Section). Masoretic Studies, No. 8. Missoula, MT: Scholars Press, 1992.

________. "The Orthography of Karaite Hebrew Bible Manuscripts in Arabic Transcription." *Journal of Semitic Studies* 38 (1993) 49–70.

________. "The Syllabic Nature of Tiberian Hebrew Vocalization." *Semitic Studies In Honor of Wolf Leslau*, Vol. I. Ed. Alan S. Kaye. Wiesbaden: Harrassowitz, 1991.

Kittel, R., ed. *Biblia Hebraica 1*. Stuttgart: Privileg. Württ. Bibelanstalt, 1912.

________, ed. *Biblia Hebraica 3*. 7th ed. Stuttgart: Privileg. Württ. Bibelanstalt, 1952.

Klein, M.L. "Manuscripts of the Proto–Massorah to Onqelos." *Estudios Masoreticos: Proceedings of the 10th Congress of IOMS*. Madrid: Instituto de Filología, CSIC, Departamento de Filología Bíblica y de Oriente Antiquo, 1993.

Knauf, E.A. "*Chatef Patach* in geschlossener Silbe in Codex Leningradensis." *Biblische Notizen* 19 (1982) 57–58.

Kogut, S. "The Authority of Masoretic Accents in Traditional Biblical Exegesis." *Shaarei Talmon*. Ed. M. Fishbane, et al. Winona Lake, IN: Eisenbrauns, 1992.

Kristianpoller, A. "Masorah and Masoretes." *Universal Jewish Encyclopedia*, Vol. VII. New York, NY: Universal Jewish Encyclopedia, Inc., 1942.

Laberge, L. "Texte de l'Ancien Testament." *Eglise et Théologie* 7 (1976) 295–331.

Langlamet, F. "Les divisions massorétique du livre de Samuel: à propos de la publication du Codes du Cairo." *Revue Biblique* 91 (1984) 481–519.

________. "Le Seigneur dit à Moïse: une clé de lecture des divisions massorétiques." *Mélanges bibliques et orientaux*. Alter Orient und Altes Testament 215. Ed. A Caquot, et al. Kevelaer, Germany: Butzon and Bencker, 1985.

LaSor, W.S. "An Approach to Hebrew Poetry through the Masoretic Accents." *Essays on the Occasion of the Seventieth Anniversary of the Dropsie University*. Ed. A. Katsh and L. Nemoy. Philadelphia: Dropsie University, 1979.

Lehman, I.O. "A Study of the Oldest Dated Oriental Bible Texts." *1972 and 1973 Proceedings of IOMS*. Masoretic Studies, No. 1. Missoula, MT: Scholars Press, 1974.

Lehmann, M.R. "Further Study of the Pe'in Lefufot." *Proceedings of the Eleventh Congress of IOMS*. Jerusalem: Magnes Press, 1994.

Leiman, S.Z., ed. *The Canon and Masorah of the Hebrew Bible*. New York, NY: Ktav, 1974.

________. "The Inverted Nuns at Numbers 10:35–36 and the Book of Eldad and Medad." *Journal of Biblical Literature* 93/3 (1974) 348–55.

Levene, J. "Elijah Levita." *Jewish Encyclopedia*, vol. VIII. New York, NY: Funk and Wagnalls Co., 1905.

Levin, S. "Defects, Alleged or Real, in the Tiberias Pointing. *Hebrew Studies* 23 (1982) 67–84.

Levy, K. *Zur Masoretischen Grammatik*. Bonner Orientalistische Studien, No. 15. Stuttgart: Kohlhammer, 1936.

Lieberman, A.A. " לֹא/לוֹ : An Analysis of a Kethib–Qere Phenomenon." *VIII International Congress of the International Organization for Masoretic Studies (1988)*. Masoretic Studies, No. 6. Missoula, MT: Scholars Press, 1990.

Lipschütz, L. "Kitab al–Kilaf, the book of Hillufim." *Textus* 4 (1964) 1–29.

________. *Kitab al–Kilaf, the book of Hillufim*. Jerusalem: Magnes Press, 1965.

________. "Mishael ben Uzziel's Treatise on the Differences Between Ben Asher and Ben Naphtali." *Textus* 2 (1962) 1–58.

Lizowsky, G. *Konkordanz zum Hebräischen Alten Testament*. Stuttgart: Württembergische Bibelanstalt, 1958.

Loewe, R.J. "The Medieval History of the Latin Vulgate." *Cambridge History of the Bible* 2 (1969) 102–54.

Loewinger, D.S. "The Aleppo Codex and the Ben Asher Tradition." *Textus* 1 (1960) 59–111.

________. *Cairo Codex of the Bible* (Facsimile). Jerusalem: Makor Publishing, 1971.

________. *Codex Leningrad B19a* (Facsimile). Jerusalem: Makor Publishing, 1970.

________. *The Masora Magna to the Bible: Ochla ve–Ochla Codex Paris* (Facsimile). Jerusalem: Makor Publishing, 1978.

Lowenstamm, S.E. "The Nouns זער, זעור (Ketib) זעיר (Qere)." *Tarbiz* 36 (1966–67) #2, I–II.

Lyons, D. "The Collative Tiberian Masorah: a Preliminary Study." *1972 and 1973 Proceedings of IOMS*. Masoretic Studies, No. 1. Missoula, MT: Scholars Press, 1974.

________. "Exhaustive and Cumulative Categories in the Masora." *Proceedings of the Eleventh Congress of IOMS* (Hebrew Section). Jerusalem: Magnes Press, 1994.

Malone, J.L. "Textually Deviant Forms as Evidence for Phonological Analysis: A Service of Philology to Linguistics." *The Journal of the Ancient Near Eastern Society* 11 (1979) 71–79.

Mansoor, M. "The Massoretic Text in the Light of Qumran." *Supplements to Vetus Testamentum* 9 (1963) 305–21.

Mandelkern, S. *Concordance on the Bible*. 2 vols. New York, NY: Shulsinger Brothers, 1955.

Marx, A. "Notes to JQR." *Jewish Quarterly Review* 18 (1905–6) 567–70.

Mashiah, R. "Between Great and Little *Telisha*." *Proceedings of the Eleventh Congress of IOMS* (Hebrew Section). Jerusalem: Magnes Press, 1994.

McCarthy, C. "Emendations of the Scribes." *The Interpreter's Dictionary of the Bible, Supplementary Volume*. Nashville, TN: Abingdon Press, 1976.

________. *The Tiqqune Sopherim and Other Theological Corrections in the Masoretic Text of the Old Testament*. Orbis Biblicum et Orientalis 36. Göttingen: Vandenhoeck and Ruprecht, 1981.

McKane, W. "Observations on the Tikkune Sopherim." *On Language, Culture, and Religion: In Honour of Eugene A. Nida*. Ed. Matthew Black and W. A. Smalley. The Hague: Mouton, 1974.

Meyer, R. "Die Bedeutung des Codex Reuchlinianus für die hebräische Sprachgeschichte." *Zeitschrift der deutschen morgenländischen Gesellschaft* 113 (1963) 51–61.

Miletto, G. "Il Kethib–Qere nella tradizione babilonese." *Biblische und Judaistische Studien*. Judentum and Umwelt 29. Ed. A. Vivian. Frankfurt am Main: Peter Lang, 1990.

Minkoff, H. "The Aleppo Codex: Ancient Bible from Ashes." *Bible Review* 7 (1991) 22–27, 38–40.

Mitchell, H.G. "A Hebrew Manuscript." *Journal of Biblical Literature* 5 (1885) 20–27.

Montgomery, J.A. "Notes on Two Syriac MSS." *Journal of Biblical Literature* 39 (1920) 113–117.

Moore, G.F. "The Vulgate Chapters and Numbered Verses in the Hebrew Bible." *Journal of Biblical Literature* 12 (1893) 73–78.

Morag, S. "On the Historical Validity of the Vocalization of the Hebrew Bible." *Journal of the American Oriental Society* 94 (1974) 307–35.

________. "On Some Terms of the Babylonian Massora." *1972 and 1973 Proceedings of IOMS*. Masoretic Studies, No. 1. Missoula, MT: Scholars Press, 1974.

________. "The Vocalization of Codex Reuchlinianus: Is the 'Pre-Masoretic' Bible Pre-Masoretic?" *Journal of Semitic Studies* 4 (1959) 216–37.

________. *The Vocalization Systems of Arabic, Hebrew, and Aramaic*. The Hague: Mouton, 1962.

________. "The Yemenite Tradition of the Bible: the Transition Period." *Estudios Masoreticos: Proceedings of the 5th Congress of IOMS*. Textos y Estudios "Cardenal Cisneros", 33. Madrid: Instituto "Arias Montano" CSIC, 1983.

Morrow, W.S. "Kethib and Qere." *The Anchor Bible Dictionary*, Vol. 4. New York, NY: Doubleday, 1992.

________ and E.G. Clark. "The Ketib/Qere in the Aramaic Portions of Ezra and Daniel." *Vetus Testamentum* 36 (1986) 406–22.

Mulder, M.J. "The Transmission of the Biblical Text." *Mikra: Text, Translation, Reading, and Interpretation of the Hebrew Bible in Ancient Judaism and Early Christianity*. Ed. Martin Jan Mulder. Philadelphia: Fortess, 1990.

Murtonen, A.E. *Materials for a Non–Masoretic Hebrew Grammar*. Helsinki, 1 (1958), 2 (1960), 3 (1962).

Mynatt, D.S. "Causes for the Masorah Parva Errors in the Leningrad Codex (B19a)." *Proceedings of the Eleventh Congress of IOMS*. Jerusalem: Magnes Press, 1994.

________. *The Sub Loco Notes of the Torah in BHS*. Fort Worth, TX: Bibal Press, 1994.

Norzi, S.Y. *Sefer Minhat Shay*. Vienna: Holfinger, 1813.

Ognibeni, B. "La collezione massoretica 'klh w'klh." *Tradition of the Text*. Orbis Biblicus et Orientalis 109. Ed. G. Norton and S. Pisano. Fribourg, Switzerland: Universitätsverlag, 1991.

Orlinsky, H.M., ed. *1972 and 1973 Proceedings of IOMS*. Masoretic Studies, No. 1.

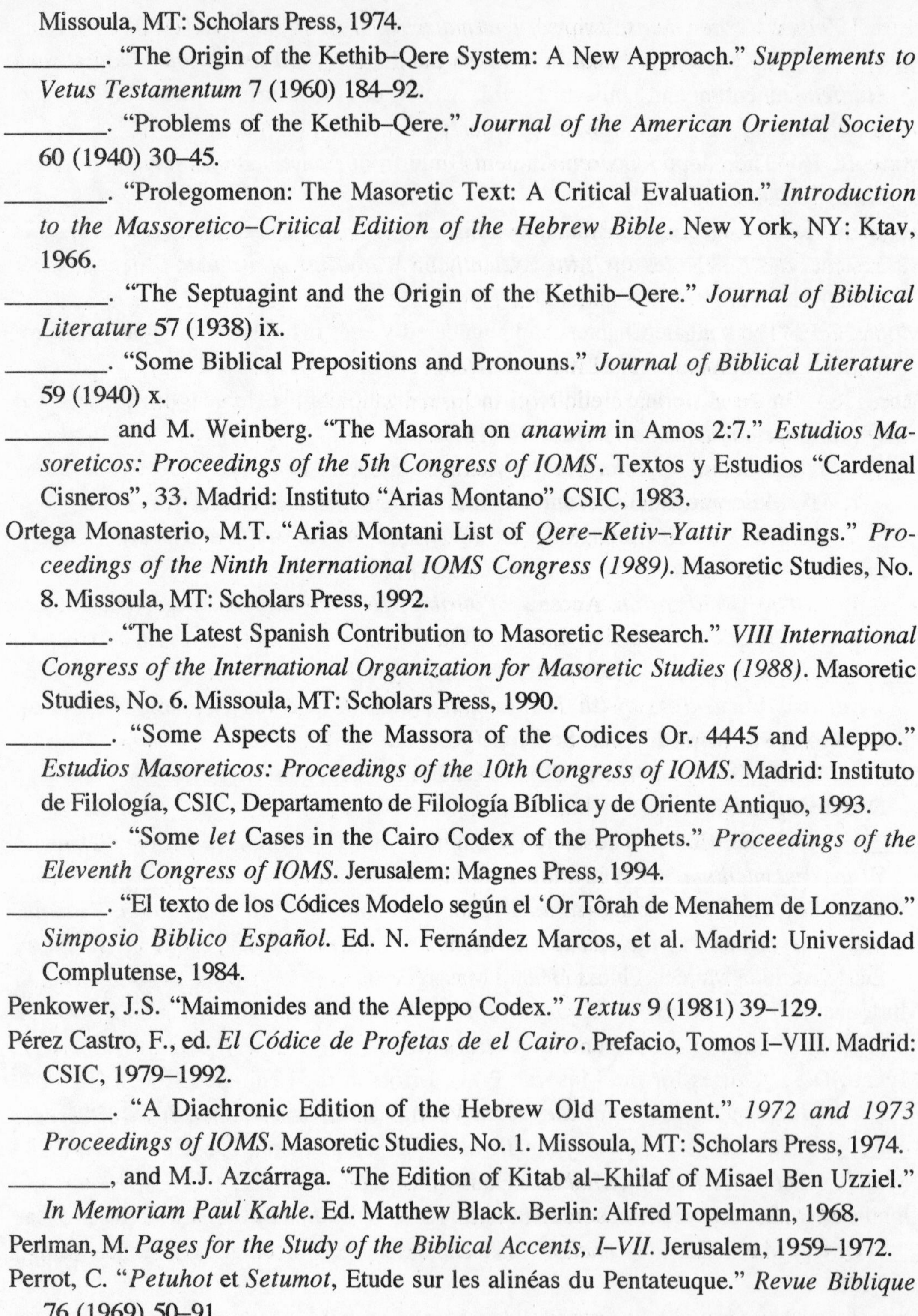

Missoula, MT: Scholars Press, 1974.

________. "The Origin of the Kethib–Qere System: A New Approach." *Supplements to Vetus Testamentum* 7 (1960) 184–92.

________. "Problems of the Kethib–Qere." *Journal of the American Oriental Society* 60 (1940) 30–45.

________. "Prolegomenon: The Masoretic Text: A Critical Evaluation." *Introduction to the Massoretico–Critical Edition of the Hebrew Bible*. New York, NY: Ktav, 1966.

________. "The Septuagint and the Origin of the Kethib–Qere." *Journal of Biblical Literature* 57 (1938) ix.

________. "Some Biblical Prepositions and Pronouns." *Journal of Biblical Literature* 59 (1940) x.

________ and M. Weinberg. "The Masorah on *anawim* in Amos 2:7." *Estudios Masoreticos: Proceedings of the 5th Congress of IOMS*. Textos y Estudios "Cardenal Cisneros", 33. Madrid: Instituto "Arias Montano" CSIC, 1983.

Ortega Monasterio, M.T. "Arias Montani List of *Qere–Ketiv–Yattir* Readings." *Proceedings of the Ninth International IOMS Congress (1989)*. Masoretic Studies, No. 8. Missoula, MT: Scholars Press, 1992.

________. "The Latest Spanish Contribution to Masoretic Research." *VIII International Congress of the International Organization for Masoretic Studies (1988)*. Masoretic Studies, No. 6. Missoula, MT: Scholars Press, 1990.

________. "Some Aspects of the Massora of the Codices Or. 4445 and Aleppo." *Estudios Masoreticos: Proceedings of the 10th Congress of IOMS*. Madrid: Instituto de Filología, CSIC, Departamento de Filología Bíblica y de Oriente Antiquo, 1993.

________. "Some *let* Cases in the Cairo Codex of the Prophets." *Proceedings of the Eleventh Congress of IOMS*. Jerusalem: Magnes Press, 1994.

________. "El texto de los Códices Modelo según el 'Or Tôrah de Menahem de Lonzano." *Simposio Biblico Español*. Ed. N. Fernández Marcos, et al. Madrid: Universidad Complutense, 1984.

Penkower, J.S. "Maimonides and the Aleppo Codex." *Textus* 9 (1981) 39–129.

Pérez Castro, F., ed. *El Códice de Profetas de el Cairo*. Prefacio, Tomos I–VIII. Madrid: CSIC, 1979–1992.

________. "A Diachronic Edition of the Hebrew Old Testament." *1972 and 1973 Proceedings of IOMS*. Masoretic Studies, No. 1. Missoula, MT: Scholars Press, 1974.

________, and M.J. Azcárraga. "The Edition of Kitab al–Khilaf of Misael Ben Uzziel." *In Memoriam Paul Kahle*. Ed. Matthew Black. Berlin: Alfred Topelmann, 1968.

Perlman, M. *Pages for the Study of the Biblical Accents, I–VII*. Jerusalem, 1959–1972.

Perrot, C. "*Petuhot* et *Setumot*, Etude sur les alinéas du Pentateuque." *Revue Biblique* 76 (1969) 50–91.

Pick, B. "Lost Hebrew Manuscripts." *Journal of Biblical Literature* 2 (1882) 122–27.

________. "The Masoretic Piska in the Hebrew Bible." *Journal of Biblical Literature* 6 (1886) 135–39.

Porges, N. "Notes on JQR." *Jewish Quarterly Review* 18 (1905–6) 149–50.

Price, J.D. *The Syntax of Masoretic Accents in the Hebrew Bible*. Lewiston, NY: Edwin Mellen Press, 1990.

Prijs, J. "Über Ben Naftali–Bibelhandschriften und ihre paläographischen Besonderheiten." *Zeitschrift für die Alttestamentliche Wissenschaft* 69 (1957) 171–84.

Ratzabi, Y. "Massoretic Variants to the Five Scrolls from a Babylonian-Yemenite MS." *Textus* 5 (1966) 93–113.

Rabin, C. "Massorah and 'Ad Litteras.'" *Hebrew Studies* 26 (1985) 81–91.

Reed, S.A. "A Puzzling Masoretic Note in Joshua 21:35." *Textus* 15 (1990) 77–85.

Reich, N. "*Alphabetarin*-the Evolution of a Masoretic Term." *Proceedings of the Eleventh Congress of IOMS* (Hebrew Section). Jerusalem: Magnes Press, 1994.

Reiner, F.N. "Masoretes, Rabbis, and Karaites: a Comparison of Biblical Interpretations." *1972 and 1973 Proceedings of IOMS*. Masoretic Studies, No. 1. Missoula, MT: Scholars Press, 1974.

Revell, E.J. "Aristotle and the Accents." *Journal of Semitic Studies* 19 (1974) 19–35.

________. "Biblical Punctuation and Chant in the Second Temple Period." *Journal for the Study of Judaism* 7 (1976) 181–98.

________. *Biblical Texts with Palestinian Pointing and Their Accents*. Masoretic Studies, No. 4. Missoula, MT: Scholars Press, 1977.

________. "The Conditioning of Stress Position in *Waw* Consecutive Perfect Forms in Biblical Hebrew." *Hebrew Annual Review* 9 (1985) 277–300.

________. "Conjunctive Dagesh: A Preliminary Study." *VIII International Congress of the International Organization for Masoretic Studies (1988)*. Masoretic Studies, No. 6. Missoula, MT: Scholars Press, 1990.

________. "Dehiq: Exceptions to the Standard Pattern." *Proceedings of the Ninth International IOMS Congress (1989)*. Masoretic Studies, No. 8. Missoula, MT: Scholars Press, 1992.

________. "The Hebrew Accents and Greek Ekphonetic Numes." *Studies in Eastern Chant* 4 (1974) 140–70.

________. *Hebrew Texts with Palestinian Vocalization*. Toronto: University of Toronto Press, 1970.

________., ed. *VIII International Congress of the International Organization for Masoretic Studies (1988)*. Masoretic Studies, No. 6. Missoula, MT: Scholars Press, 1990.

________. "Masorah." *The Anchor Bible Dictionary*, Vol. 4. New York, NY: Doubleday, 1992.

________. "Masoreten des Westens II, Ms M, and other Palestinian Mss with Defective

Accentuation." *1972 and 1973 Proceedings of IOMS*. Masoretic Studies, No. 1. Missoula, MT: Scholars Press, 1974.

________. "Masoretes." *The Anchor Bible Dictionary*, Vol. 4. New York, NY: Doubleday, 1992.

________. "Masoretic Accents." *The Anchor Bible Dictionary*, Vol. 4. New York, NY: Doubleday, 1992.

________. "Masoretic Studies." *The Anchor Bible Dictionary*, Vol. 4. New York, NY: Doubleday, 1992.

________. "Masoretic Text." *The Anchor Bible Dictionary*, Vol. 4. New York, NY: Doubleday, 1992.

________. "Nesiga and the History of the Masorah." *Estudios Masoreticos: Proceedings of the 5th Congress of IOMS*. Textos y Estudios "Cardenal Cisneros", 33. Madrid: Instituto "Arias Montano" CSIC, 1983.

________. "A New Biblical Fragment with Palestinian Vocalization." *Textus* 7 (1969) 59–75.

________. "A New Subsystem of 'Tibero–Palestinian' Pointing." *Fifth World Congress of Jewish Studies* 4 (1973) 91–107.

________. "The Oldest Evidence for the Hebrew Accent System." *Bulletin of John Rylands Library* 54 (1971) 214–22.

________. "Pausal Forms and the Structure of Biblical Poetry." *Vetus Testamentum* 31 (1981) 186–199.

________. "Pausal Forms in Biblical Hebrew: Their Function, Origin, and Significance." *Journal of Semitic Studies* 25 (1980) 60–80.

________. "The Placing of the Accent Signs in the Biblical Texts with Palestinian Pointing." *Studies on the Ancient Palestinian World*. Ed. J.W. Wevers and D.B. Redford. Toronto: University of Toronto Press, 1972.

________. "The Reading Tradition as a Basis for Masoretic Notes." *Estudios Masoreticos: Proceedings of the 10th Congress of IOMS*. Madrid: Instituto de Filología, CSIC, Departamento de Filología Bíblica y de Oriente Antiquo, 1993.

________. "The Relation of the Palestinian to the Tiberian Massora." *1972 and 1973 Proceedings of IOMS*. Masoretic Studies, No. 1. Missoula, MT: Scholars Press, 1974.

________. "Studies in the Palestinian Vocalization of Hebrew." *Essays on the Ancient Semitic World*. Ed. J. W. Wevers and D. B. Redford. Toronto: University of Toronto Press, 1970.

________. "Syntactic Semantic Structure and the Reflexes of Original Short *A* in Tiberian Pointing." *Hebrew Annual Review* 5 (1981) 75–100.

________. "The Voweling of the 'I Type' Segolates in Tiberian Hebrew." *Journal of Near East Studies* 44 (1985) 319–28.

Ribera, J. "The Babylonian Masoretic Tradition Reflected in the Mss of the Targum to the Latter Prophets." *VIII International Congress of the International Organization for Masoretic Studies (1988)*. Masoretic Studies, No. 6. Missoula, MT: Scholars Press, 1990.

________. "Relationship Between Semantics and Vocalization." *Estudios Masoreticos: Proceedings of the 10th Congress of IOMS*. Madrid: Instituto de Filología, CSIC, Departamento de Filología Bíblica y de Oriente Antiquo, 1993.

Richter, G. "Concerning the Hebrew Text of the Old Testament and the Masoretic Text Tradition." *Bible Magazine* 3 (1915) 923–38.

Riviere, P. and M. Serfaty. "Etude critique des Paseq des livres en prose à la lumière des nouvelles théories sur les chaines de la cantilation." *Estudios Masoreticos: Proceedings of the 5th Congress of IOMS*. Textos y Estudios "Cardenal Cisneros," 33. Madrid: Instituto "Arias Montano" CSIC, 1983.

Roberts, B.J. "The Divergences in the Pre-Tiberian Massoretic Text." *Journal of Jewish Studies* 1 (1948–49) 147–55.

________. "The Emergence of the Tiberian Massoretic Text." *Journal of Theological Studies* 49 (1948) 8–16.

________. "The Hebrew Bible Since 1937." *Journal of Theological Studies* 15 (1964) 253–264.

________. "Old Testament Text." *The Interpreter's Dictionary of the Bible*, Vol. IV. Nashville, TN: Abingdon Press, 1962.

________. *The Old Testament Text and Version*. Cardiff: University of Wales Press, 1951.

________. "The Textual Transmission of the Old Testament, including Modern Critical Editions of the Hebrew Bible." *Tradition and Interpretation*. Ed. G. Anderson. Oxford: Clarendon Press, 1979.

Robertson, E. "Points of Interest in the Massoretic Text." *Journal of Near Eastern Studies* 2 (1943) 35–39.

Rosowsky, S. *The Cantillation of the Bible: The Five Books of Moses*. New York, NY: The Reconstructionist Press, 1957.

Rubinstein, A. "A Kethib–Qere Problem in Light of the Isaiah Scroll." *Journal of Semitic Studies* 4 (1959) 127–33.

________. "The Problem of Errors in the Massorah Parva of Codex B19a." *Sefarad* 25 (1965) 16–23.

________. "Singularities in the Massorah of the Leningrad Codex (B19a)." *Journal of Jewish Studies* 12 (1961) 123–31.

________. "The Terms משתבשין and דחזי in the Babylonian Massorah." *Vetus Testamentum* 10 (1960) 198–212.

Saebo, M. "From Pluriformity to Uniformity: Some Remarks on the Emergence of the Massoretic Text." *Annual of the Swedish Theological Institute* XI (1978) 127–37.

Sanders, J.A. "Text and Canon: Concepts and Method." *Journal of Biblical Literature* 98 (1979) 5–29.

Schillinger, F.W. "A Concise History of Bible Manuscripts (A Conference Paper)." *Theologische Zeitblätter, Theology Magazine* 5 (1915) 67–72.

Schoville, K. "An Introduction to the Masoretic Text." *Bible Review* 9 (1993) 12.

Schramm, G. *The Graphemes of Tiberian Hebrew*. Near Eastern Studies 2. Berkeley, CA: University of California Publications.

Scott, W.R. *A Simplified Guide to BHS*. Berkeley: Bibal Press, 1987.

Seeligmann, I.L. "Researches into the Criticism of the Masoretic Text of the Bible." *Tarbiz* 25 (1956–7) #2, I–II.

Segal, J.B. *The Diacritical Point and the Accents in Syriac*. Oxford: Oxford University Press, 1953.

Segal, M.H. "The Promulgation of the Authoritative Text of the Hebrew Bible." *Journal of Biblical Literature* 72 (1953) 35–47.

Serfaty, M. "Un fragment de catalogue massorétique: T–S NS 287–15 (Contribution à l'histoire des méthodes de classification des anciennes listes massorétiques)." *Proceedings of the Ninth International IOMS Congress (1989)*. Masoretic Studies, No. 8. Missoula, MT: Scholars Press, 1992.

________. "L'indispensable comparison des *massorot* en vue de leur compréhension." *Estudios Masoreticos: Proceedings of the 10th Congress of IOMS*. Madrid: Instituto de Filología, CSIC, Departamento de Filología Bíblica y de Oriente Antiquo, 1993.

________. "Nouveau fragments de *`Okhla we–`Okhla*: T–S NS 287–18, 28, 39." *Proceedings of the Eleventh Congress of IOMS*. Jerusalem: Magnes Press, 1994.

Shereshevsky, E. "The Accents in Rashi's Commentary." *Jewish Quarterly Review* 62 (1971–72) 277–87.

Shoshany, R. "Methodological Problems in the Study of the Babylonian Accentuation System." *Proceedings of the Eleventh Congress of IOMS* (Hebrew Section). Jerusalem: Magnes Press, 1994.

Siegal, J.P. "An Orthographic Convention of 1QIs[a] and the Origin of Two Masoretic Anomalies." *1972 and 1973 Proceedings of IOMS*. Masoretic Studies, No. 1. Missoula, MT: Scholars Press, 1974.

________. "The Severus Scroll and 1QIs[a]." *1972 and 1973 Proceedings of IOMS*. Masoretic Studies, No. 1. Missoula, MT: Scholars Press, 1974.

________. *The Severus Scroll and 1QIsa*. Masoretic Studies, No. 2. Missoula, MT: Scholars Press, 1975.

Sierra, S.J. "Hebrew Codices with Miniature Belonging to the University of Bologna." *Jewish Quarterly Review* N.S. 63 (1952–53) 229–48.

Ska, J.L. "*BHS*: Corrigenda." *Biblica* 64 (1983) 343.

Skehan, P.W. "Qumran and the Present State of the Old Testament Text Studies: The

Masoretic Text." *Journal of Biblical Literature* 78 (1959) 21–25.

Slotki, I.W. "'Breaks in the Midst of Verses' or 'פִּסְקָא בְּאֶמְצַע פָּסוּק.'" *Journal of Theological Studies* 22 (1920–21) 263–65.

Smith, H.P. "Biblical Manuscripts in America." *Journal of Biblical Literature* 42 (1923) 239–50; 44 (1925) 188–89.

Snaith, N.H. "The Ben Asher Text." *Textus* 2 (1962) 8–14.

________. "Bible: Printed Editions." *Encyclopedia Judaica*, Vol. IV. Jerusalem: Macmillan Co., 1972.

Sperber, A. *Codex Reuchlinianus, no. 3 of the Badische Landesbibliothek in Karls–ruhe...with a General Introduction: Masoretic Hebrew.* Corpus Hebraicorum Medii Aevi 2/1. Copenhagen: Munksgaard, 1956.

________. *A Grammar of Masoretic Hebrew: A General Introduction to the Pre-Masoretic Bible.* Copenhagen: Ejnar Munksgaard, 1959.

________. *A Historical Grammar of Biblical Hebrew.* Leiden: Brill, 1966.

________. *Problems of the Masora.* Philadelphia: Jewish Publication Society, 1943.

________. "Problems of the Masora." *Hebrew Union College Annual* 17 (1942–3) 293–394.

________. *The Prophets According to Codex Reuchlinianus.* Leiden: Brill, 1969.

________. "The Targum Onkelos in its Relation to the Masoretic Hebrew Text." *Proceedings of the American Academy for Jewish Research* 6 (1934–5) 309–51.

Sperber, D. "Some Tannaitic Biblical Variants." *Zeitschrift für die Alttestamentliche Wissenschaft* 79 (1967) 79–80.

Stevenson, W.B. "History and Sources of the Jewish Masorah." *Glasgow University Oriental Society, Transactions* 6 (1929–33) 22–23.

Strack, H.L. *The Hebrew Bible–Latter Prophets: The Babylonian Codex of Petrograd* (Facsimile). New York, NY: Ktav, 1971.

Straus, J. "Requests and Replies." *ET* 4 (1892–3) 80.

Szinessy, S. "The Prideaux Pentateuch." *Society of Biblical Archaeology, Transactions* 1 (1872) 263–270.

Szyszman, S. "La famille des massorètes karaïtes Ben Asher et le Codex Alepensis." *Revue Biblique* 73 (1966) 531–51.

Ṭalmon, S. "The Three Scrolls of the Law that were Found in the Temple Court." *Textus* 2 (1962) 14–27.

Teicher, J.L. "The Ben Asher Bible Manuscripts." *Journal of Jewish Studies* 2 (1950) 17–25.

Trever, J.C. "A Report on Some Important Hebrew Manuscripts in England." *Journal of Biblical Literature* 71 (1952) ix.

Van Der Heide, A. "A Biblical Fragment with Palestinian-Tiberian ('Pseudo-Ben Naftali') Punctuation in the Leyden University Library (Hebr. 259–1)." *Museon* 87 (1974)

415–23.

Vasholz, R.I. *Data for the Sigla of BHS*. Winona Lake, IN: Eisenbrauns, 1983.

Waldman, N.M. "The Hebrew Tradition." *Current Trends in Linguistics 13*. Ed. T. Sebeok. The Hague: Mouton, 1975.

________. *The Recent Study of Hebrew*. Winona Lake, IN: Eisenbrauns, 1989.

Warfield, B.B. "The Massora Among the Syrians." *American Journal of Semitic Languages and Literature* 2 (1885–86) 13–23.

Weil, G.E. "L'Archetype du Massoret ha–Massoret d'Elie Lévita." *Revue d'Historie et de Philosophie Religieuses* 41 (1961) 147–58.

________. "La Bible de l'Université hébraique de Jerusalem." *Revue d'Histoire et de Philosophie Religieuses* 43 (1963) 193–99.

________. "Les decomptes de versets, mots et lettres du pentateuque selon le manuscrit b 19a de Leningrad." *Mélanges Dominique Barthélemy*. Orbis Biblicus et Orientalis 38. Ed. Pierre Casetti, et al. Göttingen: Vandenhoeck and Ruprecht, 1981.

________. "Le Development de l'Oeuvre Massoretic. Recherches Nouvelles en Matière de Critique Textuelle de l'Ancien Testament." *Bulletin d'Information de l'Institute Rechercher et d'Histoire des Textes* 9 (1962–3).

________. *Elie Lévita humaniste et massorète (1469–1549)*. Leiden: E. J. Brill, 1963.

________. "La formation du commentaire de la Mm marginale dans les grands codex biblique. Etude comparée des listes de Dt 28,17 à 34,12 dans les manuscrits A et L." *Revue d'Histoire des Textes* I (1971) 1–48.

________. "Un fragment de Okhlah Palestinienne." *Annual of the Leeds University Oriental Society* 3 (1963) 68–80.

________. "Fragment d'une Massorah alphabétique du Targum Babylonien du Pentateuch." *Annual of the Leeds University Oriental Society* 5 (1963) 114–34.

________. *Initiation á la Massorah: l'introduction au Sefer Zikhronot d'Élie Lévita*. E. J. Brill, 1964.

________. *Massorah Gedolah*, Vol. 1. Rome: Pontifical Biblical Institute, 1971.

________. *Le Massoret ha–Massoret*. Strassbourg: Committee for Research at the University of Strassbourg, 1956.

________. "La Massorah." *Revue des Etudes Juives* 131 (1972) 5–104.

________. "La Massorah Magna babylonienne des Prophetes." *Textus* 3 (1963) 163–70.

________. "Massorah, massorètes et ordinateurs: les sources textuelles et les recherches automatisées." *Bible et informatique*. Trauvaux de linguistique quantitative 37. Paris: Champion-Slatkine, 1986.

________. "Nouveau fragment de la Massorah Magna du Targum de Babylone: Ms heb d 62 Fol 45 Bodleian Library-Oxford." *In Memoriam Paul Kahle*. Ed. Matthew Black. Berlin: Alfred Topelmann, 1968.

________. "Nouveaux fragments inédits de la Massorah Magna babylonienne." *Textus*

6 (1968) 75–105.

________. "La nouvelle édition de La Massorah et l'histoire de la Massorah." *Supplements to Vetus Testamentum* 9 (1962) 267–84.

________. "Propositions pour une étude de la Tradition massorétique babylonienne." *Textus* 2 (1962) 103–19.

________. "Qere–Kethib." *The Interpreter's Dictionary of the Bible, Supplementary Volume*. Nashville, TN: Abingdon Press, 1976.

________. "Quatre fragments de la Massorah Magna babylonienne." *Textus* 3 (1963) 74–120.

________. "Quelques Motivations de la Nouvelle Edition de la Massorah dans la Bible Hébraique de Stuttgart." *Wort und Geschichte*. Alter Orient und Altes Testament 18. Ed. H. Gese and H. P. Rüger. Neukirchen–Vluyn: Neukirchener Verlag, 1973.

________, P. Riviere, and M. Serfaty. *Concordance de la cantilation du Pentateuque et des cinq Megillot*. Paris: Editions du CNRS, 1978.

________, P. Riviere, and M. Serfaty. *Concordance de la cantilation des premiers prophetes Josue, Juges, Samuel, et Rois*. Paris: Editions du CNRS, 1981.

________, and N. Weil. "Un fragment de la Massorah Magna du Targum du Pentateuque dans la collection D. Kaufmann de Budapest (MS KG 592 BM6)." *Jubilee Volume of the Oriental Collection*. Ed. E. Apor. Budapest: Library of the Hungarian Academy of Sciences, 1978.

Weinberg, M. "Some Problems of the Masorah on Isaiah." *1972 and 1973 Proceedings of IOMS*. Masoretic Studies, No. 1. Missoula, MT: Scholars Press, 1974.

________. "A Study of וַ־יֹּאמַר in the Masora Finalis." *VIII International Congress of the International Organization for Masoretic Studies (1988)*. Masoretic Studies, No. 6. Missoula, MT: Scholars Press, 1990.

Weisberg, D. "The Rare Accents of the Twenty–One Books." *Jewish Quarterly Review* 56 (1965–66) 315–36; 57 (1966–67) 57–70, 227–38.

Wernberg–Møeller, P. "Aspects of Masoretic Vocalization." *1972 and 1973 Proceedings of IOMS*. Masoretic Studies, No. 1. Missoula, MT: Scholars Press, 1974.

________. "Observations on the Old Accusative Ending in Massoretic Hebrew." *VIII International Congress of the International Organization for Masoretic Studies (1988)*. Masoretic Studies, No. 6. Missoula, MT: Scholars Press, 1990.

Werner, E. "Masoretic Accents." *The Interpreter's Dictionary of the Bible*, Vol. III. Nashville, TN: Abingdon Press, 1962.

Wickes, W. *A Treatise on the Accentuation of the Three So–Called Poetical Books of the Old Testament*. Oxford: Clarendon Press, 1881.

________. *A Treatise on the Accentuation of the Twenty-one So–Called Prose Books of the Old Testament*. Oxford: Clarendon Press, 1887.

Widawsky, L. "The Main Divider in the Prose Books Accents." *Proceedings of the*

Eleventh Congress of IOMS (Hebrew Section). Jerusalem: Magnes Press, 1994.

________. "*Paseq's* Characteristics in Units of Two, Three, or more Words." *Proceedings of the Ninth International IOMS Congress (1989)* (Hebrew Section). Masoretic Studies, No. 8. Missoula, MT: Scholars Press, 1992.

Wiener, H.M. "Samaritan Septuagint Massoretic Text," *Expositor, 8th Ser.* 2 (1911) 200–19.

Wilensky, M. "About Manuscripts." *Hebrew Union College Annual* 12 & 13 (1937–38) 559–72.

________. "Additions and Corrections." *Hebrew Union College Annual* 16 (1941) 243–249.

Wilson, G.H. "The Qumran Psalms Manuscripts and the Consecutive Arrangement of Psalms in the Hebrew Psalter." *Catholic Biblical Quarterly* 45 (1983) 377–88.

Wilson, R.D. "The Textual Criticism of the Old Testament." *Princeton Theological Review* 27 (1929) 36–59.

Wonneberger, R. *Understanding BHS: A Manual for the Users of the Biblia Hebraica Stuttgartensia.* Rome: Biblical Institute Press, 1984.

Wood, J. "A Syriac Masora." *Glasgow University Oriental Society, Transactions* 14 (1950–52) 35–42.

Würthwein, E. *The Text of the Old Testament.* 2nd ed. Grand Rapids, MI: Eerdmans, 1995.

Yannai, Y. "Elisha and the Shunammite (II Kings 4:8–37): A Case of Homoeoteleuton, or a Text Emendation by Ancient Masoretes?" *Estudios Masoreticos: Proceedings of the 5th Congress of IOMS.* Textos y Estudios "Cardenal Cisneros", 33. Madrid: Instituto "Arias Montano" CSIC, 1983.

Yarkoni, R. "The Ben Buyaa Pentateuch Manuscript: Evidence concerning the Tiberian Massorah prior to its General Acceptance." *Studies in Judaica, 1991.* Teudah 7. Ed. M. Friedman. Tel Aviv: Tel Aviv University Publishing Projects, 1991.

________. "Yequti'el ha-Naqdan—One of the Last Masoretes or an Early Ashkenazi Grammarian?" *Estudios Masoreticos: Proceedings of the 10th Congress of IOMS.* Madrid: Instituto de Filología, CSIC, Departamento de Filología Bíblica y de Oriente Antiquo, 1993.

Yeivin, I. *The Aleppo Codex of the Bible: A Study of Its Vocalization and Accentuation.* Jerusalem: Magnes Press, 1968.

________. "A Babylonian Fragment of the Bible in the Abbreviated System." *Textus* 2 (1962) 120–39.

________. "A Biblical Fragment with Tiberian Non-Masoretic Vocalisation." *Tarbiz* 29 (1959–60) #4, III–IV (Hebrew).

________. "A Closed Syllable with a Long Vowel." *Proceedings of the Eleventh Congress of IOMS* (Hebrew Section). Jerusalem: Magnes Press, 1994.

________. "The Dageshed Alefs in the Bible." *Studies in the Bible and the Ancient Near East*. Jerusalem: E. Rubinstein, 1978.

________. "The Division in Sections in the Psalms." *Textus* 7 (1969) 76–102.

________. "Fragment of a Massoretic Treatise." *Textus* 1 (1960) 185–208.

________, ed. *Geniza Bible Fragments with Babylonian Massorah and Vocalization, 1. Pentateuch*. 2 Vols. Leiden: Brill, 1973.

________. *Introduction to the Tiberian Masorah*. Trans. and Ed. E. J. Revell. Masoretic Studies, No. 5. Missoula, MT: Scholars Press, 1980.

________. "The New Edition of the Biblica Hebraica." *Textus* 7 (1969) 114–23.

________. "Notes and Communications. 1. A Unique Combination of Accents." *Textus* 1 (1960) 209–10.

________. "A Palestinian Fragment of Haftereth and Other Mss. with Mixed Pointing. *Textus* 3 (1962) 121–27.

________. "Two Terms of the Babylonian Masora to the Bible." *Leshonenu* 30 (1965–66) #1, n.p.n.

________. "The Vocalization of Qere–Kethiv in A." *Textus* 2 (1962) 146–49.

Zeitlin, S. "The Masora and the Dead Sea Scrolls." *Jewish Quarterly Review* N.S. 49 (1958–9) 161–63.

Zimmermann, F. "The Edited Masoretic Text." *Journal of Biblical Literature* 61 (1942) x.

________. "The Perpetuation of Variants in the Masoretic Text." *Jewish Quarterly Review* N.S. 34 (1943–44) 459–74.

Zipor, M.A. "The Masoretic 'Eighteen Tiqqune Sofrim': the Birth and Transformations of a Tradition." *Fifth World Congress of Jewish Studies* 1 (1990) 51–58.

Reviews of *BHS*

Barr, J. Review of *Biblia Hebraica Stuttgartensia*, ed. by K. Elliger and W. Rudolph. *Journal of Semitic Studies* 25 (1980) 98–105.

________. Review of *Biblia Hebraica Stuttgartensia*, ed. by K. Elliger and W. Rudolph. *Journal of Theological Studies* 30 (1979) 212–16.

Boccaccio, P. Review of *Biblia Hebraica Stuttgartensia*, ed. by K. Elliger and W. Rudolph. *Biblica* 61 (1980) 126–30.

Dahood, M. Review of *Biblia Hebraica Stuttgartensia*, ed. by K. Elliger and W. Rudolph. *Catholic Biblical Quarterly* 32 (1970) 254–55.

Emerton, J.A. Review of *Biblia Hebraica Stuttgartensia*, ed. by K. Elliger and W. Rudolph. *Theologische Literaturzeitung* 98 (1973) 514–16.

Klein, R.W. Review of *Biblia Hebraica Stuttgartensia*, ed. by K. Elliger and W. Rudolph.

Concordia Theological Monthly 42 (1971) 471.

Lys, D. Review of *Biblia Hebraica Stuttgartensia*, ed. by K. Elliger and W. Rudolph. *Etudes Théologiques et Religieuses* 45 (1970) 91–92.

________. Review of *Biblia Hebraica Stuttgartensia*, ed. by K. Elliger and W. Rudolph. *Etudes Théologiques et Religieuses* 46 (1971) 79–80.

________. Review of *Biblia Hebraica Stuttgartensia*, ed. by K. Elliger and W. Rudolph. *Etudes Théologiques et Religieuses* 47 (1972) 230–31.

Roberts, B.J. Review of *Biblia Hebraica Stuttgartensia*, ed. by K. Elliger and W. Rudolph. *Journal of Theological Studies* 25 (1974) 465–68.

________. Review of *Biblia Hebraica Stuttgartensia*, ed. by K. Elliger and W. Rudolph. *Expository Times* 80 (1969) 214–15.

Sanders, J.A. Review of *Biblia Hebraica Stuttgartensia*, ed. by K. Elliger and W. Rudolph. *Journal of Biblical Literature* 98 (1979) 417–19.

Skehan, P.W. Review of *Biblia Hebraica Stuttgartensia*, ed. by K. Elliger and W. Rudolph. *Catholic Biblical Quarterly* 31 (1969) 615–16.

Scripture Index

Exodus

Leviticus

Numbers

Judges

2 Chronicles